OXFORD TECHNOLOGY LAW AND POLICY

Series Editors

FRANK PASQUALE

Professor of Law, Cornell Tech and Cornell Law School

JULIA POWLES

Associate Professor of Law and Technology, The University of Western Australia

Artificial Justice

OXFORD TECHNOLOGY LAW AND POLICY

Series Editors
Frank Pasquale, Cornell University and
Julia Powles, The University of Western Australia

The Oxford Technology Law and Policy series aims to publish scholarly works of the highest quality, focusing on research that combines rigorous social, political, and ethical theory with a practical sense of the policy implications of critical thought. The series welcomes works exploring contemporary controversies over technology (including automation, robotics, artificial intelligence, data policy, privacy, digital rights, and platform capitalism), as well as those that develop historical methods to reinterpret technological advancements, focused on the role of law and policy in channelling the development of technology. The series does not favour any single approach and invites works rooted in both long-standing and emerging traditions of critical technology studies, from both established and new voices. The Series Editors welcome innovative and interdisciplinary approaches that advance the discussion on technology law and policy.

OTHER TITLES IN THIS SERIES

Artificial Justice
Tatiana Dancy

Ethical Data Science
Prediction in the Public Interest
Anne L. Washington

Artificial Justice

TATIANA DANCY

OXFORD
UNIVERSITY PRESS

Great Clarendon Street, Oxford, OX2 6DP,
United Kingdom

Oxford University Press is a department of the University of Oxford.
It furthers the University's objective of excellence in research, scholarship,
and education by publishing worldwide. Oxford is a registered trade mark of
Oxford University Press in the UK and in certain other countries

© Tatiana Dancy 2023

The moral rights of the author have been asserted

First Edition published in 2023

All rights reserved. No part of this publication may be reproduced, stored in
a retrieval system, or transmitted, in any form or by any means, without the
prior permission in writing of Oxford University Press, or as expressly permitted
by law, by licence or under terms agreed with the appropriate reprographics
rights organization. Enquiries concerning reproduction outside the scope of the
above should be sent to the Rights Department, Oxford University Press, at the
address above

You must not circulate this work in any other form
and you must impose this same condition on any acquirer

Public sector information reproduced under Open Government Licence v3.0
(http://www.nationalarchives.gov.uk/doc/open-government-licence/open-government-licence.htm)

Published in the United States of America by Oxford University Press
198 Madison Avenue, New York, NY 10016, United States of America

British Library Cataloguing in Publication Data

Data available

Library of Congress Control Number: 2023944490

ISBN 978-0-19-284689-1

DOI: 10.1093/oso/9780192846891.001.0001

Printed and bound by
CPI Group (UK) Ltd, Croydon, CR0 4YY

Links to third party websites are provided by Oxford in good faith and
for information only. Oxford disclaims any responsibility for the materials
contained in any third party website referenced in this work.

Contents

1. Introduction ... 1
   - The English Convict ... 1
   - Statistical Algorithms ... 5
   - Algorithmic Justice ... 7
     - Relevance ... 9
     - Equality ... 11
     - Choice ... 13

2. Relevance ... 21
   - The Fire Tells the Story ... 21
   - The Lure of Blame ... 27
   - The Phantom of Heilbronn ... 33

3. Equality ... 41
   - Guilty as Sin ... 41
   - Puzzle People ... 45
   - A Big Honking Book ... 48
   - Guinea-Chasing Treatments ... 51
   - Bumps in Boston ... 54
   - The Quirky Guy from the Morgue ... 58

4. Choice ... 71
   - Born Criminal ... 71
   - An Ideal Crime-Fighting World ... 78
   - Relentless Pursuit ... 86
   - The Worst-Case Scenario ... 90
   - Every Parent's Nightmare ... 97
   - A Blizzard of Prescriptions ... 100

5. Transparency ... 115
   - A Chilling Conclusion ... 115
   - The Determinative Factor ... 118

6. Concluding Remarks ... 129
   - Summary ... 129
   - The English Convict ... 132
   - Algorithmic Justice ... 134
   - The Value of Choice ... 137

Criminal Justice 139
Transparency 140
Policy and Prediction 142
Conclusion 144

Index 149

Acknowledgements

I owe extensive thanks to Emmanuel Voyiakis, for his painstaking efforts to help me clarify my earlier thoughts on the subject of algorithmic justice—without which I could not have got this far. I also owe thanks to attendees of the Surrey Centre for Law & Philosophy discussion forum and the Melbourne Law School faculty research seminar series—in particular, to Lulu Weis for her conscientious comments during the latter presentation.

I have been fortunate enough to have several (official and unofficial but always generous) mentors throughout my academic career, each of whom has encouraged me, educated me, and generally supported me in innumerable ways. This includes James Edelman, David Kershaw, Tom Poole, and Erika Rackley.

Finally, I owe a personal debt of gratitude to several people: to my grandparents, John and Angela Dancy, for nurturing the intellectual curiosity of their wayward grandchild; to my younger sister Natasha, who produced the fantastic image for the front cover, and who continues to inspire me with her creativity and determination; to Nickie and Tom, for their endless support and encouragement along the way; and to the many friends, near and far, who have made the process of navigating two big international moves during this project a lot of fun, amidst a lot of chaos.

Last but by far from least, I owe thanks to Mike, my husband—who has put up with countless, often impatiently introduced and over-ebullient, conversations on this topic, who always roots for me, and who makes every challenge seem surmountable. And a final nod to the extra little human who pushed me to meet this particular deadline...

1
Introduction

The English Convict

In 1913, as tension was building amongst Eurasian powers towards the end of the Balkan Wars, Charles Buckman Goring published his magnum opus: *The English Convict: A Statistical Study*.[1] Medic and pioneering criminologist, Goring wanted to figure out (in his words) 'whether the criminal is born or made'.[2] And he believed that a robust statistical enquiry could reveal the answer: 'We owe much to the experimental methods of investigating natural phenomena in plants and animals', he wrote, 'but in future our debt will be as great to the statistical method'.[3]

Through a decade-long research programme funded by the British government, Goring conducted a study of some 2000 male prisoners housed at Pankhurst Prison in London. He reported that prisoners demonstrated a strong propensity for 'mental defect',[4] including low intelligence and 'degenerate' psychology,[5] and were generally of 'inferior stature'[6] and 'defective physique'.[7] There was, he concluded, a 'criminal diathesis'—a diagnosable criminal condition, defined by a set of psychological and physical characteristics that were 'so potent' in some people 'as to determine for them, eventually, the fate of imprisonment'.[8] Goring even linked certain characteristics to specific types of crime—lower intelligence to petty theft, muscular weakness to crimes of violence, and short stature to sexual offences.[9]

The history of the statistical method has an uneasy relationship with eugenics, and Goring's research hardly bucked that trend. Having found 'no evidence of any significant relationship' between crime and certain 'environmental' factors such as education, socio-economic status, and family background,[10] he concluded that the criminal diathesis was fundamentally hereditary.[11] The 'crusade against crime' could, he argued, be conducted by 'modifying opportunity for crime by segregation and supervision of the unfit'.[12] But he thought that the only way of 'attacking the evil at its very root' was to 'regulate the reproduction of those degrees of constitutional qualities – feeble-mindedness, inebriety, epilepsy, deficient social instinct, insanity, which conduce to the committing of crime'.[13]

Mercifully, Goring's wider policy ambitions for criminal justice were met with little enthusiasm by those who were not already affiliated with the eugenics lobby. But the central thesis of his research—that there is a diagnosable criminal 'type' of person, who is predisposed to antisocial activity—is echoed in various features of modern criminal justice systems. These features have been magnified by the growing use of statistical algorithms—decision-making rules developed on the basis of insights gleaned from patterns in population data. These algorithms, and their use in public and private decision-making, are the focus of this book.

Statistical algorithms are used widely across criminal justice, to make population-level decisions about the distribution of policing resources, and to make targeted decisions about surveillance and punishment. For instance, the 'Correctional Offender Management Profiling for Alternative Sanctions' (COMPAS) system, developed and owned by Equivant,[14] is a suite of algorithmic tools that are used to predict recidivism rates for individuals and wider communities. Since 1998, COMPAS has been used by law enforcement and judicial officers in multiple US states to shape decisions about how to treat the criminal accused and convicted. As of 2022, more than a million defendants have received COMPAS risk scores,[15] and many of those scores have been used to determine whether particular defendants should be incarcerated, and (if so) what the nature and duration of incarceration and any post-release supervision should be.[16]

Though the literature often refers to 'the COMPAS algorithm',[17] COMPAS is not a single algorithm that produces one type of risk-score; rather, the COMPAS software includes a range of tools that use algorithms to predict risk, which are described by Equivant as 'configurable for the user'.[18] The tools available include 'Pre-Trial Services',[19] which principally concern the risk that the accused will flee the jurisdiction, and three assessments (the General Recidivism Risk scale (GRR), the Violent Recidivism Risk scale (VRR), and the 'full assessment') that involve predictions about recidivism.[20]

The facts that count towards Equivant's 'full assessment' of a given individual include: whether they were raised by their 'natural' parents, and whether and when those parents separated;[21] the involvement of family or friends in 'antisocial' activities; neighbourhood crime rates;[22] access to medical insurance;[23] residential instability;[24] and financial stress.[25] These facts inform individual risk scores, and a set of generalized criminal 'typologies'.

Like Goring, Equivant uses these typologies to drill down into specific categories of offence. For instance, the COMPAS Practitioners' Guide tells us that the 'socially marginalized—poor, uneducated, stressed, habitual offenders' tend towards 'instrumental crime for financial gain', 'family disorganization and inadequate parenting' lead to 'minor non-violent offences', whilst 'young antisocial poorly educated women' are most likely to commit certain kinds of violent offence.[26]

COMPAS is designed to operate as a way of facilitating the individual 'diagnosis' of criminality, to inform decisions about how to reduce the incidence of crime in general and recidivism in particular. The Practitioners' Guide begins with a medical analogy:

> Think about the different steps taken in the medical field to find a solution to an illness or a problem. When you don't feel well and you go to the doctor, what is the first thing that the doctor does? Asks about symptoms: When did they start? How severe are they? She asks about your medical history: Are you taking any medications? Have you had this or a similar problem before? And, she runs tests, takes your temperature, takes your blood pressure, takes blood samples, orders MRIs, etc. What does she do with all of this information? She makes a diagnosis and prescribes an effective treatment.[27]

This, Equivant tells us, is how we should understand criminal risk assessment: practitioners are 'connecting the dots' that chart the path from facts about individual history to criminal activity,[28] in order to inform a diagnosis and corresponding decision about the most 'effective treatment'.[29] Despite Equivant's assertions that 'treatment' should be oriented towards needs-based rehabilitation rather than punishment, it is standard practice in many jurisdictions for risk and needs-based assessments to feed a composite pre-sentence evaluation,[30] which judges are trained to use in the context of sentencing and related decisions.[31]

Policing algorithms often use similarly expansive assessments about social and family history to make predictions about criminal activity, which in turn inform decisions about how to focus resources. In Florida, in the United States, the Pasco County Sheriff's Office (PCSO) uses an algorithm to identify 'at-risk youth who are destined to a life of crime', described as 'targets'.[32] Points are assigned for various factors that include: socio-economic deprivation;[33] 'adverse childhood experiences';[34] including 'poor rearing as a child';[35] having 'delinquent friends';[36] and being a victim of or witness to personal crime.[37] An individual who receives a score above a certain threshold will be captured by a dedicated programme of 'relentless pursuit',[38] in which deputies apply high-intensity surveillance tactics to targets, and to their friends and family.[39]

The COMPAS and the PCSO algorithms belong to a wider category of tools that are used by policymakers and practitioners to diagnose individuals as criminal, antisocial, or otherwise unsuitable for certain important benefits because of facts about their social or family circumstances, or the way in which they have been treated at the hands of others. These tools extend throughout many spheres of our public and private lives, including criminal punishment, policing, healthcare, education, finance, recruitment, and social welfare.

For instance, the Opioid Risk Tool (ORT)[40] is a medical protocol that is used to make decisions about whether to prescribe opioids to patients, on the basis of a range of facts about the patient and their family. The algorithm, which is now the second-line medical standard for opioid prescription decisions across the world, gathers data via a questionnaire with ten scoreable components. These include: a family or personal history of substance abuse; patient age range; history of psychological disorder; and (if the patient is female) a history of preadolescent sexual abuse.[41] The output is a numerically expressed prediction about the likelihood that, if prescribed opioids, a given patient will go on to misuse their prescription, or to engage in aberrant drugs-related behaviours. A higher score indicates a higher risk, and contra-indicates prescription.

There is a good deal of evidence to suggest that even simple statistical algorithms can produce more accurate predictions than highly specialized and individualized clinical assessment.[42] Computers can now access and process vast quantities of data at speed, and algorithms are capable of using that data to produce a precise set of predictive rules, which are not derailed by the sorts of problems that plague human decision-making—a lack of sustained cognitive focus, the potential to be swayed by personal preference or pressure, systematic tendencies to make irrational deductive leaps, and so on.[43] Equipped with better predictions about how a particular outcome will be influenced by the presence or absence of certain facts, we can make decisions that are better aligned with our policy goals.

But there are also important concerns that arise from the use of statistical algorithms to help us to allocate the benefits and burdens of social policies, some of which have been captured by conversations about 'algorithmic justice'. The dominant theme of these conversations, across a range of (academic, policy, and media) spheres, has been upon whether and how we can minimize algorithmic 'bias' and discrimination.[44] These dialogues are geared towards inequality: they capture the various reasons that we may have to object to differences between people—what they have, and how they are treated—and to try to minimize these differences.[45]

In this book, I unpack the different sorts of reasons that we might draw upon when we object to policies of decision-making on the grounds of 'algorithmic injustice'. I argue that these reasons extend beyond egalitarian considerations, and cannot be addressed by reducing or eliminating unjustifiable differences between people. Importantly, they encompass the value of having the chance to influence what happens to us by exercising meaningful choices, and of giving people the benefit of the doubt about their ability to choose well.

Statistical Algorithms

Statistical algorithms are useful when we make decisions against a backdrop of uncertainty: will this person reoffend, and (if so) will the nature of a future offence be violent or non-violent? How will a patient respond to a particular course of treatment, and what will happen if they are left untreated? Of a given pool of candidates, who is likely to do the best job, if hired for a specific role? Answering these questions may (for better or worse) help us to decide whether and how to allocate certain benefits and burdens—whether to send someone to prison, which course of medical treatment to prescribe, which candidate to hire, and so on.

In the absence of knowledge that will allow us to arrive at answers deductively, we might instead attempt to make an inference from what we can observe about others. Perhaps the pathology of a particular condition is poorly understood, but a treating physician has noticed that other patients with that condition have responded well to a certain combination of medication and psychological therapy. We can do this in a more systematic way, by gathering data from a representative subset of our target population—the population amongst whom we need to make selective decisions—and identifying correlations between certain characteristics and the outcomes that we want.

If we have sufficient confidence that there is a relationship between some target variable and certain facts about individuals within that subset, and that this relationship will hold true when we apply our conclusions to the wider population, we are in a position to make predictions about how our target variable will be affected by the presence of certain facts amongst that population. When we reduce these perceived correlations to a predictive rule, we arrive at something that we might call a 'statistical algorithm'.

The term 'algorithm' describes a set of rules that guide decisions about what to do. It crops up most often in the context of computer programs, which are rules that computers follow to achieve a specified objective. But it is also used to describe rules that people can follow to make decisions, typically when variables are translated into numeric inputs. For instance, the Vaginal Birth after Caesarean (VBAC) calculator is a medical protocol that is widely used to predict the risk posed by vaginal birth for women who have already undergone one or more caesarean sections. The calculation, which can be made by a human or by an automated program, allocates points according to factors such as: age, pre-pregnancy weight, height, prior vaginal delivery, and the presence of certain co-morbidities such as chronic hypertension. A higher score means a higher predicted chance of a successful VBAC, which influences the treatment recommendations made by obstetric physicians.

I use the term 'statistical algorithm' inclusively, in a way that captures tools like the VBAC (which can be accessed as a formula for humans to use, or via a computer interface) and tools like COMPAS (which are accessible only via a computer interface). For the purposes of this book, a statistical algorithm is a decision-making protocol for computers or people to follow, which has been developed on the basis of inferences drawn from large pools of data.

Statistical algorithms have been a key part of policymaking in a range of spheres for several decades: amongst a broad range of other decisions, we use them to allocate organs, match DNA, rank students, grant visas, and distribute much-needed social resources. But predictive tools are rapidly expanding into new realms of decision-making, which can be life-changing for those affected. This includes policing and criminal punishment, educational ranking and admissions, recruitment, and a range of aberrations in contractual counter-performance, such as loan default, plagiarism detection, and 'toxic' behaviour in the workplace.

New tools can distil greater volumes of data at speed. Given a clear objective, learning algorithms can develop their own rules to determine the likelihood that two or more facts will coincide, on the basis of patterns distilled from datasets that are often too large or cumbersome to process using traditional means. From some of their earliest applications, such as spam filters and recommendation engines, learning algorithms are now used to perform a range of tasks that can affect our lives in far-reaching ways—from voter modelling and the triaging of public resourcing needs, to credit scoring, recruitment, and predictive policing and sentencing.

As predictive tools capture more areas of public and private decision-making, pressing questions arise about the nature and magnitude of the burdens that we can reasonably expect people to bear when we implement policies that aim to achieve some wider social benefit. These are the sorts of questions that arise under the heading of 'algorithmic fairness', or 'algorithmic justice'.

Algorithmic Justice

Literature addressing algorithmic justice has largely focused on egalitarian considerations: variously termed 'equality', 'bias', and 'discrimination', the concern dominating discussion has been the presence of unjustified differences between the way in which groups of individuals are treated by policies of algorithmic decision-making.[46] Taking into account the flaws of human-led alternatives, disparate views have emerged about the extent to which we can achieve the goal of ensuring 'that algorithms are fair, i.e. that they do not exhibit a bias towards particular ethnic, gender, or other protected groups'.[47]

These conversations are supported by detailed, empiric assessments of specific decision-making tools. For instance, a study by non-profit investigative media organization ProPublica found that COMPAS was twice as likely to 'misclassify' a black defendant as high risk for recidivism than a white defendant.[48] More precisely, the study authors found that COMPAS was twice as likely to classify a black defendant as highly likely to commit another crime, where that prediction was not borne out by the evidence during the assessed period (two years). By contrast, COMPAS was almost twice as likely to 'misclassify' a white defendant as low risk.

For some, this data regarding the distribution of the risk of error is conclusive evidence of racial bias.[49] Others have argued that an equal distribution of risk of error is not an appropriate goal for algorithms that process population data which display meaningful differences in incidences of the target variable amongst individuals within that population.[50] These conversations continue, and are reflected in the criticisms levelled at policies of algorithmic decision-making that govern other key aspects of our public and private lives.

Egalitarian reasons—reasons that concern the differences between the benefits to which people have access, and for trying to reduce those differences—are important, and warrant the extensive intellectual and financial resources that have been applied to them. Yet, these are not the only concerns that count towards the conclusion about whether a policy of algorithmic decision-making is just. I argue here that there are important non-comparative reasons to object to policies that use algorithms like COMPAS, which allocate some of the most significant institutional burdens on the basis of facts over which individuals may have little or no influence.

In particular, I argue that these reasons include the value of choice—the value of having, and being seen to have, a meaningful chance to avoid the burdens of a social policy by making appropriate choices. Some of the concerns that arise from the value of choice persist even if we can find ways to reduce or eliminate the sorts of inequities that are captured by conversations about algorithmic bias.

The structure and method that I use in this book borrows from Scanlon's contractualism,[51] and his application of that thesis to ideas of inequality.[52] For Scanlon, there are moral limits to the way in which individuals may be treated in order to achieve certain desirable ends,[53] and we figure out what these limits are by 'pairwise comparison'[54] of the reasons that apply to individuals as such and from their perspective. For any given principle or policy, this means comparing the reasons that any individual burdened by the policy has for objecting to it with the reasons that any other individual has for objecting to alternative (potentially more burdensome) policies.[55] The strength of the case for objecting to a given policy can be affected both by the costs imposed on individuals, and by how those costs are imposed.[56]

There are various reasons for embracing a contractualist strategy, some of which concern the way in which we factor in reasons that stem from individual interests.[57] Unlike utilitarianism and many other forms of consequentialism, intolerable costs imposed upon some people are not easily outweighed by small but numerous benefits to others when we approach the matter from a contractualist standpoint.[58] There being 'no individual who enjoys these benefits and would have to forgo them if the policy were disallowed', the 'sum of smaller benefits' does not allow us to require some people to make overwhelming sacrifices.[59]

But there is also a non-partisan methodological case for adopting this sort of framework, which has been the primary motivation for structuring the book around certain organizing ideas that emerge from Scanlon's contractualism, and its application to problems of comparative and non-comparative justice. This approach encourages us to 'look beneath' concepts such as equality, fairness, and justice, to 'uncover the reasons that people have to want or to object to certain forms of treatment'.[60] And in doing so, it allows a diverse set of reasons to count towards the outcome of the moral equation, without reducing them to a single concern (well-being, happiness, and so on).[61]

So, the focus of this book is upon the justification for using statistical algorithms to make policy decisions that benefit some at the expense of others. And the goal is to unpack and evaluate some of the reasons that individuals might have for wanting or objecting to policies that use these algorithms. Of these reasons, I discuss three: a rational relationship between the policy and some social benefit (Chapter 2, Relevance); objectionable differences between the benefits to which individuals have access (Chapter 3, Equality); and the value of opportunities to avoid the burdens of social policies by choosing appropriately (Chapter 4, Choice).

The rest of the book is about the information that we need to have about the relevant algorithm in order to make these assessments, and the role of human 'supervision' of algorithmic decisions (Chapter 5, Transparency). In Chapter 6 (Concluding Remarks), I draw conclusions and make some policy recommendations.

Relevance

We may be able to justify adopting a policy that requires some people to bear certain costs, if this will bring about some benefit—perhaps by allowing others to avoid the weightier costs that they would suffer under a different policy.[62] For instance, once a COVID-19 vaccine had been developed and produced at levels that could support public distribution, many national governments instituted vaccination schemes that required the majority of citizens to wait longer to receive a vaccine (with associated risk of intermediate harm) to allow the most vulnerable to be protected against the more significant mortality risks that they faced. Those vulnerable groups were identified by certain risk factors, such as age and/or certain kinds of comorbidity.

But we can only justify a policy on this basis—that it brings about some benefit—if it actually has that effect, or (*ex ante*) we have good reason to believe that it will. This is the focus of Chapter 2—the requirement to demonstrate that there is a rational link between the selection criteria that we use to divvy up burdens, and the cost that we avoid by making the decision on the basis of these criteria. In the context of COVID-19 vaccination, this meant proving some sound deductive or inductive basis for thinking that: (1) the relevant criteria (eg age and/or comorbidity) did in fact put individuals at a greater risk of harm; and (2) priority vaccination was an effective means of mitigating that risk.

Often, we lack the information that we need to be confident about the different variables that affect some outcome. This can include information of the sort that we need to make decisions about how to distribute much-needed medical resources: how will a patient with particular characteristics fare when exposed to a particular virus, and will vaccination be effective at protecting them against the risk of serious harm? Given this sort of uncertainty, our best route to an optimal decision about how to treat that patient is often to rely upon statistical inferences. We might, for instance, have (or be able to source) data that can reveal which patient characteristics are generally associated with poor outcomes amongst a representative subset of our target population, or whether vaccination has been associated with positive outcomes in other patients with these characteristics.

In this way, statistics help us to do a better job of figuring out how to meet some policy objective, such as improving rates of morbidity and mortality. Thus, to meet the demands of relevance, we do not always need to have a good understanding of the causal mechanism behind the correlations that inform our selection criteria. Rather, we simply need to show that we have good reason to think that the correlations that we perceive amongst the sample population are reliable—that they will help us to achieve the relevant benefit when we make decisions that affect our target population.

To do this, it is enough that we have either: (1) retrospective evidence that a policy based on these criteria is in fact associated with some avoided cost amongst that population (the gold standard); or (2) a sound basis for believing that these correlations between certain facts and the cost that we want to avoid will hold true amongst our target population, and a reliable prospective strategy for avoiding that cost. This basis is far from guaranteed; it depends, amongst other things, upon the way in which we populate and analyse the sample data.

From the early 1990s, 'Shaken Baby Syndrome'[63] was defined by the presence of a 'triad' of symptoms in a young child, absent evidence of external trauma:[64] bleeding in the outer membranes of the brain; bleeding at the back of the eye; and a disturbance of brain function. Throughout the decades that followed, police and medical professionals were trained to look for these symptoms, which became a 'proxy for guilt',[65] sometimes for the most serious criminal charges of murder and attempted murder. If the triad was present, 'doctors would routinely testify to complete certainty' that the child had been shaken deliberately.[66]

Despite this confidence, and the significant impact that it had upon criminal trials, the studies from which the triad was constructed were poor: they used small datasets, lacked suitable controls, and adopted inclusion criteria that matched the diagnostic criteria that they sought to validate.[67] In 2003, a study of fifty-seven articles led to the conclusion that the evidence linking the triad to Shaken Baby Syndrome was 'analogous to an inverted pyramid, with a small database (most of it poor-quality original research, retrospective in nature, and without appropriate control groups) spreading to a broad body of somewhat divergent opinions'.[68] The result was a serious risk of misdiagnosis in children and wrongful conviction for caregivers prosecuted by reference to the three features of the triad. In the United Kingdom, the Crown Prosecution Service (CPS) now advises that the triad should be 'approached with caution', and not in any case treated as conclusive evidence that a crime has occurred.[69]

The use of large datasets is no panacea for this risk, that we will draw false inferences from apparent correlations; to the contrary, a bigger data pool means a higher number of plausible correlations, which can fail to hold true once we apply our conclusions to the target population. But we can minimize the risk of this concern by gathering and processing data properly. This means taking steps to ensure that our sample data is sufficiently broad and representative of the wider target population, adopting suitable controls and proxies, and testing the algorithm thoroughly against new data. It also means ensuring that we ascribe the outputs of those processes an appropriate weight and role in our reasoning process, as we navigate the distance between the algorithmic prediction and the eventual decision.

Equality

Egalitarian reasons are reasons to object to differences between the benefits to which people have access, and to try to eliminate or minimize these differences.[70] Chapter 3, Equality discusses two egalitarian reasons that we might have to object to the use of statistical algorithms to make policy decisions, which relate to the way in which we take into account the interests of others, the social status that they occupy, and the attitudes and treatment that follow from that status.

The first reason concerns the duty of equal concern—the duty that certain individuals and institutions owe to have and show equal regard for the interests of everyone within a certain group.[71] That group is defined by the remit of their allocative responsibility: the general obligation arises where an individual or institution owes a duty to provide some good to all members of a particular group,[72] and applies axiomatically (though not exclusively) to the State, to parents, and to those in quasi-parental roles.

Discharging this duty does not require proof of equal treatment; to the contrary, equal treatment may involve a failure of equal concern, if there are good reasons to treat individuals differently from one another. Instead, it requires that departures from equal treatment be justified by some sufficiently compelling reason. For instance, a school should generally require all pupils to sit their examinations under identical conditions, but may decide to allocate more time or different apparatus for pupils with exceptional needs.

The second is status inequality: a set of persistent beliefs about the characteristics or capabilities of certain people or groups of people may lead others to treat them as less entitled to important social or economic benefits. This is the distinctive feature of 'discrimination', as that term is often used, and it is a problem of justice when it results in the exclusion of those affected from opportunities without justification.[73] It hardly needs to be said that these beliefs, and the treatment that they prompt, can often be pervasive and enduring, and can lead to sustained disadvantage.

Problems of status inequality can be coincident with failures of equal concern, but are not circumscribed by the presence of those duties. For instance, a company hiring new employees will rarely owe a duty of equal concern for the interests of all possible candidates. Yet, a practice of limiting the recruitment pool to men may evidence or reinforce a set of unjustified beliefs about the competence of women. That practice is a matter of (in)justice in that women are excluded from valuable opportunities—to be considered for, or to obtain, jobs for which they may be well qualified.

Statistical algorithms can generate inequalities of both kinds. Even if an algorithm produces outcomes that correlate to some worthwhile social goal at a population level, it may nevertheless concentrate the risk of error unjustly upon certain individuals or groups, with the result that those individuals or groups are more likely to be denied benefits for no good reason. This may reveal a failure of equal concern, and/or an underlying set of stigmatizing beliefs and practices. And an algorithm that distributes the risk of error fairly can nevertheless advance the goals of a social policy that is unjust in these ways.

Take a different example, from the sphere of medical treatment: the Model for End State Liver Disease (MELD) is a protocol that is used to prioritize patients for liver transplants. Years after its adoption, studies revealed that the MELD has much higher rates of waitlist mortality for women than for men, a fact that has been attributed to the use of data that were insufficiently nuanced to take account of relevant differences in the characteristics of women.[74] In the context of these predictive and treatment failures, there is a good case for concluding that the development and use of the MELD protocol demonstrates a failure to have and show equal concern for the interests of women.

In a different context, statistical algorithms have been used to guide a range of recruitment decisions that do not involve this kind of predictive failure, but which nevertheless support a set of practices that both reflect and reinforce stigmatizing differences in status. In 2018, Amazon decommissioned a tool that was designed to help uncover passive candidates for recruiters to solicit.[75] The company had used natural language processing to sift resumés, by identifying linguistic features that correlated to hiring success. The algorithm did exactly what it was supposed to do (predict hiring outcomes), with a high level of accuracy for all groups. Yet, because the data upon which it was trained revealed a clear pattern of prioritizing men over equivalently qualified women, the algorithm achieved this goal by identifying a range of adjectival features that were typical of male resumés, and using those features to promote male candidates. The result was a policy that reflected pre-existing practices of discrimination, and reinforced a set of beliefs and practices that involved the systematic exclusion of women from professional opportunities.

Thus, there are a range of ways in which decision-making policies that use statistical algorithms can stem from or reinforce stigmatizing differences in status, and/or demonstrate a failure to show equal concern for the interests of a particular group. These are egalitarian concerns, in that they relate to differences between individuals—the way in which they are perceived and treated, and the benefits to which (in consequence) they have access.

Choice

Chapter 4, Choice is about what else might be wrong with policies that use algorithms like COMPAS to divvy up the burdens of social policies. The reasons considered in this chapter concern the value of choice—of having the chance to influence what happens to us, by responding appropriately when presented with different options about what to do.[76]

The argument of this chapter is not that there is a basic value to freedom or autonomy, which can sometimes require us to make policy burdens contingent upon the exercise of choice. Rather, it is that we can have good reasons to want to have the opportunity to choose, and these reasons can count against policies that make the imposition of burdens contingent on facts that we cannot (or cannot easily) influence. Accordingly, the focus is not upon the choices that we make, but upon the quality of the choices with which we are provided.

Having a choice can be valuable for different sorts of reasons. We will likely enjoy our meal at a restaurant more if we get to choose what we have to eat,[77] and may have a better time on holiday if we choose the destination. These sorts of reasons are instrumental: they concern the way in which (depending on our background, experience, and the position in which we find ourselves), having a choice can improve aspects of our lives, in small or significant ways.

There are also non-instrumental reasons to value choice, some of which are reasons for 'wanting to see features of ourselves manifested in actions and their results'.[78] For instance, we may want to be able to choose how to dress or furnish our living spaces, how to celebrate important moments with our loved ones, or when and how to protest decisions to which we are opposed. These reasons can apply to us even if exercising these choices does not make our lives go better (I might have terrible fashion or décor sense, a dreadful sense of occasion, or an overzealous sense of injustice), because these are ways of expressing our personality, tastes, and preferences.[79]

Finally, denying some people the opportunity to make certain choices—choices that others may be expected to make as a matter of course—can signal that they do not have the maturity or competence to choose well, or otherwise lack the standing in society that other adults hold.[80] For instance, the widespread disenfranchisement of women prior to the mid-twentieth century communicated a general view about the ability of women to participate in public life in a meaningful way. This sort of practice can be objectionable on its own terms, and where it tends to make things worse for people in other ways, including by reinforcing the perception that these individuals are less suitable candidates for certain professional or social opportunities.[81]

These reasons can have particular force in certain contexts that are captured by algorithmic decision-making, including policies of criminal punishment. We have clear instrumental reasons to want punishment to turn on behaviours in which we can choose not to engage, and to be informed and equipped to exercise these choices well. We have representative reasons, to want to have and maintain a range of opportunities for individual expression, which can be curtailed in significant ways by certain forms of punishment. And we have symbolic reasons to want criminal punishment to be related to our status as rational choosers.

Giving people these opportunities, by making punishment contingent upon how people behave when confronted with different options, signals that they have a certain sort of rational competence—that they are able to guide their decisions in accordance with the rules, for their own good and the good of others. By contrast, denying these opportunities, by making punishment contingent upon characteristics over which individuals have little or no influence, signals the contrary—that those who have these characteristics are less competent to choose well, and less deserving of the trust that this competence justifies.

These reasons make a powerful case for wanting our policies of criminal punishment to be responsive to the way in which we behave when we are presented with adequate choices about what to do. The claim is not that we can justify punishing someone who chooses badly, or (vice versa) that we cannot justify punishing someone who has failed for whatever reason to exercise a choice. Rather, it is that we can have good reasons for wanting meaningful opportunities to choose to avoid the burdens of criminal punishment, in light of the various background (social and economic) conditions that shape the availability of routes to a satisfactory life on the right side of the law.[82]

This is what else is wrong with the use of tools like COMPAS to divvy up the burdens of social policies. Policies of algorithmic decision-making use these tools to make actuarial predictions—predictions about the choices that people will make in the future, which in turn affect the burdens that are assigned to them. Yet, these predictions are often informed by a range of facts that have nothing to do with the choices that they have made in the past—facts such as socio-economic circumstances, adverse childhood experiences, or family involvement in crime.

So, when we use these facts to allocate burdens, we not only deny people opportunities that they have significant instrumental reason to value; we also mark them out as less capable of choosing well, and (in light of this shortcoming) less deserving of certain privileges to which others are entitled. As Equivant would have it, those to whom these facts apply—like Goring's Pankhurst prisoners—just belong to a certain sort of criminal 'type', whose base proclivities warrant a certain sort of institutional response.

We have a decision to make about the sort of system that we want to adopt, which must not be obscured by technological advances towards predictive accuracy.[83] One version of that system gives appropriate weight to reasons that we have to want meaningful opportunities to avoid or minimize the burdens of criminal punishment by choosing appropriately. Another version treats criminal proclivity as a fact to be diagnosed from family background and socio-economic circumstance, and criminality as a fait accompli.

Notes

1. Charles Buckman Goring, *The English Convict: A Statistical Study* (His Majesty's Stationery Office 1913) 26.
2. ibid.
3. ibid 27.

4. ibid 7.
5. ibid 24.
6. ibid 157 and 370.
7. ibid 370.
8. ibid 26
9. ibid 371.
10. ibid.
11. See generally Piers Beirne, 'Heredity Versus Environment: A Reconsideration of Charles Goring's The English Convict (1913)' (1988) 28 The British Journal of Criminology 315 and Edwin D Driver, 'Pioneers in Criminology XIV: Charles Buckman Goring (1870–1919)' (1957) 47 Journal of Criminal Law and Criminology 515.
12. Goring (n 1) 373.
13. Goring (n 1) 373, quoted by Gina Lombroso-Ferrero in 'The Results of an Official Investigation Made in England by Dr Goring to Test the Lombroso Theory' (1914) 5 Journal of the American Institute of Criminal Law and Criminology 207, 222.
14. Previously Northpointe.
15. Alexandra Taylor, 'AI Prediction Tools Claim to Alleviate an Overcrowded American Justice System … But Should they be Used' *Stanford Politics* (September 13 2020) <https://stanfordpolitics.org/2020/09/13/ai-prediction-tools-claim-to-alleviate-an-overcrowded-american-justice-system-but-should-they-be-used/> accessed 20 January 2023.
16. See eg Brief of Defendant-Appellant, *State v Loomis* (2015) Ws Ct App AP157-CR, 2015 WL 1724741, 10.
17. See eg Ellora Israni, 'Algorithmic Due Process: Mistaken Accountability and Attribution in *State v Loomis*' *JOLT Digest* (31 August 2017) <https://jolt.law.harvard.edu/digest/algorithmic-due-process-mistaken-accountability-and-attribution-in-state-v-loomis-1> accessed 20 January 2023; Leah Wisser, 'Pandora's Algorithmic Black Box: The Challenges of Using Algorithmic Risk Assessments in Sentencing' (2019) 56 American Criminal Law Review 1811.
18. Northpointe Institute for Public Management, *Measurement and Treatment Implications of COMPAS Core Scales* (Northpointe Institute 2009) 4.
19. ibid.
20. ibid.
21. ibid 13.
22. ibid 10.
23. ibid 22.
24. ibid 10, 16.
25. See generally Equivant, *Practitioner's Guide to COMPAS Core* (Equivant 2019) and Northpointe Institute for Public Management (n 18).
26. Equivant (n 25) Ch 5, 52–61.
27. ibid 3.
28. ibid.
29. ibid.
30. See eg 'COMPAS—Potential Decision Points (County Adult)' in *Electronic Case Reference Manual* (State of Wisconsin Department of Corrections) <https://doc.helpdocsonline.com/arrest-and-adjudication> accessed 12 July 2022.

31. Brief of Defendant-Appellant, *State v Loomis*, 2015AP157-CR (Wis Ct App 2015), 2015 WL 1724741, 29.
32. Pasco County Sheriff's Office, *Intelligence-Led Policing Manual* (Revised edn, PCSO 2018) 14.
33. ibid 13.
34. ibid 72.
35. ibid 13.
36. ibid.
37. ibid 17.
38. ibid.
39. ibid 18.
40. Lynn R Webster and Rebecca M Webster, 'Predicting Aberrant Behaviors in Opioid-Treated Patients: Preliminary Validation of the Opioid Risk Tool' (2005) 6 Pain Medicine 432.
41. ibid.
42. See eg Daniel Kahneman, *Thinking, Fast and Slow* (Penguin 2012) 222 and Theodore R Sarbin, 'A Contribution to the Study of Actuarial and Individual Methods of Prediction' (1943) 48 American Journal of Sociology 593.
43. See generally Kahneman (n 42).
44. See eg Julia Angwin and others, 'Machine Bias' *ProPublica* (23 May 2016) https://www.propublica.org/article/machine-bias-risk-assessments-in-criminal-sentencing accessed 20 January 2023; Safiya Noble, *Algorithms of Oppression: How Search Engines Reinforce Racism* (NYU Press 2018); Sandra Wachter, Brent Mittelstadt, and Chris Russell, 'Counterfactual Explanations Without Opening The Black Box: Automated Decisions and the GDPR' (2018) 31 Harvard Journal of Law & Technology 841, 853; Matthew Le Bui and Safiya Umoja Noble, 'We're Missing a Moral Framework of Justice in Artificial Intelligence: On the Limits, Failings, and Ethics of Fairness' in Markus D Dubber, Frank Pasquale, and Sunit Das (eds), *The Oxford Handbook of Ethics of AI* (OUP 2020); European Commission, *White Paper On Artificial Intelligence—A European Approach to Excellence and Trust* (2020).
45. TM Scanlon, *Why does Inequality Matter?* (OUP 2017) 1. As Binns puts it, '"fairness" as used in the fair machine learning community is best understood as a placeholder term for a variety of normative egalitarian considerations': see Reuben Binns, 'Fairness in Machine Learning: Lessons from Political Philosophy' (2018) 81 Proceedings of Machine Learning Research: Conference on Fairness, Accountability, and Transparency 146.
46. See eg Cathy O'Neil, *Weapons of Math Destruction: How Big Data Increases Inequality and Threatens Democracy* (Broadway Books 2016); Solon Barocas and Andrew D Selbst, 'Big Data's Disparate Impact' (2016) 104 California Law Review 671; Sara Wachter-Boettcher, *Technically Wrong: Sexist Apps, Biased Algorithms, and Other Threats of Toxic Tech* (WW Norton & Co 2017); Virginia Eubanks, *Automating Inequality: How High-Tech Tools Profile, Police and Punish the Poor* (St Martin's Press 2018); Noble (n 44); Le Bui and Noble (n 44); Annette Zimmermann, Elena Di Rosa, and Hochan Kim, 'Technology can't Fix Algorithmic Injustice' *Boston Review* (9 January 2020) <http://bostonreview.net/science-nature-politics/annette-zimmermann-elena-di-rosa-hochan-kim-technology-cant-fix-algorithmic> accessed 20 January 2023.

47. Wachter, Mittelstadt, and Russell (n 44) 853.
48. Julia Angwin and others, 'How We Analyzed the COMPAS Recidivism Algorithm' *ProPublica* (23 May 2016) <https://www.propublica.org/article/how-we-analyzed-the-compas-recidivism-algorithm> accessed 20 January 2023.
49. ibid.
50. William Dieterich, Christina Mendoza, and Tim Brennan, *COMPAS Risk Scales: Demonstrating Accuracy Equity and Predictive Parity* (Northpointe 2016).
51. TM Scanlon, *What We Owe to Each Other* (HUP 1998).
52. ibid 268.
53. TM Scanlon, 'Contractualism and Justification' in Markus Stepanians and Michael Frauchiger (eds), *Reason, Justification, and Contractualism: Themes from Scanlon* (De Gruyter 2021) 38–39.
54. See Thomas Nagel, 'Equality' in *Mortal Questions* (CUP 1979).
55. Scanlon (n 53) 45, 56–57.
56. See eg Scanlon (n 51) 195.
57. Unlike utilitarianism and many other forms of consequentialism, intolerable costs imposed upon some people cannot be outweighed by small but numerous benefits to others: ibid 230. Though on aggregation cf Scanlon (n 53) 57.
58. Scanlon (n 51) 230. Though Scanlon now allows that the number of individuals affected can feed into the justification for a principle or policy in specific ways: Scanlon (n 53) 57.
59. Scanlon (n 51) 230–31.
60. Scanlon (n 53) 44.
61. Scanlon (n 51) 212.
62. See eg Scanlon (n 53) 58 and Scanlon (n 51) 196.
63. Now termed 'non-accidental head injury'. See eg Crown Prosecution Service, 'Non Accidental Head Injury Cases (NAHI, formerly referred to as Shaken Baby Syndrome [SBS])—Prosecution Approach' (*Crown Prosecution Service*, 5 November 2021) <https://www.cps.gov.uk/legal-guidance/non-accidental-head-injury-cases-nahi-formerly-referred-shaken-baby-syndrome-sbs> accessed 20 January 2023.
64. Deborah Tuerkheimer, *Flawed Convictions: 'Shaken Baby Syndrome' and the Inertia of Injustice* (OUP 2014) xi.
65. ibid 4.
66. ibid 298.
67. Mark Donohoe, 'Evidence-based Medicine and Shaken Baby Syndrome: Part I: Literature Review, 1966–1998' (2003) 24 The American Journal of Forensic Medicine and Pathology 239.
68. ibid.
69. See eg Crown Prosecution Service (n 63).
70. Scanlon (n 45) 1.
71. ibid ch 2.
72. ibid 11.
73. ibid 26.
74. CynthiaA Moylan and others, 'Disparities in Liver Transplantation before and after Introduction of the MELD Score' (2008) 300 Journal of the American Medical Association 2371.

75. Jeffrey Dastin, 'Amazon scraps secret AI recruiting tool that showed bias against women' *Reuters* (11 October 2018) <https://www.reuters.com/article/us-amazon-com-jobs-automation-insight-idUSKCN1MK08G> accessed 20 January 2023.
76. Scanlon (n 51) 255.
77. ibid 251; Emmanuel Voyiakis, *Private Law and the Value of Choice* (Bloomsbury 2017) 106.
78. Scanlon (n 51) 252.
79. Voyiakis (n 77) 120.
80. Scanlon (n 51) 253. See also Voyiakis (n 77) 120.
81. Scanlon (n 51) 252–53; Voyiakis (n 77) 107.
82. Scanlon (n 51) 264.
83. See eg Bernard E Harcourt, *Against Prediction* (University of Chicago Press 2008) 31.

2
Relevance

The Fire Tells the Story

In 1962, Gerald Hurst blew up his laboratory at Cambridge University.[1] Hurst's research involved 'high-energy' chemistry—explosives, incendiaries, and rocket propellants—and one of his early fluorochemical experiments was a little too successful.[2] Hurst was hauled in front of his college dean, and nearly lost the chance to complete his doctoral thesis. But complete it he did, before moving on to an illustrious military career. Working on what he calls 'the dark side of arson', Hurst created an explosive to retrofit napalm bombs, and developed new ways for undercover agents in Vietnam to build bombs using materials that could be sourced locally.[3]

Yet, as the years passed, Hurst began to feel uncomfortable with his earlier career choices. A new post as the Atlas Powder Company's chief scientist gave him an unfamiliar commodity—free time, and the chance to use it for good. Hurst spent much of it providing pro bono consulting services to those who had been convicted of arson using unreliable forensic techniques.[4]

In 2004, Hurst came across Cameron Todd Willingham's case. Willingham had been convicted of the murders of his three young children, each of whom fell victim to a house fire in 1991. Willingham maintained his innocence throughout his arrest and detention, and refused to accept a plea deal. He was sentenced to capital punishment, and Hurst received the case file just a few weeks before Willingham was due to be executed.[5]

At trial, investigators cited several pieces of evidence that had been widely accepted as indicators of arson throughout the 1980s:[6] a 'V-shape' scorch mark on the walls of Willingham's house, supposedly signalling the sort of 'fast-developing, hot fires' typical of arson; a 'pour pattern' and puddle-shaped burn line, thought to be caused by liquid fire accelerant; and other marks that the investigators treated as clear evidence of multiple points of origin, an indication that the fire had been started deliberately.[7]

Certain witness remarks stood out to Hurst: the neighbours had described a forceful explosion, flames suddenly bursting from the shattered windows of

Artificial Justice. Tatiana Dancy, Oxford University Press. © Tatiana Dancy 2023.
DOI: 10.1093/oso/9780192846891.003.0002

the house.[8] This is called a 'flashover',[9] and it occurs when a fire becomes so hot (about 550 degrees Celsius) that the contents of the building spontaneously combust. This was the evidence that put Hurst in mind of the Lime Street Fire, which had marked a turning point in arson investigation a year before Willingham's arrest.

In 1990, arson expert John Lentini had been called in by police to assist with a criminal investigation.[10] At that time, Gerald Wayne Lewis was suspected of deliberately starting a fire in which six people had died, including Lewis' wife. Lewis claimed that the fire had been started accidentally, when his young son dropped matches on the couch. But the evidence of arson seemed to be mounting: a V-shape burn, puddle configurations, and a flashover burn.

To disprove Lewis' version of events, the prosecution purchased a condemned house next door to the site of the investigation, and set about recreating the fire scene. They installed a similar couch, and set it on fire using matches. At the time, the prevailing theory was that an accidental fire would burn more slowly, so that flashover temperatures would take longer to reach. This fire reached flashover in less than five minutes. After it, the 'arson' signs were all there—a V-shaped mark, and the pour patterns and puddle configurations that investigators had attributed to fire accelerant. In one moment, Lentini went from being (in his words) 'prepared to testify and send this guy to Old Sparky' to the horrified realization that he had 'almost sent a man to die based on theories that were a load of crap'.[11] The charges against Lewis were dropped.

As Lentini later put it, the Lime Street experiment 'changed the books on fire science'.[12] In 1992, he published a short paper in the main industry circular that was widely read by investigators and researchers in arson and related fields of forensic science.[13] Very soon, it was 'common knowledge' amongst arson investigators that flashover and post-flashover burning, however caused, could produce patterns that looked identical to those caused by liquid fire accelerant.[14]

Lentini went on to write the *Scientific Protocols for Fire Investigation*,[15] a new manual for fire investigators. That book, now in its third edition, contains extensive commentary on the 'myths' about arson indicators that had developed over the years leading up to the Lime Street fire: 'crazed glass indicated rapid heating';[16] shiny alligator blisters or spalling (broken cement, brick, or concrete) was 'incontrovertible evidence of the presence of an ignitable liquid';[17] a sharp V-angle burn mark meant that 'the fire had to have been set because of its speed';[18] and a puddle-shaped line of demarcation meant a liquid fire accelerant.[19] Lentini connects each of these arson indicators to a single 'major misconception'—that accelerated fires burn hotter and faster than natural fires.[20]

Lentini argues that these myths and misconceptions stem from the human tendency to make 'unwarranted generalizations' from limited data.[21] For example, he says, 'an investigator might observe that in a garage fire, a pattern of spalling surrounds the remains of a gasoline container and make an association of gasoline with spalling. The next time that spalling is observed, he infers that gasoline must have been involved.'[22] Lentini explains that this practice is then reinforced by the repetition of these false conclusions by practitioners, creating the appearance of legitimacy.[23]

In cognitive science, the term 'bias' doesn't connote inequality; rather, it describes any deviation from logically sound reasoning that is commonly observed amongst humans.[24] Two biases are particularly relevant in this context: 'illusory correlation',[25] the tendency to overestimate the strength and/or significance of relationships between two groups of facts; and 'causal thinking',[26] the tendency to attribute causal explanations, however implausible, to those perceived correlations. These biases are often at work in commonplace situations. For instance, a survey of 2,400 US sports fans found that 62 per cent had blamed themselves (often for clothing or seating choices) for their team's loss,[27] and half of those had blamed friends or family—often banishing them from the room for the duration of an important game.[28]

Humans are not alone in our overeager tendency to draw causal conclusions from limited data. In the early twentieth century, a young orangutan named Julius was subjected to one of the first systematic experiments on primate intelligence.[29] Julius was required to navigate through a maze by following a series of directional instructions. If he navigated the route successfully and entered the designated box, he would receive a reward (Julius was partial to peanuts). Failure meant confinement, or a long route back to start again.

On one occasion, his observers, a team led by American psychologist Robert Yerkes, recorded 'a curiously interesting bit of behaviour'.[30] Julius, perhaps understandably bored with the whole ordeal, made a neat pirouette before entering the correct box. Success! Julius received his reward. Yet, on subsequent attempts, he would simply spin around and stop, entering a box at random, or none at all. Yerkes later wrote that Julius' association between route choice and reward had been replaced with a new belief about the causal mechanism: pirouettes = peanuts.

Three decades later, psychologist and pioneering behaviourist Burrhus Frederic Skinner developed an experiment to test for this kind of behaviour, this time in domestic pigeons. In an article aptly named 'Superstition in the

Pigeon',[31] Skinner recounted an experiment in which hungry pigeons were fed by clockwork. Skinner noted they began to perform odd rituals, such as swinging their bodies from side to side like a pendulum, and nodding their heads vigorously. He described these activities as 'a sort of superstition': 'The bird behaves as if there were a causal relation between its behavior and the presentation of food, although such a relation is lacking.'[32]

Some of Skinner's later experiments with pigeons, including his attempt to develop a pigeon-guided glide bomb during the Second World War, were a little less successful.[33] But this one made waves in the then-nascent field of cognitive science. Other have since criticized the anthropomorphic label 'superstition' and the conscious processing attributed to it, as well as Skinner's explanation for the precise mechanism generating the conditioned response.[34] Nevertheless, the broad account has passed into general use, as an example of the way in which the perception of the conditions and mechanisms for a particular outcome can be influenced by a few propitious coincidences.

The arson investigators at whom Lentini directed his criticisms had developed decision-making principles from precisely the same sort of cognitive mistakes as those made by Julius, the acrobatic orangutan and Skinner's hungry pigeons: they drew general inferences about burn patterns from localized correlations and attributed (in this case sinister) causal explanations to them. The Lime Street experiment showed with absolute clarity that the very same burn patterns that had been identified as indicators of arson could, in fact, stem from accidental or natural fires.

Willingham was convicted in 1992,[35] the same year in which Lentini's groundbreaking paper was published. The damning evidence was provided by two investigators: assistant fire chief Douglas Fogg and deputy fire marshal Manuel Vasquez. At trial, Vasquez testified that 'most all of' the 1500 fires that he had investigated involved arson—this compared with rates of around 50 per cent for the State of Texas.[36] According to Vasquez, this simply showed that he was better than the average investigator at mediating the truth. 'The fire tells the story',[37] he told the court; 'I am just the interpreter'.[38]

The evidence provided by Fogg and Vasquez mirrored the evidence in the Lime Street fire almost perfectly. Yet, the investigators were either unaware or unmoved by Lentini's publication and the shifting discourses and arson investigation practices in other parts of the country. For Fogg and Vasquez, the V-shaped 'origin' mark, pour patterns, and puddle configurations pointed to only one explanation: the fire burned with 'intense heat' because of a liquid accelerant.[39] The jury deliberated for less than an hour before returning a verdict: Willingham, the only suspect, was guilty.

Hurst wrote a 'scathing report', condemning the evidence as 'a whole series of old wives' tales' that had been disproved by Lentini's research.[40] The investigators, he said, had ignored contradictory evidence and failed to rule out innocent explanations.[41] When the Innocence Project later hired John Lentini and three other leading fire investigators to conduct an independent review of the evidence, they agreed: 'each and every one' of the indicators of arson relied upon to convict Willingham had been 'scientifically proven to be invalid'.[42]

Hurst's report was sent to the Texas Board of Pardons and Paroles. The Board convenes in private, and does not publish its deliberations. Board members are under no obligation to review materials sent to them, and usually cast their votes by fax. Between 1976 and 2004, when Willingham's petition was filed, only one application for clemency was approved by the State of Texas. It wasn't Willingham's. At 4pm on 17 February 2004, Cameron Todd Willingham received his final meal—barbequed pork ribs, onion rings, fried okra, beef enchiladas, and lemon cream pie. At 6.20pm, his heart stopped beating.

It is now estimated that hundreds, perhaps thousands, of people have been wrongfully convicted and imprisoned because of fire investigation 'mythology'.[43] And arson investigation is not the only forensic method that has such a marked effect on the dispensation of justice in particular cases. In 1995, Kennedy Brewer was convicted of the murder of Christine Jackson, the three-year-old daughter of Brewer's girlfriend.[44] This time, the damning testimony came from one Michael West, a forensic odontologist (an individual with specialist training in the application of dentistry to forensics). West testified that several bite marks on Jackson's body were 'without a doubt' indentations from Brewer's top two teeth.[45] In 2001, advanced DNA testing excluded Brewer as a possible suspect, and a panel of forensic experts who had been called in to re-examine the evidence concluded that the victim's wounds were not human bites at all; they were caused by crayfish 'nibbling on the corpse'.[46] In 2008, Brewer was exonerated after fifteen years in prison.

We may be able to justify adopting a policy that requires some people to bear certain costs, for the sake of some comparative benefit—a way of allowing others to avoid the weightier costs that would be imposed by a different policy.[47] For instance, once a COVID-19 vaccine had been developed and earmarked for widespread public distribution, many national governments instituted a vaccination scheme that required the majority of citizens to wait longer to receive a vaccine (with associated risk of intermediate harm) to allow the most vulnerable to be protected as a matter of priority against the more significant mortality risks that they faced. Those vulnerable groups were identified by specific criteria, such as age and/or certain kinds of co-morbidity.

But we can only justify a policy on the basis that it brings about some benefit if it actually has that effect, or (*ex ante*) we have good reason for believing that it will. So, we must show that there is a rational link between the selection criteria that we use to distribute burdens and the avoided cost, whatever it is. For COVID-19 vaccination programmes, this meant proving some sound deductive or inductive basis for thinking that: (1) age and/or co-morbidity did in fact put individuals at a greater risk of harm; and (2) priority vaccination was an effective means of mitigating that risk.

In the context of criminal punishment, the costs that decision-subjects must bear are amongst some of those most significant that a public institution can impose—the loss of personal freedom and associated privileges, the right to important forms of civil participation, and (under certain conditions in some jurisdictions) the loss of life. Those costs are imposed for the sake of avoiding a range of personal and property harms, and providing the reassurance and social stability that comes with making this protection available. Justifying a particular policy of criminal punishment requires us to show that this policy will in fact avoid those costs, and that (if avoided) they outweigh the costs of punishment.

This chapter is concerned with the first, simpler, task: to justify a policy that singles some people out to bear some burden for the sake of certain benefits, we must show that there is a rational link between the selection criteria—the people to whom and conditions under which those burdens are allocated—and the benefits at which we aim. And to justify a particular decision made by reference to a justified policy, we must show that the policy has been applied with sufficient accuracy—in a way that singles out the right people, in the right way.

Vasquez, Fogg, and West were making a contribution to this evidential component of the decision: their role was to supply an opinion about the likelihood that the scene in question involved deliberate harm (in Willingham's case), or that a particular individual was involved (in Brewer's). There were answers to these questions, but that knowledge was not available to those tasked with making that decision—law enforcement, and later jury members as part of the judicial process. The forensic experts were brought in to supply that missing link in the chain.

With the benefit of hindsight, we can see that they failed to do this: the burn patterns upon which Vasquez and Fogg based their conclusions were not the sinister markers of arson, but rather the random effects of a post-flashover accidental fire; the 'dental impressions' that West identified were merely the marks of opportunistic crustaceans. There was no rational connection between these facts and the social goal designed to be served by criminal incarceration and (in Willingham's case) execution, and no good reason *ex ante* for believing that such a connection existed.

But the experts didn't misidentify that connection for any unusual or surprising reason. They were culpable, but not of ill-motivation or wilful blindness; rather, they simply took insufficient care to ward against ordinary cognitive mistakes, and the hubris with which they gave testimony influenced a judicial process that led to the most severe consequences for those affected. We face risks that sit somewhere on this spectrum whenever we make decisions about how to treat others in situations of uncertainty, risks that can only be mitigated to a certain degree by professional training and context.[48]

In this chapter, we will see that statistics and rules developed on the basis of statistical inferences can help us to conduct more rigorous assessments about the likelihood that our target variable will coincide with certain facts, and therefore to reach better decisions about how to treat others when we are otherwise unsure about the rational significance of certain facts. In the context of forensics, this includes DNA matching—scientific techniques for isolating genetic markers, supported by simple statistical rules that allow experts to draw (more or less) reliable conclusions about the probability that a given individual was the source of some blood sample. But we will also see that whether they do have this effect in practice depends upon our techniques for gathering and processing data, and translating our predictions into conclusions about what to do.

The Lure of Blame

In the early hours of 15 August 2016, Craig Stillwell and Carla Roberts woke to the sounds of their baby daughter, Effie, screaming.[49] By the time the paramedics arrived, she was pale, limp, and barely responsive. The hospital found no external injuries, but identified what had come to be known as the 'triad' of symptoms that defined Shaken Baby Syndrome (SBS): subdural haematoma (bleeding in the outer membranes between the brain and the skull); retinal haemorrhage (bleeding at the back of the eye); and encephalopathy (a disturbance of brain function).[50] At around 3pm, officers from the Thames Valley Police arrived at the hospital, and Craig was placed under arrest for grievous bodily harm. Effie was discharged into foster care a month after her admission to hospital.

In 1971, paediatric neurosurgeon Arthur Norman Guthkelch published the thesis that would be the foundation of SBS.[51] He reviewed thirteen cases of infant subdural haematoma, five of which showed no signs of physical violence. Guthkelch thought that the bleeding identified in these cases could have been caused by physical shaking, and recommended that doctors pursue further enquiries 'however guardedly or tactfully' with the parents of children presenting with these symptoms, even when there were 'no marks of injury at all'.[52]

Shortly afterwards, American paediatric radiologist John Caffey published two articles on the 'whiplash-shaking and jerking of abused infants',[53] in which he sought to explain 'an extraordinary diagnostic contradiction'—bleeding and swelling in the brain and eyes, 'in the absence of signs of external trauma to the head'.[54] Caffey's answer lay in the 'indirect acceleration-deceleration traction stresses such as whiplash-shaking of the head'.[55] Caffey proposed a 'nationwide educational campaign', and even wrote some rhyming couplets to go with it: 'Guard well your baby's precious head; Shake, jerk and slap it never; Lest you bruise his brain and twist his mind; Or whiplash him dead, forever.'[56]

Caffey did not conclude that subdural haemorrhage could only be caused by shaking, merely that it was almost always due to trauma of some kind—whether intentional or accidental.[57] He noted that 'the evidence on which our concepts of the pathogenicity of infant-shaking is based does not lend itself to satisfactory statistical analysis'.[58] Nevertheless, when the nationwide campaign that Caffey envisaged finally took place in 1993,[59] the American Academy of Pediatrics recommended a 'medical presumption of child abuse when a child younger than 1 year of age' presented with the triad.[60] The result was striking: SBS cases involved doctors establishing whether an illegal act had occurred. It was, in essence, 'the diagnosis of a crime'.[61]

Prosecutors across the United States were given extensive training on the steps of identifying, investigating, and pursuing charges in cases of subdural and retinal bleeding.[62] And the presumption of child abuse quickly became something more: if the three features of the triad were present, doctors would 'routinely testify to complete certainty' that the child had been deliberately shaken.[63] By 2015, the triad had become a 'proxy for guilt',[64] with 1600 convictions for crimes based on SBS in the United States alone,[65] and at least three capital punishment sentences.[66]

Yet, two decades of accumulated evidence has challenged the accepted explanation of the mechanism behind SBS. In 2003, Mark Donohoe assessed the quality of the prevailing evidence at that time—54 articles, citing a total of 307 cases.[67] Donohoe noted that many of these studies 'made the obvious logical error of selecting cases by the presence of the very clinical findings and test results they seek to validate as diagnostic'.[68] He added that the 'gold standard'—some method of identifying cases of in which shaking had occurred, and appropriate control groups involving accidental or natural harm—had been achieved in none.[69]

Donohoe's conclusion was damning: the evidence linking SBS to the triad was 'analogous to an inverted pyramid, with a small database (most of it poor-quality original research, retrospective in nature, and without appropriate control groups) spreading to a broad body of somewhat divergent opinions'.[70] Echoing Lentini's concerns about appearance of validity that repetition lent to arson mythology, he wrote that 'one may need reminding that repeated opinions based on poor-quality data cannot improve the quality of evidence'.[71] In 2016, Donohue's findings were verified by a large-scale review, assessing 1065 research papers on the subject of SBS. Researchers did not doubt that SBS could be caused by shaking, but found 'very low-quality scientific evidence' for the hypothesis that the triad alone evidenced deliberate harm.[72]

In 2017, Carla Andrews received the results of a series of blood tests: Carla and Effie both had Ehlers-Danlos Syndrome (EDS), and Effie had a type of EDS that results in a collagen deficit affecting formation of the vascular system, which is known to cause spontaneous bleeds.[73] In April 2017, Buckinghamshire County Council sought to withdraw its application for a care order for Effie. Emphasizing Effie's predisposition to 'vascular fragility',[74] the judge gave her permission, and Effie was returned to her parents' care.

Justice is sometimes described as an 'individualistic' exercise, concerned with the 'assessment of individual outcomes by individualized criteria'.[75] This looks like a very poor fit for the practice of using statistics to make decisions about how to treat other people. As a science, 'statistics' is concerned with amassing numerical data about a subset of some population, for the purpose of making inferences about the wider population from which it was drawn. Accordingly, when we use statistics to make decisions about how to treat certain people, we are by definition basing that decision on facts about people other than the decision-subject—facts about the group to which they belong, with whose characteristics they share. And in Scanlon's words: 'statistical facts about the group to which a person belongs do not always have the relevant justificatory force'.[76]

But we should be clear about the nature of this objection. We are often justified in making decisions about how to treat people on the basis of those characteristics that the decision-subject shares with some wider group. For instance, the United Kingdom's COVID-19 vaccination distribution programme contained a set of clear priority rules, which were based on statistical evidence about risk factors for serious illness and mortality—largely, age and comorbidity. The decision about whether to offer a vaccine to a particular person was an 'individual' assessment, which was also about the characteristics (eg age or the presence of a particular medical condition) that this patient shared with others.

So, the task of 'assessing individual outcomes by individualised criteria' does not require us to ignore facts about people other than the decision-subject that are rationally related to the social benefit at which we aim. Nor does it require us to consider information about the decision-subject that does not bear on that goal: those charged with distributing and administering COVID-19 vaccines did not have to take into account hair colour, musical preferences, or artistic skills. Rather, we must ensure that decision-making policies and practices capture facts that are relevant to the justification for a particular policy, pitched at a level of granularity that can capture both individual reasons for action, and the systemic effects of adopting a particular policy.

'Relevant', here, does not mean that we must provide a causal explanation for how and why our selection criteria bear on that goal. Indeed, this is precisely the logical gap that we often seek to fill when we turn to statistics. We show that a fact is relevant when we show that a decision made by incorporating it helps us to avoid some cost. Or, absent direct evidence of this kind, relevant criteria may be those that correlate to a higher incidence of some cost that we have a reliable strategy for avoiding. For instance, if a justified policy of distributing COVID-19 vaccines limits the risk of mortality and serious illness without imposing intolerable costs on those who are deprioritized, relevant criteria are those that (when vaccines are distributed by reference to those criteria) correlate to lower incidences of mortality and serious illness, or which correlate to higher incidences of mortality and serious illness that we expect to be able to mitigate through vaccination.

This distinction between deduction from what we know and inference from what we perceive maps a philosophical debate about whether we are ever justified in believing conclusions that are merely derived by inference from patterns that we observe in the world around us. Bertrand Russell gave a famous example of the chicken who expects to be fed each morning, having experienced nothing else for the duration of its short life. One day, the farmer instead comes to wring the chicken's neck.[77] Russell concluded that 'more refined views as to the uniformity of nature would have been useful to the chicken'[78] (although precisely how the better-informed chicken would have avoided its fate is not altogether clear).

But our quest is not the epistemologist's: we are not concerned with belief or knowledge for its own sake, but rather with the best route to justified decisions in the realm of uncertainty. Like Russell's chicken, we are often required to shape our actions on the basis of limited information. Unlike the chicken, we have meaningful choices about what to do on the basis of this information—choices that may include how to treat others in light of some benefit at which we aim. In this context, uncertainty (quite a lot of it) is tolerable, as long as we are able to make a better assessment of the conditions under which we will achieve that benefit than we would if we relied upon unaided human decision-making. And at this juncture, it bears emphasis that even fairly simplistic rules developed on the basis of statistical inferences can do a better job of predicting how a target variable will be influenced by the presence of certain facts than nuanced and individualized human judgement.

In 1943, Sarbin published the results of a study comparing the success of 'actuarial' and 'clinical' methods of making predictions.[79] The goal of the exercise was to determine which method would predict academic achievement more accurately. To conduct the experiment, Sarbin chose a sample of 162 college freshmen, and recorded honour-point ratios at the end of the first quarter of their freshman year.[80] The actuarial assessments adopted in the study were made on the basis of a limited and basic set of statistical rules—by entering high school percentile rank and college aptitude test score into a two-variable regression equation. Individual assessments were made by the university's clinical counsellors, and included a far broader range of variables: an interviewer's form and impressions; test scores for aptitude, achievement, vocation, and personality; and the counsellor's own impressions.

Sarbin found that the actuarial method was, by a small margin, more successful than the clinical method at predicting academic achievement. He concluded that 'any jury sitting in judgment on the case of the clinical versus the actuarial methods must on the basis of efficiency and economy declare overwhelmingly in favour of the statistical method for predicting academic achievement'.[81]

Many other studies have produced similar results across a range of different areas of decision-making.[82] Conrad and Satter compared statistical and discretionary predictions about the success of naval trainees in an electrician's mate school.[83] They pitted the output of a two-variable regression equation (electrical knowledge and arithmetic reasoning test scores) against the predictions of interviewers on the basis of test scores, personal history data, and interview impressions. Their conclusions favoured the statistical method.

So, statistics and statistical rules can help us to make predictions about the coincidence of some individual characteristic and our target variable, which can help us to formulate a policy that achieves some benefit. But this is far from guaranteed; whether they do so in a given case turns on whether the apparent correlations upon which we rely to do so are, or are sufficiently likely to be, repeated across our target population. We have already seen that humans are prone to hallucinating patterns in data, and imbuing those perceived patterns with undue significance. Those risks are not eliminated by the use of statistics, nor by a wider data-sample; on the contrary, the more data we have, the greater are the number and range of possible coincidences.

We can reduce these risks by taking a number of steps to ensure that the processes that we use to gather and analyse data are sufficiently robust. Some of these steps relate to the justification for extrapolating from our sample population; this includes ensuring that our dataset is sufficiently broad and representative of the target population, and that any proxies are justified in their own turn by some deductive or inductive relationship to the target variable(s). Others relate to the reasons that we have for ruling out a number of other possible explanations for an apparent correlation; this includes identifying and incorporating appropriate controls.

The temptation to short-circuit these processes in pursuit of answers can be particularly strong in cases that, like SBS, involve serious harm to those most vulnerable. Deborah Tuerkheimer calls this the 'lure of blame': 'Rather than confront the absence of a wrongdoer, we identify a perpetrator who can be held responsible for awful circumstances. This tendency often results in misperceptions of causation.'[84] No doubt, many of those accused of SBS-related crimes were guilty. But the triad of facts used to secure convictions lacked the statistical foundation necessary to demonstrate the requisite connection. In the absence of reliable inclusion criteria and controls for the studies from which the triad was drawn, it was not possible to be sufficiently confident that serious wrongdoing corresponded in all or most cases to the presence of subdural haematoma, retinal haemorrhage, and encephalopathy.

So, statistical facts about the group to which our decision-subject belongs often *do* have the relevant justificatory force. But the strength of this connection to our social goal depends on a range of factors that concern the quality of our processes of data-gathering and interpretation. Unless we are rigorous about these processes, we will make the same mistakes as those that we considered above—drawing causal inferences from insufficient data, sometimes with life-changing consequences for those affected.

The Phantom of Heilbronn

From 1993 until 2009, police agencies across multiple European countries pursued a suspected serial killer and prolific thief, dubbed the 'Phantom of Heilbronn'. Her DNA had been recovered from a range of items from forty diverse crime scenes, including: a toy pistol after the 2004 robbery of Vietnamese gemstone traders in Arbois, France; the remnants of a cookie in a trailer that had been broken in to on the night of 24 October 2001 in Budenheim, Germany; and a teacup in Schlenger, Austria, at the scene of a murder involving ligature strangulation. Investigators were unable to agree upon any characteristics that united these crimes, let alone a possible motive for them.

After sixteen years of resource-intensive investigative work, a clue was uncovered: investigators found the Phantom's DNA in fingerprints on a male asylum seeker's application.[85] That was the first sign that something had gone amiss in the process of DNA gathering and analysis. Heilbronn's Phantom, it turned out, was a female employee at the factory that manufactured the cotton swabs used to collect DNA samples. Her DNA had survived the sterilization process, remaining in sufficient quantity to confound investigators.

DNA (deoxyribonucleic acid) is a biological code that programmes how we develop, grow, and function. A small difference in DNA goes a long way: humans share 50 per cent of our DNA with trees, 80 per cent with cows, and 90 per cent with the Abyssinian domestic cat. Human DNA is 99.9 per cent identical, but the remaining 0.1 per cent marks us out as unique—and it is this unique part of our DNA that is used to generate a DNA profile for the purposes of genealogy and forensics.

In the summer of 1984, Alec Jeffreys, then a young researcher at Leicester University, was searching for ways to trace genetic profiles through family lineages. Jeffreys discovered a small fragment of DNA that was repeated at the same position ('locus') on different chromosomes. This fragment turned out to be a 'completely individual specific pattern'.[86] With this pattern, researchers could for the first time produce 'DNA "fingerprints"': a DNA profile that was either completely unique, or shared only by identical twins.[87]

Jeffreys wrote later that he spent the afternoon of his discovery 'running round the lab pricking my finger and leaving blood spots all over the place— a sort of mock "scene of the crime"' to test whether DNA could be sampled by police for the purposes of human identification.[88] Needless to say, that experiment was a success, and the next decade saw a rapid expansion of DNA testing methods, which have been used both to convict and exonerate criminal defendants. Since 1989, 500 DNA exonerations have taken place in the

United States alone.[89] Half of those convictions were secured by other forensic methods, including bite-mark, blood spatter, and hair follicle analysis.[90]

DNA matching uses a simple equation. Let us suppose that a DNA sample (sample 1) has been retrieved from a crime scene and processed by a laboratory. The police have identified a suspect (X), and ask the laboratory to compare a sample of X's DNA (sample 2) to sample 1. The laboratory returns a match: samples 1 and 2 correspond at every locus tested. To use that information as part of a criminal prosecution, we might wish to figure out the chances of a coincidence—just how likely it is that such a match could be returned even if sample 1 did not contain X's DNA.

Because each DNA locus is independent, we can apply the product rule for probabilities: if someone has the DNA type ABC, the probability of someone having a matching DNA type is A x B x C. This gives the RMP (Random Match Probability) of the genotype—the probability that a person, selected at random from the population, has a matching profile. The smaller that probability, the greater the likelihood that the two DNA samples tested came from the same person. This rule can be expressed as an equation (A x B x C = RMP), or as a set of instructions for a human or computer to follow.

When performed correctly on samples derived from a single source, DNA matching can be highly accurate. Yet, contamination and processing errors occur in around 0.5 per cent of cases, and are not always detected at the time at which the match result is returned.[91] Given the relative weight that is attributed to DNA evidence, this can have disastrous effects for suspects and defendants.

In 2017, Roy Verret was arrested for the murder of Howard Poche, after the victim's blood was found on Verret's washing machine.[92] Verret had only a passing acquaintance with Poche, and the blood sample was the only physical evidence tying him to the crime. The defendant's lawyer, Mr Singer, noticed something odd about the laboratory DNA results: when the murder weapon (a knife) and the washing machine were processed by the lab, only the latter showed evidence of blood. Singer offered an explanation, which would take three years to prove: a crime lab analyst had mixed up the two DNA samples. Singer was eventually vindicated, and Verret exonerated—but only after the latter had spent three years in a maximum-security prison.

Even if there are no processing errors, and we conclude that there is a high probability that samples 1 and 2 derive from the same person, we cannot necessarily be confident that sample 1 arrived at the crime scene by physical contact with the suspect. The increasing sensitivity of DNA gathering processes has created a heightened risk that the incriminating DNA was in fact transported indirectly (so-called 'DNA transfer'). In one study, researchers considered whether DNA transfer might confound evidence in investigations concerning child abuse. Researchers washed underwear with sheets containing bodily fluids, and found that sufficient amounts of DNA to yield complete genetic profiles could be innocently deposited onto a child's clothing through laundry.[93]

When it comes to perceptions of accuracy, there is clear evidence that jurors tend to have too much confidence in DNA matching as a forensic tool, attributing 'greater weight to it than it is capable of bearing'.[94] The disparity between the accuracy of DNA match statistics and human perception can be aggravated when numbers are small, or when jurors are not given specific information about laboratory error rates.[95] These mistakes are remarkably persistent: post-trial judicial instructions have a negligible impact on jurors' perceptions of culpability.[96]

Moreover, the use of DNA match statistics in the context of a criminal trial requires a relatively sophisticated understanding of the role that statistics play in decisions about guilt or innocence. The RMP must be combined with the laboratory accuracy rate and any background probability (given the presence of other information pertinent to the trial), and then used to navigate the distance between predictions about the defendant's involvement with the crime scene and conclusions about their role in any wrongdoing.

Accordingly, there are many ways in which a set of accurate DNA results can be misused by those tasked with translating predictions into decisions. In one study, a number of participants committed the 'prosecutor's fallacy', which can be exemplified as follows: if a defendant and perpetrator share a blood type found in 10 per cent of the population, there is a 10 per cent chance the defendant would have this blood type if innocent and thus a 90 per cent chance that they are guilty.[97] That conclusion is, of course, false; there will be a great deal of other information pertinent to the question of guilt, which we ignore when we make such simple leaps of judgement.

On the flipside, there is a great deal of evidence that many people underestimate the importance of incidence rate statistics when dealing with forensic information. Let us suppose that we have evidence that a wrongdoer has a particular blood type. That blood type is shared by 10 per cent of the local population, including our suspect. In a city with a population of 100,000, that means around 10,000 people can be expected to share the same blood type. In consequence, many people will conclude that there is very little probative value to the evidence.[98] This mistake is part of a broader tendency to overlook base-rate statistics. In fact, if the prior probability of guilt was 20 per cent, application of Bayes' theorem (an accepted formula for calculating probability) to the new evidence increases that probability to 0.71 (71 per cent).[99]

When translating evidence about RMP to probability of guilt, we also have to grapple with the 'anchoring' effect of numbers: once read or heard, a number can have an undue influence upon the conclusion that we reach, even in a professional context.[100] In one experiment, professional judges were asked to roll dice before recommending a sentence for a particular shoplifting offence.[101] The judges were not aware that the dice were loaded: they would only reveal a combined total of three or nine. On average, those who rolled a 9 recommended a sentence of eight months, whilst those who rolled a 3 recommended a sentence of five months. This anchoring effect can make us particularly vulnerable to overestimating the likelihood of guilt when the RMP is low.

So, when we aim at relevance—at the case for thinking that a given policy of algorithmic decision-making brings about the social good at which we aim—we should not only ensure that our data-gathering and analysis are rigorous; we should also be concerned with the way in which the algorithmic output is used by those who have the task of translating it into a decision about what to do. Even if the algorithm does its job well, the decision may be unjust if we fail to assign appropriate weight to the output, given what we know about the limitations of its accuracy, or the way in which it relates to the question at hand.

Notes

1. David Grann, 'Trial by Fire: Did Texas Execute an Innocent Man?' *New Yorker* (31 August 2009) <https://www.newyorker.com/magazine/2009/09/07/trial-by-fire> accessed 20 January 2023.
2. Gerald Hurst, 'Death by Fire' *Frontline* (15 January 2010) <https://www.pbs.org/wgbh/pages/frontline/death-by-fire/interviews/gerald-hurst.html> accessed 20 January 2023.
3. ibid.
4. ibid.
5. Grann (n 1).
6. See eg John F Boudreau and others, *Arson and Arson Investigation Survey and Assessment* (National Institute of Law Enforcement and Criminal Justice, United States Department of Justice 1977).
7. Statement of Facts in *State of Texas v Cameron Todd Willingham* (1991) Tex13th D 24240–CR XI, 159–268; Grann (n 1).
8. Statement of Facts in *State of Texas v Cameron Todd Willingham* (1991) Tex13th D 24240–CR XI, 60.
9. See eg Hurst (n 2).
10. Grann (n 1).
11. Phoebe Judge, 'Lime Street', This is Criminal, Episode 135. https://thisiscriminal.com/episode-135-527-lime-street-3-6-2020/ accessed 20 January 2023.
12. Hurst (n 2).

13. John Lentini, 'Lime Street Fire: Another Perspective' (1992) 43 Fire and Arson Investigator' 52.
14. Hurst (n 2).
15. John Lentini, *Scientific Protocols for Fire Investigation* (1st edn, Taylor & Francis 2006).
16. John Lentini, *Scientific Protocols for Fire Investigation* (3rd edn, CRC Press 2018) 450.
17. ibid 482.
18. ibid 469.
19. ibid 456.
20. ibid 470.
21. ibid 445.
22. ibid 445–46.
23. ibid 446.
24. Keith E Stanovich and Richard F West, 'Individual Differences in Reasoning: Implications for the Rationality Debate?' (2000) 23 Behavioral and Brain Sciences 645, 646. See also Jonathan Evans, 'Heuristic and Analytic Processes in Reasoning' (1984) 75 British Journal of Psychology 451, 462: 'a bias is a source of error which is systematic rather than random'.
25. Loren J Chapman, 'Illusory Correlation in Observational Report' (1967) 6 Journal of Verbal Learning & Verbal Behavior 151.
26. Daniel Kahneman, *Thinking, Fast and Slow* (Penguin 2012) 77.
27. 'Sports Fans Admit They're So Superstitious They've Asked "Bad Luck"' Family Members to Leave During Game' *People* (2021) <https://people.com/sports/sports-fans-superstitions-survey/#:~:text=Two%2Dthirds%20of%20sports%20fans,willing%20to%20take%20any%20chances> accessed 20 January 2023.
28. ibid.
29. Robert M Yerkes, *The Mental Life of Monkeys and Apes: A Study of Ideational Behaviour* (Behaviour Monographs 1916).
30. ibid ch 5.
31. Burrhus F Skinner, 'Superstition in the Pigeon' (1948) 38 Journal of Experimental Psychology 168.
32. ibid 171.
33. Burrhus F Skinner, 'Pigeons in a Pelican' (1960) 15 American Psychologist 28.
34. See eg Eduardo J Fernandez and William Timberlake, 'Superstition Revisited: Sex, Species, and Adventitious Reinforcement' (2020) 170 Behavioral Processes 1.
35. *State of Texas v Cameron Todd Willingham* (1991) Tex13th D 24240–CR XI.
36. Statement of Facts in *State of Texas v Cameron Todd Willingham* (1991) Tex13th D 24240–CR XI, 228.
37. ibid 244.
38. ibid.
39. ibid 241–44.
40. Hurst (n 2).
41. Grann (n 1).
42. ibid.
43. José Almirall and others, 'Forensic Science Assessments: A Quality and Gap Analysis' (2017) American Association for the Advancement of Science 5.

44. *Kennedy Brewer v State of Mississippi* (1995) Supreme Court of Mississippi 95-DP-00915-SCT.
45. Innocence Project, 'Kennedy Brewer' <https://innocenceproject.org/cases/kennedy-brewer/> accessed 20 January 2023.
46. '2 Men Freed in Child Death Bite-Mark Cases' *NBC News* (1 March 2008) <https://www.nbcnews.com/id/wbna23411936> accessed 20 January 2023.
47. See eg TM Scanlon, 'Contractualism and Justification' in Markus Stepanians and Michael Frauchiger (eds), *Reason, Justification, and Contractualism: Themes from Scanlon* (De Gruyter 2021) 58; TM Scanlon, *What We Owe to Each Other* (HUP 1998) 196.
48. Kahneman (n 26) 125–26.
49. Will Storr, 'We Believe You Harmed Your Child: The War Over Shaken Baby Convictions' *The Guardian* (8 December 2017) <https://www.theguardian.com/news/2017/dec/08/shaken-baby-syndrome-war-over-convictions> accessed 20 January 2023.
50. Deborah Tuerkheimer, *Flawed Convictions: 'Shaken Baby Syndrome' and the Inertia of Injustice* (OUP 2014) xi.
51. ArthurN Guthkelch, 'Infantile Subdural Haematoma and its Relationship to Whiplash Injuries' (1971) 2 British Medical Journal 430.
52. ibid 431.
53. John Caffey, 'On the Theory and Practice of Shaking Infants. Its Potential Residual Effects of Permanent Brain Damage and Mental Retardation' (1972) 124 American Journal of Diseases of Children 161; John Caffey, 'The Whiplash Shaken Infant Syndrome: Manual Shaking by the Extremities With Whiplash-Induced Intracranial and Intraocular Bleedings, Linked With Residual Permanent Brain Damage and Mental Retardation' (1974) 54 Pediatrics 396.
54. Indeed 'no history of trauma of any kind': Caffey, 'The Whiplash Shaken Infant Syndrome' (n 53) 402.
55. ohnCaffey, 'On the Theory and Practice of Shaking Infants' (n 53) 169.
56. ohnCaffey, 'The Whiplash Shaken Infant Syndrome' (n 53) 403.
57. ohnCaffey, 'On the Theory and Practice of Shaking Infants' (n 53) 168.
58. ibid.
59. The National Center on Child Abuse and Neglect funded a three-year nationwide campaign to raise awareness about SBS in 1993.
60. Tuerkheimer (n 50) 4.
61. Storr (n 49).
62. Tuerkheimer (n 50) 219.
63. ibid 270.
64. ibid 4.
65. Radley Balko, 'Dr John Plunkett, RIP. He Told the Truth About Bad Forensics—And Was Prosecuted for It' *Washington Post* (10 April 2018) <https://www.washingtonpost.com/news/the-watch/wp/2018/04/10/dr-john-plunkett-rip-he-told-the-truth-about-bad-forensics-and-was-prosecuted-for-it/> accessed 20 January 2023.
66. Andy Coghlan, 'Evidence of 'Shaken Baby' Questioned by Controversial Study' *New Scientist* (9 November 2016) <https://www.newscientist.com/article/mg23230994-100-evidence-of-shaken-baby-questioned-by-controversial-study/> accessed 20 January 2023.

67. Mark Donohoe, 'Evidence-based Medicine and Shaken Baby Syndrome: Part I: Literature Review, 1966–1998' (2003) 24 The American Journal of Forensic Medicine and Pathology 239.
68. ibid.
69. ibid 241.
70. ibid.
71. ibid.
72. Coghlan (n 66).
73. *F(A minor) v Buckinghamshire County Council* [2017] 4 WLUK 452 [14].
74. ibid [160].
75. Jeremy Waldron, 'The Primacy of Justice' (2033) 9 Legal Theory 269, 284.
76. See eg TM Scanlon, *Why does Inequality Matter?* (OUP 2017) 27.
77. Bertrand Russell, *The Problems of Philosophy* (Sanage 2020, originally published 1912) 41–42.
78. ibid.
79. Theodore R Sarbin, 'A Contribution to the Study of Actuarial and Individual Methods of Prediction' (1943) 48 American Journal of Sociology 593.
80. The ratio of credits to grades that have been converted into honour points.
81. Sarbin (n 79) 600.
82. See eg Kahneman (n 26) 222.
83. HerbertS Conrad and GeorgeA Satter, 'Use of Test Scores and Quality Classification Ratings in Predicting Success in Electrician's Mates School' (1945) Office of Social Research and Development Report No 5667.
84. Tuerkheimer (n 50) 13.
85. Claudia Himmelreich, 'Germany's Phantom Serial Killer: A DNA Blunder' *Time* (27 March 2009): <https://content.time.com/time/world/article/0,8599,1888126,00.html> accessed 20 January 2023.
86. AlecJ Jeffreys, Victoria Wilson, and SweeLay Thein, 'Individual-Specific 'Fingerprints' of Human DNA' (1985) 316 Nature 76.
87. ibid.
88. 'The Man Behind the DNA Fingerprints: An Interview with Professor Sir Alec Jeffreys' (2013) Investigative Genetics 21.
89. 'Exonerations by year: DNA and non-DNA' (2023) National Registry of Exonerations, <https://www.law.umich.edu/special/exoneration/Pages/Exoneration-by-Year.aspx> accessed 20 January 2023.
90. Innocence Project, 'DNA Exonerations in the United States': <https://innocenceproject.org/dna-exonerations-in-the-united-states/> accessed 20 January 2023.
91. Ate Kloosterman, Marjan Sjerps, and Astrid Quak, 'Error Rates in Forensic DNA Analysis: Definition, Numbers, Impact and Communication' (2014) 12 Forensic Science International: Genetics 77.
92. Heather Murphy, 'A DNA Mix-Up Involving a Washing Machine Kept a Man in Jail for 3 Years' *New York Times* (26 June 2020) <https://www.nytimes.com/2020/06/26/us/louisiana-dna-washing-machine.html> accessed 20 January 2023.
93. Sarah Noël and others, 'DNA Transfer During Laundering May Yield Complete Genetic Profiles' (2016) 23 Forensic Science Int Genet 240.

94. Kimberly Schweitzer and Narina Nuñez, 'What Evidence Matters to Jurors? The Prevalence and Importance of Different Homicide Trial Evidence to Mock Jurors' (2018) 25 Psychiatry Psychology and Law 437; Jane Goodman-Delahunty and Lindsay Hewson, 'Improving Jury Understanding and Use of Expert DNA Evidence' (2010) Australian Government, Australian Institute of Criminology AIC Reports Technical and Background Paper 37, 2.
95. ibid.
96. Stephanie Dartnall and Jane Goodman-Delahunty, 'Enhancing Juror Understanding of Probabilistic DNA Evidence' (2006) 38 Australian Journal of Forensic Sciences 85.
97. William C Thompson and Edward L Schumann, 'Interpretation of Statistical Evidence in Criminal Trials: The Prosecutor's Fallacy and the Defense Attorney's Fallacy (1987) 11 Law and Human Behavior 167, 170.
98. See Pedro Domingos, *The Master Algorithm: How the Quest for the Ultimate Learning Machine Will Remake Our World* (Penguin 2017) 147–48.
99. Thompson and Schumann (n 97) 171.
100. Kahneman (n 26) 125–26.
101. Birte English, Thomas Mussweiler, and Fritz Strack, 'Playing Dice with Criminal Sentences: The Influence of Irrelevant Anchors on Experts' Judicial Decision Making' (2006) 32 Personality and Social Psychology Bulletin 188.

3
Equality

Guilty as Sin

On 30 November 1983, eighteen-year-old Pamela Pope told the police that she had been abducted from a shopping centre in Bibb County, Alabama, and violently raped multiple times by two black men.[1] She subsequently identified her assailants from a police line-up: two brothers and local tradesmen, Dale and Ronnie Mahan. DNA testing was not yet available, but the Mahan brothers' blood type matched semen found on the victim.

The brothers had a robust alibi: numerous friends and family members testified that they had been celebrating their sister's birthday at a local bar. Nevertheless, they were arrested and charged with rape and kidnapping. At trial, the jury found them guilty, and the sentencing judge awarded Dale a thirty-five-year sentence, and Ronnie a life sentence without parole.[2] During almost fourteen years of imprisonment, Dale was denied parole three times for refusing to acknowledge his guilt and show remorse.[3]

In 1997, tests revealed that the brothers' DNA did not match that of the semen sample recovered in 1983. At this point, Pope changed her story several times, naming two other men, one of whose DNA did match the sample. Nevertheless, Assistant District Attorney Arthur Green, refused to abandon the case against the Mahan brothers. He argued that they must have prevented themselves from ejaculating during the alleged incidences of rape. To the media, he said 'These sons of bitches are guilty as sin. There's no question in my mind. This is not a case of innocence ... These two bastards are guilty. I just can't prove it.'[4]

One final discovery gave Green little choice: DNA from a pubic hair recovered from Pope's clothing didn't match the Mahan brothers' DNA either. The prosecution dropped the case, and Dale and Ronnie were released from prison in December 1997. The brothers made a beeline to their local diner for a double round of cheeseburgers, fries, and Coca-Cola. A beaming thirty-six-year-old Dale told reporters: 'I was never bitter or nothing. You've just got to be hopeful.'[5]

A 2017 report by the National Registry of Exonerations ('Race and Wrongful Convictions in the United States') demonstrates that the Mahans' case is, in one significant respect, far from exceptional: black defendants in the United States are much more likely than white defendants to have their convictions overturned.[6] Whilst black people constitute only 13 per cent of the American population, they make up 47 per cent of the 1900 cases listed in the National Registry of Exonerations.[7] For sexual assault, black defendants are 3.5 times more likely to be exonerated.[8] And black people also make up the vast majority of more than 1800 defendants who were framed by police in fifteen large-scale corruption scandals and later cleared in 'group exonerations'.[9]

Despite clear evidence of inequality in access to appropriate legal protection, data concerning rates of incarceration have been used to justify significant and lasting policies of racial segregation. In 1896, Frederick Ludwig Hoffman published *The Race Traits and Tendencies of the American Negro*,[10] the first in-depth statistical assessment of the health, lifespan, and criminal activity of black people in the United States.[11] Hoffman treated criminality as a fact to be laid bare by judicial and prison-population data. 'The negroes are responsible for 82.09 per cent of the homicides' in Charleston, he wrote, 'while they form but 56.4 per cent of the whole population'.[12] Hoffman even pointed to the high proportion of black victims of extrajudicial killings for evidence of criminality, labelling these killings 'summary justice'.[13] He wrote: 'the crime of lynching is the effect of a cause, removal of which lies in the power of the colored race'.[14]

Hoffman downplayed environmental factors by pointing to evidence of higher weight amongst black children,[15] blaming negative social outcomes on a 'low standard of sexual morality', a tendency towards 'self-destruction', and 'easy conditions of life and liberal charity'.[16] He argued for the termination of systems of social support, and rules for 'race purity' in marriage and cohabitation.[17] 'It is not in the conditions of life, but in race and heredity', he concluded, that we find the reason for the 'superiority of one race over another, and of the Aryan race over all'.[18]

For policymakers who shared Hoffman's reprehensible views and the policy goals to which they gave rise, the text provided a timely and convenient case for a legislative programme of social, political, and economic segregation. Over the next fifty years, rights and freedoms were stripped from black people across the United States via a set of state and federal mandates that would come to be known collectively as the 'Jim Crow' laws. Those laws, which governed many aspects of public and private life throughout the mid-twentieth century, included: banning inter-racial marriages, courtships, and cohabitation; introducing segregated schooling, hospital care, and transport; and the removal of a range of property and civil-service rights, including jury participation and the right to vote in general and local elections.

The effect is perverse: evidence of white violence and institutional discrimination, repackaged and presented as hereditary weakness of black character, was used to support policies of systemic racism. In this context, black people suffered twice—once at the hands of policies and practices that supplied inadequate and unequal access to critical legal protections, and a second time from policies of social segregation that were justified by the very inequities to which those failures led.

In the previous chapter, we saw that there are reasons to object to policies that single some people out to bear a burden for no good reason, where we lack proof that there is a rational connection between the policy and social goal at which it aims. These reasons are not always comparative: all members of a community might have good reason to object to the closure of their local hospital because of baseless suspicions about groundwater contamination. Their objection would be to the unjustified denial of a benefit, rather than to the fact that a neighbouring town has better access to hospital care. But there are also significant egalitarian reasons to object to policies that single people out for no good reason, two of which I consider here: first, a failure of equal concern; second, stigmatizing differences in status.

Certain institutions and individuals owe a duty to show equal concern for the interests of all members of a certain group when making decisions that affect those individuals.[19] That general duty is owed axiomatically by the State to its citizens, but it also arises in other contexts in which the agent in question owes a duty to provide some good to all members of a given class. This includes parents and teachers, and we will also see that it may include certain organizations established to represent and support its members, such as trade unions.

The duty of equal concern rarely requires equal treatment. For instance, during the COVID-19 pandemic, a policy of dishing out vaccines or other limited medical resources to everyone within a given community on a 'first come first served' basis would have demonstrated a manifest failure to show equal concern for the interests of those who were must vulnerable. Demonstrating equal regard for the interests of others requires decision-makers to treat those concerned (equally or unequally) in accordance with good reasons.

The racial policies of the Jim Crow era evidence a non-comparative failure to give black people sufficient access to certain key benefits (including political participation and legal protection), and a comparative failure, to treat the interests of all citizens as equally important. We will see that governments can breach the duty of equal concern by actions that fall short of this sort of outright racism. But a failure to show equal concern is often precipitated by enduring ideas about the status that people should hold because of characteristics with which they were born.

This brings us to the second sort of egalitarian objection to these laws and policies. Race-based policies can be objectionable because of the immediate disadvantages that they cause people—a set of exclusions that are not justified by the policy goal. But they may also be objectionable for a more fundamental reason, where they stem from or promote a form of status inequality—a social and political environment in which certain groups are *systematically* denied important benefits for no good reason, because of a set of unjustified beliefs about the characteristics of members of those groups.[20] These beliefs can be pervasive and enduring, affecting attitudes towards, and opportunities available to, individuals across the breadth of their lives.

The race-based policies of the Jim Crow era also demonstrate this sort of failure: they gave legislative credence to a cultural environment in which black people were generally regarded as less deserving of certain goods, and thus excluded from those goods across many aspects of their personal and professional lives. This included socio-political benefits, such as the right to vote, travel, and participate in key social activities, and what Scanlon terms 'associational goods'—the opportunity to have and maintain meaningful relationships with others on equal terms.[21]

Thus, there are three ways in which we might object to the 'discriminatory' effect of the policies that developed from Hoffman's statistical research. There is a non-egalitarian objection, which isolates the lack of a rational connection between race as a criterion for segregation and any plausible advantage that might be formulated as a justificatory goal. And there are two critical egalitarian objections: these policies evidenced an abject failure to accord the interests of black citizens the same weight as the interests of white citizens, and entrenched a long-standing culture of socio-political stratification.

In the rest of this chapter, we will see that each of these egalitarian objections can apply with significant force to policies that are shaped by the outputs of statistical algorithms, across a range of different areas of public and private decision-making.

Puzzle People

'Do you think that in the next decade a puzzle man with a heart, liver, and pancreas taken from other human beings might be feasible?'[22] This was the question posed by an Italian journalist to Thomas Starzl, the pioneer of liver transplantation. In 1963 Starzl had performed the first liver transplant surgery on Bennie, a three-year-old child born with biliary artresia. Bennie's liver was, as Starzl put it, 'incomplete': it could build and break down proteins, sugars, and fats, but could not collect bile, the waste by-product of that process. Bile would pass into Bennie's blood stream, causing jaundice—the yellow pigment that shows in a patient's skin and eyes—and damaging Bennie's healthy liver cells.

When Bennie arrived on Starzl's operating table, he had very little time left to live; after three years of suffering, peppered by a series of failed surgical interventions, a liver transplant was his last chance. The operation was fraught with complications from the outset. Bennie's liver was already encased in scar tissue, and had fused to his stomach and intestines. His failing liver was unable to produce the proteins needed to clot blood, and he eventually lost so much blood that he could not be resuscitated. In his memoir, Starzl recalled that 'the surgeons stayed in the operating room for a long time after, sitting on the low stools around the periphery, looking at the ground and saying nothing'.[23]

Following a three-year self-imposed moratorium on experimental transplant surgery, surgeons returned to the problem equipped with new solutions for bleeding and clotting. On 27 July 1967, Starzl performed the first successful liver transplantation on a nineteen-month-old girl, Julie Rodriquez. Julie survived for fifteen months after surgery, eventually dying of a cause unrelated to the liver transplant.[24]

The survival rate for liver transplants improved dramatically over the course of the late twentieth century, to more than 90 per cent by 1984. But this success created a new problem: the demand for organs far outstripped supply.[25] By the mid-1980s and early 1990s, difficult decisions about organ allocation were being confronted across the United States, which was then home to some of the most experienced surgeons and advanced surgical techniques in the nascent field of liver transplant surgery.

These decisions were initially resolved by reference to patient need, with level of care as a proxy: patients in the intensive care unit were prioritized for treatment; hospitalized patients who were not in intensive care were next in line; and outpatients were the last to receive organs, once the needs of patients in the other categories had been met (if they could be met). There is evidence that this system was sometimes abused by physicians, who would keep patients in the ICU to maintain priority status.[26]

In 1996, a medical conference was organized with the goal of instituting a new set of consensus criteria for liver transplants. The result was the Child–Pugh–Turcotte (CTP) score.[27] The CTP score is based on the severity of three objective variables relating to the body's effectiveness at building and breaking down molecules and clotting blood, and two subjective variables relating to fluid collection and brain disease. The CTP score was widely accepted, and still governs decisions about how to prioritize and treat patients with liver disease that has not yet reached the most advanced stages.

But decisions about organ allocation for patients with end-stage liver disease—the most serious cases, with the poorest outcomes—fall outside this system. Until 2002, allocative decisions in this category were largely made according to the length of time that patients had spent on the waiting list. The Model for End-Stage Liver Disease (MELD) was introduced in February 2002,[28] and is now the prevailing protocol for calculating pre-treatment survival rates in patients with advanced liver disease, thereby informing decisions about relative priority for transplant.

The MELD calculation is made on the basis of factors such as levels of bilirubin and creatinine in the blood.[29] Bilirubin (a by-product of the breakdown of red blood cells) is used to assess liver function, whilst creatinine (a muscle metabolism by-product) is used to assess kidney function. The higher the MELD score assigned to a patient, the more likely a patient is to receive a liver from a deceased donor when an organ becomes available.

Overall patient survival rates have improved since the MELD was instituted. Yet, recent studies show that women have a 19 per cent increased risk of waitlist mortality compared to men with the same MELD scores.[30] Multiple factors contribute to these differences, most notably the use of creatinine as a variable: women typically have less muscle than men, and produce less creatinine. Moreover, women are typically smaller than men, and therefore eligible for fewer of the available livers.[31]

These differences in treatment outcome were not discovered for years after the MELD had been adopted, largely because the MELD was developed on the basis of studies that either did not report sex data, or which reported a statistical make-up of 70 per cent men, without disaggregating results by sex.[32] It was only once this disaggregation had finally taken place that it was possible to see that overall rates of success concealed a difference in the way in which those rates of accuracy in decision-making were being distributed amongst patients with different characteristics. Call this the burden of the risk of error: between men and women, the latter were much more likely to have their case downgraded for reasons that did not relate to the predictive goal of pre-treatment survival.

These failures—to include women in research studies, and to take account of gender differences in patient data—are common and systemic in medical research. Criado-Perez describes many other examples of large-scale failures in the diagnosis and treatment of women due to a lack of sex-specific data, even for diseases that primarily affect women.[33] In her words:

> For millennia, medicine has functioned on the assumption that male bodies can represent humanity as a whole. As a result, we have a huge historical data gap when it comes to female bodies, and this is a data gap that is continuing to grow as researchers carry on ignoring the pressing ethical need to include female cells, animals and humans, in their research .... Women are dying, and the medical world is complicit.[34]

When we develop decision-making policies according to prevailing knowledge, there is always a risk that we will make mistakes about which criteria will best advance the social goal at which we aim. Even if statistical algorithms can help us to identify those criteria, producing predictions that are more accurate overall than unaided human decision-making, they may yet have the effect of distributing the risk of error unevenly amongst affected groups. This is far more likely if data are not representative of the target population, so that relevant information about certain groups within that population is not captured by the data upon which the predictions are based.

When systemic failures to capture and process gender-specific data mean that key responsibilities of the State, which include the provision of public healthcare, are discharged in a way that denies critical benefits to certain people for no good reason, the relevant policy may be objectionable on both non-comparative and comparative grounds. The State must provide healthcare at a certain minimum threshold for all citizens, and it must have and show equal concern for all citizens. The latter duty requires that departures from equal treatment be justified by some sufficiently compelling reason. And in this case, that departure is attributable to a systemic failure to capture data that can reflect relevant differences between individuals, because of an unjustified assumption that these differences are not medically significant. It cannot be justified by the goal that the MELD was designed to serve, of achieving better healthcare outcomes for those with end-stage liver disease.

A Big Honking Book

Eight-year-old Chad Bradford could only imagine one future—playing professional baseball.[35] By 1994, when Bradford was scouted for Major League Baseball (MLB) by the Chicago White Sox, he looked set to achieve that dream. There was just one obstacle: Bradford's technique hardly fit the mould of top-tier baseball. As Michael Lewis later wrote in his now-infamous book *Moneyball: The Art of Winning an Unfair Game*, 'the guy looked funny when he threw, no question about it'.[36] In fact, Bradford's throw was so far underhand that his knuckles would sometimes scrape the dirt as he threw.[37] And, at 84mph, his pitching fastball just wasn't that fast.[38]

So, for the next five years of his career, Bradford was treated as a 'just-in-case' player, overlooked by managers, coaches, and scouts.[39] By 2002, the clock seemed to be ticking fast towards the end of Bradford's baseball career, and he had all but given up any hope of professional advancement. What Bradford did not know is that his fate was bound up with the fortunes of one of the major league underdogs, the Oakland Athletics, some 2000 miles away.

Before 2002, recruitment decisions in baseball relied heavily upon human discretion—specifically, the opinion of baseball scouts. Scouts attended 'scout school', in which they were taught to make decisions according to their subjective evaluation of 'speed, arm strength, hitting ability and mental toughness',[40] looking for players with a 'fluid arm action and easy release',[41] 'a live, active lower body, quick feet, agility, instinct',[42] aggression, confidence, and alertness.[43]

Scouting decisions were often ill-supported by playing outcomes. As scouts were often 'overly influenced by a guy's most recent performance', and any scout with a playing background would often 'generalize wildly from his own experience'.[44] These tendencies correspond to a cognitive bias known as the 'availability heuristic':[45] predictions about the likelihood that some future event will come to pass can be influenced by 'the ease with which relevant instances come to mind'.[46] Events may come to mind easily for a number of reasons, only some of which justify conclusions about the probability that they will happen again. For instance, an event may have been observed to happen frequently, or it may simply have happened relatively recently, reflect an individual's own experiences, or stand out because of some exceptional feature.

At the start of the 2002 major league baseball season, the Oakland Athletics ('As') faced a funding crisis. Billy Beane, the As' General Manager, knew that the team stood no chance of league success if they relied on traditional recruitment methods: if the Oakland As could afford a player, they could be sure that the other major league teams could afford to poach that player. So, Beane turned to his Assistant, Paul DePodesta, a Harvard Economics graduate with a keen interest in 'sabermetrics', the statistical analysis of baseball games.

Statistician Bill James had written a series of articles and books, including (in James' words) a 'big honking book' that gave a decade-by-decade history of baseball statistics,[47] arguing that it was long past time for a sea-change in the way in which recruiters thought about the game. In James' view, many players were significantly undervalued because they either looked, played, or otherwise behaved in a way that did not correspond to mainstream views about player potential. And those mainstream views simply didn't align with the facts about player performance. For James, 'The essential measure of a hitter's success' was 'how many runs he has created',[48] a variable that could be forecast reliably with a simple equation.[49]

DePodesta passionately agreed, and proposed that the As base their recruitment decisions around a simple insight: 'A player's ability to get on base—especially when he got on base in unspectacular ways—tended to be dramatically underpriced in relation to other abilities.'[50] DePodesta created his own formula, focusing on slugging percentage (total bases divided by at-bats) and on-base percentage (the ratio of the number of the times the batter reaches base to their number of plate appearances), with particular weight attached to the latter.[51]

For Beane and DePodesta, one of the players most critical to success was 'a mild-mannered Baptist whose delivery resembled no other pitcher in the major leagues'[52]—Chad Bradford. Bradford was what the Oakland As would come to call an 'undervalued player': despite his unconventional pitching style, his playing statistics were exceptional.[53] According to DePodesta's algorithm, Bradford was their dream player: he 'hardly ever walked a batter; he gave up virtually no home runs; and he struck out nearly a batter an inning'.[54]

The rest is a history well told by Lewis' book and subsequent movie adaptation:[55] Bradford played a key role in the Oakland As' record-breaking twenty-game winning streak between August and September of 2002. This success sowed the seeds of an enduring change in baseball recruitment practice, in which subjective scouting observations gave way to empirically tested sabermetrical algorithms.

Since 2002, hiring algorithms have spread far beyond the domain of high-profile sports recruitment.[56] They crop up in a range of fields and at all stages of the hiring process, from attracting or curating a candidate pool and conducting an initial sift, to interviewing and final selection. And they are used to perform a range of predictive tasks, including: identifying the profile of candidates most likely to interact with a particular job advert; reproducing the historic hiring practices of organizations at scale; and providing risk scores for certain behaviours, particularly those behaviours deemed high-risk by the hiring individual or organization. These behaviours range from well-defined (eg bullying and harassment) to altogether nebulous (eg 'toxic' behaviour,[57] 'bad attitudes', 'grit, rigor and teamwork',[58] initiative, curiosity, and 'polish' in communication).[59]

The use of statistical algorithms in recruitment practices may disadvantage potential employees in various ways. On occasion, they prevent candidates from obtaining jobs for which they have applied and are best qualified. More often, they simply prevent candidates from coming into contact with opportunities for which they are well suited. For instance, by applying broad generalizations about historical browsing behaviours of certain groups, advertising algorithms built into social media platforms affect the number and type of employment opportunities that are presented to candidates. One study revealed that Facebook adverts for supermarket cashier positions were shown to an audience of 85 per cent women, while jobs with taxi companies went to an audience that was approximately 75 per cent black.[60] Similar results were recorded in a study of Google adverts: high-paying jobs were far more often shown to a male audience than a female audience.[61]

Employee-sourcing algorithms have had a similar effect, bypassing certain groups of people with qualifications that are equivalent to those who pass the sourcing threshold. For instance, a LinkedIn algorithm designed to match candidates with particular opportunities was found to refer far more men to recruiters. The algorithm reflected the regularity with which certain types of candidate reach out to recruiters and/or apply for positions—and men, it turns out, are often 'more aggressive at seeking out new opportunities'.[62]

In 2018, Reuters reported that Amazon had decommissioned a tool that was designed to help uncover passive candidates for recruiters to solicit.[63] Amazon had used natural language processing to sift resumés, by identifying linguistic features that correlated to hiring success. The algorithm did exactly what it was supposed to do, and did it well. However, as the data upon which the algorithm was trained revealed a clear pattern of hiring men over equivalently qualified women, it achieved this goal by identifying a range of adjectival features that were typical of male resumés, and using those features to promote male candidates.

It is important to be clear about the nature of objections that might be captured by the language of 'algorithmic bias' in this context. In the previous chapter, I addressed the relationship between the relevant selection criteria and the social goal at which we might aim by implementing a particular policy. The first objection relates to this requirement: using algorithmic recruitment tools to rule out any particular candidate on the grounds of gender may not be rationally related to the goal of hiring those candidates who will best support the company in achieving some worthwhile objective.

The second objection is more directly egalitarian. It concerns the reasons that we have for eliminating unjustified differences between people—the way in which they are perceived and treated, and thus the benefits to which they have access. Problems of status inequality can be coincident with failures of equal concern, but are not circumscribed by the presence of those duties. Institutions and individuals who advertise a job rarely owe potential employees a duty to have and show equal concern for their interests.[64] But there are reasons to object to hiring policies and practices that stem from, or contribute to, an environment in which certain groups of people—though they have the aptitude and inclination necessary for success in a particular role, and have qualifications that rival or exceed those of other candidates—are generally deemed less suitable for certain opportunities.

These objections do not only apply as a static feature of the opportunities available to certain groups at a particular moment in time. The view that individuals (both employers and would-be candidates) have about the type of person capable of performing a particular job is 'heavily dependent on who, in their experience, has generally done this'.[65] Thus, policies that steer jobs, job adverts, and associated benefits towards certain groups and away from others can have an enduring impact on the range of professional opportunities that are made available to individuals with particular characteristics.

This is what's at stake for individuals when decisions are made that involve the exclusion of candidates from certain employment opportunities, or which add additional hurdles for certain candidates, for no good reason: the concern is not just that specific candidates miss out on roles for which they are well suited, but that candidates with those characteristics are excluded from similar roles throughout their careers, and face obstacles of this kind at every stage of their professional advancement.

Guinea-Chasing Treatments

'If you want to start a revolution, tell a story.'[66] Thus begins Adam Kay's introduction to AJ Cronin's novel *The Citadel*, first published in 1937. The protagonist of the semi-autobiographical story is a doctor from a small Welsh mining village, who establishes a private practice in London. The narrative contains a damning critique of healthcare provision in England and Wales, highlighting systematic failures to engage with evidence-based science, and serious inequalities between public and private treatment.[67]

Cronin lamented the lack of professionalism and scientific progress, the 'commercialism' and 'guinea-chasing treatments',[68] and—above all—the inequity of medical pay and access to medical treatment. The story and its message captured the public imagination. By November of 1937, the novel had sold over 150,000 copies, a figure unprecedented for interwar publishing.[69] In total, it sold more copies than any other hardback novel of that decade.[70]

In the early twentieth century, public health services in England and Wales were provided through a patchwork of charitable hospitals, workhouses, and public-funded hospitals, administered as part of the Poor Law Medical Service. Limited urgent care was provided by local authorities, whilst piecemeal independent primary and community care services were funded through insurance schemes linked to specific trades. In 1911, all working men had access to the 'Panel' system of local GPs. Everyone else, including family members, had to pay for private non-urgent and outpatient care.

The Citadel gave momentum to post-war calls for a 'National Health Service'.[71] In 1941, a committee was formed by the coalition Labour-Conservative government to conduct a survey of 'social insurance and allied services, including workmen's compensation'.[72] The chairman of the committee was British Economist and Liberal politician Sir William Beveridge.

Sir William and his wife, mathematician Janet Beveridge, together conducted the research necessary to support a set of policy recommendations. And the report that Sir William produced on the basis of these efforts pulled no punches. He wrote: 'In one respect only of the first importance, namely limitation of medical service, both in the range of treatment which is provided as of right and in respect of the classes of persons for whom it is provided, does Britain's achievement fall seriously short of what has been accomplished elsewhere.'[73] He recommended 'comprehensive health and rehabilitation services for all citizens who need them', regardless of employment status or ability to pay.[74]

Unsurprisingly, the report received a frosty reception by then-Chancellor Kingsley Wood. In an internal brief to Prime Minister Winston Churchill, the Chancellor highlighted the 'impracticable financial commitment' that such a scheme would require.[75] Yet, a summary version had already begun to circulate widely amongst the British public and serving armed forces, to rapturous response.[76]

Within three years, the Beveridge recommendations had become a key manifesto pledge for both major political parties.[77] The National Health Service Act was passed by Clement Attlee's government in 1948, recording a ministerial duty to 'promote the establishment ... of a comprehensive health service' in England and Wales.[78] It was a global first, and remains the world's largest publicly funded healthcare system.

The United States, by contrast, has never embraced a comprehensive system of free-at-the-point-of-service healthcare. Access to healthcare varies widely according to a range of factors that include employment status, age, military background, location, and financial means.[79] Armed service veterans have access to comprehensive government-run healthcare, the over sixty-fives are covered by Medicare, and employees may have access to health insurance via their remuneration package. Those who cannot access private healthcare or specialist federal schemes must resort to the limited state-run Medicaid system.[80]

In all categories, healthcare providers bear all or some of the burden of high costs for medical treatment, particularly emergency and critical in-patient care. Thus, there is now a burgeoning secondary risk management industry, which includes techniques for 'complex care management' that channel resources to so-called 'high-cost beneficiaries'.[81] The goal is to reduce hospital visits and stays, thus lowering the financial burden for those providers.[82]

Optum, an algorithmic service owned by UnitedHealth Group, was developed to streamline the process of identifying these beneficiaries, thereby allowing healthcare providers to introduce steps to reduce the incidence inpatient treatment for acute illness. The algorithm, which prioritizes patients for referral on the basis of factors that include total healthcare costs accrued in a twelve-month timeframe, is now applied to more than 200 million people across the United States each year.

Optum has good overall rates of predictive success. Yet, a recent study indicates that the service only refers black people to complex care programmes at the point at which they are 'considerably sicker than the average white person', with a greater prevalence of conditions such as diabetes, anaemia, kidney failure and high blood pressure'.[83]

The reason for this disparity is that the algorithm is trained on data concerning healthcare spending by providers for patients with different characteristics, rather than the actual healthcare needs of those patients, or more immediate proxies for those needs. This has the effect of deprioritizing black patients, who tend to seek care less (and thus cost less) for a given level of healthcare need than white people.[84]

The study's authors conclude that 'using traditional metrics of overall prediction quality, cost seemed to be an effective proxy for health yet still produced large biases'.[85] They suggest that the algorithm could instead be trained on hospital admissions data—predicting the need for hospital treatment from individual patient characteristics. This might encourage the conclusion that the algorithm's designers simply erred in selecting spending as their focal variable. Yet, it bears emphasis that the algorithm achieves the objective at which UnitedHealth Group and its clients aim: it reduces exposure to the risk of high-cost medical care, by allocating healthcare resources at an early stage to patients deemed likely to be expensive. Thus, spending is not a *proxy* for need; it is the policy goal that the algorithm is designed to serve.

Accordingly, this is not a situation in which the algorithm distributes the risk of predictive inaccuracy disproportionately amongst members of the relevant class. Rather, the comparative objection is that the algorithmic outputs are used to advance unjustified policy objectives—objectives that produce unjustified differences between members of the patient class.

Optum is used to set the criteria for inclusion in a range of exceptional public and private medical treatment plans. Thus, this is not a matter of how the State distributes baseline medical care. But the State also violates a comparative duty of equal concern if—rather than merely allowing people to seek additional care from private providers—it provides care beyond this basic level to some people and not others without good reason.[86] And if other variables (such as hospital admissions) can meet treatment objectives at equivalent cost without this disparate racial effect, a policy that devotes more resources to white patients cannot be justified by the goal of better healthcare outcomes.

Bumps in Boston

On 14 July 1902, the 300ft bell tower of the Patriarchal Cathedral Basilica of Saint Mark (St Mark's Basilica) in Venice collapsed. There was only one fatality—the caretaker's cat, who had taken to seeking the shade of the stone-built belfry during the hotter summer days. Following a successful international fundraising campaign, the tower was rebuilt in a perfect image of the ninth-century masterpiece, and still stands today. Yet, this episode was, it transpired, a 'sign of things to come'.[87] The campanile and basilica are now at risk from the surrounding saltwater, some colonnades held together with strands of rope and fabric.[88] And this has been part of the story of Venice from the early days of human settlement in the first century AD—a story of determination, often against long odds, to found and later maintain a community in this small cluster of islands, despite the hostility of the coastal environment.

The 118 islands that comprise the city of Venice are often associated with mercantile success, political power, and a rich artistic and cultural history. But the Venice that we know now began far more modestly: before settlement, an itinerant population of fishermen and duck-hunters arrived seasonally, using flat-bottomed boats to navigate the shallow waters of the lagoon and islands.[89] There is now reasonable consensus that the first static population of Venice was constituted largely of people fleeing Germanic and Hun invasions.[90]

After the successful defeat of a Frankish invasion in 810, the lagoon's population moved to the central islands that now comprise the city of Venice. This presented new challenges: the little land that rose above water was fragile, and had to be drained, enclosed, and filled.[91] Shorelines had to be built up and mud dug out from channels to make them passable.[92] Elizabeth Horodowich writes of the 'great degree of struggle' that these early residents faced 'to simply survive in the hostile environment of the lagoon'.[93] This, she says, is 'the same struggle that Venetians are engaged in today as they try to maintain and protect their palaces and canals against shifting ground and rising tides'.[94]

One of these challenges arises from changing modes of transportation. Since the 1950s, motorboats have largely supplanted rowing boats, increasing the underwater turbulence of the canals.[95] Combined with a rising sea level and the extraction of water from aquifers under the city, this traffic puts pressure on the canal walls, and hastens corrosion.[96] Techniques to combat underwater corrosion have included speed limits, reshaping the canal bottom, sealing crevices, and rebuilding walls. More recently, researchers have turned to technological solutions.

The Wake Turbulence Mapping device is a hardware unit designed to gather turbulence data from boats using the Venetian canals, to inform decisions about how to address the various structural vulnerabilities that may be aggravated by canal traffic.[97] It includes a vibration sensor and 'bump detector', GPS receiver, and central processing unit. That early prototype surpassed expectations, and researchers are now using the data gathered to identify areas of priority need for structural reinforcement, and to inform policy recommendations concerning infrastructure within the Venetian lagoon.

The turbulence mapping device also turned out to be particularly well suited to the solution of a different problem—one faced by city officials some 4000 miles away. Road surface defects are an expensive and burdensome problem, particularly in high-density residential areas. In the United States, the damage caused by potholes totals some US$26.5 billion per year,[98] and the City of

Boston alone employs dozens of staff with the primary task of identifying and categorizing some 20,000 potholes for priority repair each year.[99]

In 2009, Boston Mayor Thomas Menino set out to find a more efficient way to maintain the city's roads.[100] The first iteration of that solution was developed by the wake turbulence mappers, who adapted their hardware device for municipal vehicles within Boston. This led to 'Street Bump'—a second-generation smartphone app, designed to use the phone's built-in accelerometers as the user drives around the city,[101] and launched by the Mayor's Office of New Urban Mechanics (MONUM).[102] The app showed extensive initial promise as low-cost way of gathering infrastructural data. Yet, it performed poorly at distinguishing between potholes and other more innocuous road surface defects, producing far too many false positives.[103]

MONUM chose to crowdsource a solution for Street Bump. They hired a company to host a competition, offering US$25,000 in prize money, and drawing upon the judging expertise of the original developers of the Venetian solution.[104] Three winners were chosen from some 700 participants, and Street Bump 2.0 incorporates elements from each of their solutions.[105] Street Bump data is now verified by a statistical algorithm, which ranks areas of priority infrastructure repair need for city officials, with false positives at a rate of under 10 per cent.[106]

There remain some substantial obstacles to widespread data collection: in particular, the app cannot simply run in the background to an iPhone; instead, it interferes with the use of other apps, including navigation apps. Accordingly, more than three-quarters of the existing dataset has been collated from data contributed by city employees.[107] Yet, even if these obstacles can be overcome,[108] there are reasons to think that the algorithm may not communicate an accurate picture of infrastructural need amongst all city residents. In particular, the concern is that it may fail to represent the needs of lower income groups, who are unevenly distributed throughout the city.

There are several reasons for this concern. First, those in lower income groups, particularly older residents, are less likely to have smartphones and cars.[109] In consequence, they may lack the basic tools needed to contribute to the pothole dataset. Indeed, there is evidence that the quality of the data gathered may vary in more granular ways—for instance, according to the type of car in which the user travels.[110] Moreover, the app can only gather data from users who instal and run it—often (in light of the difficulty of using the phone to perform basic tasks whilst simultaneously running the Street Bump app) at personal cost. There is evidence to suggest that minority racial groups and those from lower socio-economic backgrounds may be less likely to engage with elective government services, particularly when barriers to use are otherwise high.[111]

Boston's infrastructure policy has been called 'discriminatory'.[112] I have already indicated that there may be merit to the general concerns about equality—to the way in which the app gathers the data needed to produce recommendations that reflect infrastructural need accurately throughout the city. But it is important to be clear about what we mean when we use this label. In this case, the allegation is not that the policy is itself stigmatizing, or that it reflects a persistent set of beliefs about certain groups, which results in their exclusion from certain benefits. Rather, it is that 'data sets are missing inputs from significant parts of the population — often those who have the fewest resources',[113] thereby 'increasing the social divide between neighborhoods with a higher number of older or less affluent citizens and those more wealthy areas with more young smartphone owners'.[114]

In other words, the result of failing to capture relevant data is that those who are otherwise disadvantaged are less likely to receive infrastructural resources—resources that they need just as much as others to whom the algorithm assigns greater priority. Even if the algorithm is successful overall in helping decision-makers to achieve some social goal (here, better infrastructure), the effect of using Street Bump to make infrastructural decisions—just like the use of the MELD to make healthcare decisions—is to concentrate resource-allocation mistakes upon those individuals.

Of course, we have already seen that unequal treatment is not in itself objectionable, if there is a sound justification for this disparity—a rationale for allocating benefits unevenly, by taking into account relevant differences between characteristics, needs, and so on. But in this case the reason for unequal treatment is not a lack of need; it does not reflect the social goal of improving infrastructure. Rather, it is simply a data-gathering inadequacy; it reflects a lack of suitable means of reflecting need via the chosen mechanism for gathering and processing data.

Accordingly, there are good reasons to conclude that the use of Street Bump in the face of these problems of data collection evidences a failure to demonstrate equal concern for the interests of all citizens for whom the City has allocative responsibility. To justify using Street Bump to make resource-allocation decisions, city officials should find ways not only to improve the overall data capture of the app, but also to fill those data gaps which are concentrated upon certain groups of individuals. And they are working with engineers and scientists to do just that.[115]

The Quirky Guy from the Morgue

Najeh 'Dookie' Davenport spent seven years playing professional football in the National Football League (NFL). Described as a 'bruising back'[116] and a 'power runner',[117] he was the sort of player who could create a 'huge momentum swing' in a game.[118] Davenport suffered at least ten concussions throughout his career, on one occasion crushing the bones in his eye socket. Over the months and years that followed, Davenport suffered from tinnitus, light-sensitivity, double-vision, and severe headaches.

Davenport retired at twenty-nine, moving into documentary filmmaking, educational research, and teaching. But this new stage of his career only lasted a few short years: Davenport began experiencing acute symptoms of memory loss, mood changes, depression, and progressive cognitive decline. According to Davenport, these symptoms became so severe that he was 'unable to perform basic household chores'.[119]

When Davenport took a neurological exam in 2019, a doctor found that his use of language and ability to regulate his cognitive processes were significantly impaired. The NFL initially told Davenport that he would receive compensation, but later withdrew that decision, citing a new set of race-based cognitive standards. According to the revised standards, which assumed a lower cognitive starting point for black people, Davenport simply did not 'demonstrate the requisite cognitive impairment in *any* domain'.[120]

Within the last two decades, evidence has begun to emerge that American Football can, perhaps will inevitably, cause serious and irreversible brain damage when played at professional level, at which the rate and force of impact are at their highest.[121] NFL games have a concussion rate of around 0.7 per game,[122] most occurring in running and passing plays. Players experience an average of eight serious concussions, and many more 'sub-concussion' knocks.[123]

The first report of a complete autopsy on a former NFL player was published in 2005, by a team led by Omalu Bennet. At the time of the study, Bennet's research was not widely known, and he made little effort towards self-promotion. He was just 'the quirky guy from the morgue',[124] who had taken up a role at the University of Pittsburgh to 'satisfy an intellectual curiosity'.[125] Bennet discovered what the NFL most feared—'neuropathological changes consistent with long-term repetitive concussive brain injury'.[126] His conclusion was stark: there were 'potential long-term neurodegenerative outcomes in retired professional National Football League players'.[127]

Since the publication of Bennet's research, evidence supporting those findings has snowballed: authors of a 2017 study of 202 NFL players examined posthumously reported that 99 per cent of participants suffered from chronic traumatic encephalopathy (CTE) at their death.[128] The median age at death for participants with mild CTE was forty-four (compared with a national average of seventy-eight), the most common cause being suicide.[129]

CTE is a neurodegenerative disorder that has been linked to contact sports, specifically with repeat concussions. Typical symptoms include memory loss, significant mood changes, severe mental illness (notably, depression and anxiety), confusion, difficulties in concentration, slurred speech, physical tremors, and difficulty eating or swallowing. There is no cure, and symptoms are extremely difficult to manage; few individuals diagnosed with CTE ever return to work, many struggle with basic self-care, and some become unpredictable, violent, or suicidal.

In 2021, Phillip Adams shot and killed six people, including two young children, at a house in Rock Hill, South Carolina. Adams then fled to his family home, where he turned the gun on himself.[130] Adams was a former NFL cornerback, who had been suffering from memory loss and depression since his retirement in 2016. A CTE specialist reported that an examination of Adams' brain showed 'significantly dense lesions in both frontal lobes, an abnormally severe diagnosis for a person in his 30s'.[131]

In the same year, Vincent Jackson was found dead in his hotel room. Vincent was a former wide receiver, who had been suffering from memory loss and depression since his retirement from professional football. He died alone at the age of thirty-eight, just days after his former team won the Superbowl.[132] Jackson had never been formally diagnosed with a concussion during his playing career. Yet, his brain scan also revealed CTE—a mild form, which has been strongly linked to self-harm and suicidal ideation.

These are some of the risks that footballers face, especially if they wish to join the ranks of the professional game. As the player body in charge of setting and upholding professional standards, the NFL has an acknowledged responsibility to keep players reasonably safe, and to provide support for those who have experienced long-term injury during their career. As part of that role, the NFL has instituted a scheme, the 'NFL Disability Plan', to support those who have been rendered 'totally and permanently disabled' by their participation in the sport.[133] To be eligible for meaningful financial support under the Plan, neuropsychological testing must reveal that the former player meets that disability threshold.

Until 2011, the testing standard was set by the 'Delis Norms', which were based on an assessment of a large study sample of predominantly Caucasian males.[134] In 2011, Robert Heaton's research group published a paper 'correcting' the prevailing norms for cognitive assessment, by incorporating race-based criteria.[135] They argued that race was statistically significant in determining neuropsychological performance, and made a medical case for incorporating race into testing criteria. 'Without race/ethnicity-correct scores in the clinical setting', they argued, 'a substantial number of N African-American patients might be incorrectly classified as neuropsychologically impaired, and misdiagnosed'[136]—misdiagnoses that 'have serious implications in terms of public health consequences as well as social and healthcare consequences for the patients and their families',[137] including difficulties in accessing medical insurance.

But this also provided a convenient get-out for the NFL: nearly 70 per cent of NFL players are black, and black former players constituted the vast majority of a previous settlement claim group at the time of Heaton's publication. The NFL used this new testing standard, called the 'Heaton Norms', to deny numerous claims for compensation, including that of Najeh Davenport.[138] By building in the assumption that black players have lower cognitive starting points, they attempted to evade liability for the neurophysiological injury of their former players.

We saw above that significant problems can arise when certain groups are underrepresented in medical studies from which statistical algorithms are formulated. But attempts to revise diagnostic and treatment algorithms by controlling for race have also faced objections. In particular, such efforts have been criticized for a failure to take sufficient account of genetic variation.[139] There is now reasonable scientific consensus around the notion that 'race is not a reliable proxy for genetic difference',[140] and that the lack of nuance in 'correcting' algorithms for racial factors can aggravate the disparate effects for those whose characteristics or circumstances do not correspond to the generalized norm.

The Vaginal Birth after Cesarean (VBAC) algorithm is used to predict the risk posed by vaginal birth for women who have already undergone a caesarean section (or 'C-section'). The VBAC calculator has two race-based correction factors, one for African American women and another for Hispanic women. These correction factors 'subtract' from the overall likelihood of successful VBAC, so that women in these categories are systematically assigned a lower chance of successful VBAC than white women with an equivalent age, BMI, and other relevant health markers.[141] For instance, a thirty-year-old woman with a BMI of 35 and one prior C-section will receive a 46 per cent chance of successful VBAC if she is identified as white, and a 31 per cent chance if she is identified as African American or Hispanic.

Evidence suggests that providers are strongly influenced by VBAC scores in advising patients, partly due to perceptions of liability risk.[142] This matters a great deal to women making these decisions: healthcare outcomes can be affected in significant ways by the type of delivery, particularly for women who go on to have further pregnancies. Regardless of instrumental effects for maternal and infant mortality and well-being (and here, the evidence about delivery mode is mixed) there are a number of different reasons why a woman might wish to make an informed decision about whether to pursue a vaginal birth, where possible.

Early studies offered physical explanations for a difference in vaginal birth success rates across race, which led to broad acceptance of the need to accommodate race within obstetric decisions. The 'gynecoid' pelvis, associated with white women, was described as ideally suited for childbirth, whilst the 'anthropoid' pelvis observed in black women was described as 'degraded' in character—a 'departure from the usual mammalian form'.[143] Black women were said to be 'anatomically deficient for the vital human act of giving birth'.[144]

Modern studies have found that there is no 'biological plausibility' to those distinctions,[145] which reflect 'deeply racist enterprises'.[146] These studies emphasize the danger that arises from 'accepting these categories as natural rather than historical and socially constructed'.[147] More often, they conclude, 'race is included as a proxy for other variables that reflect the effect of *racism* on health: factors like income, educational level, or access to care'—factors that have been shown to impact VBAC success rates across the United States.[148]

Thus, denying certain types of medical treatment to women on the basis of race *simpliciter* fails to reflect an accurate picture of the risks and needs of different individuals, and concentrates the risk of poor decision-making upon those whose characteristics are inadequately captured by the predictive proxy chosen. There is some evidence that the authors of the Heaton Norms were aware of these concerns: 'diagnostic sensitivity and specificity are likely to vary', they say, 'when norms are applied to people whose backgrounds differ significantly from those represented in the normative sample populations'.[149] Thus, they conclude, any clinical decisions should also take into account a range of factors relating to social, educational, and medical history. Yet that, of course, is not how the NFL chose to deploy the Heaton Norms.

The risk that the Heaton Norms will produce inaccurate assessments of cognitive disability for NFL players is acute; it has been pointed out that

NFL players in particular are a niche subset of the general population, who may be 'poorly represented by the data'.[150] It is one thing to use the best available evidence to advise patients, even if that evidence is imperfect. It is quite another to use 'race-corrected' algorithms to justify denying compensation to black players—compensation that those players would receive if they were white. In this case, the impetus for caution goes the other way: the downside risks of failing to identify cognitive impairment include a lack of much-needed financial support for those suffering a life-changing disability.

Whilst non-profit organizations rarely owe a duty of equal concern to potential beneficiaries (though they may sometimes owe these duties to those who have committed funds),[151] the NFL is a specific sort of non-profit organization—one set up and supported by members, with the goal of providing a specific sort of benefit to those members. The closest analogy is a trade or labour union; indeed, the NFL considers itself a 'trade association'.[152] There is a good case for concluding that trade unions in general, and the NFL in particular, do owe duties to give sufficient and equal weight to the interests of its members in making decisions that affect those members. If the NFL owes such a duty, the use of a set of criteria that lack the diagnostic context necessary to produce an accurate picture of individual capabilities and requirements demonstrates a manifest failure to discharge it adequately.

That failure is compounded by the tendency that these diagnostic conclusions may have to support the view that black players, and black people generally, lack cognitive capabilities that match those of white people. As Davenport's Complaint puts it: 'The NFL's enforcement of the Settlement Agreement treats the League's Black retirees as second-class citizens, or worse, by presuming that their pre-football cognitive abilities were lower than those of their White teammates.'[153] This view is part of a wider picture in which a set of unjustified social attitudes directly influence the professional and social opportunities available to black people across the breadth of their lives.

Thus, objections to the NFL's compensation policy not only concern the immediate effect upon players who are denied the funds needed to support medical and holistic treatment; they also concern the way in which these policy choices can reinforce stigmatizing differences in status between black and white players within the NFL, and between different racial groups more widely. This latter effect may be felt particularly acutely in a social context in which the NFL, and players within its structure, are highly visible.

Notes

1. Kevin Sack, 'DNA Tests Free 2 Men Convicted in '83 Rape' *The New York Times* (4 December 1997) <https://www.nytimes.com/1997/12/04/us/dna-tests-free-2-men-convicted-in-83-rape.html> accessed 20 January 2023.
2. *Dale Elize Mahan and Ronnie Benjamin Mahan v State of Alabama* (1986) 508 So 2d 1180, 6 Div 596.
3. Sack (n 1).
4. Rachel Steinback, 'The Fight for Post-Conviction DNA Testing Is Not Yet over: An Analysis of the Eight Remaining 'Holdout States' and Suggestions for Strategies to Bring Vital Relief to the Wrongfully Convicted' (1973) 98 The Journal of Criminal Law and Criminology 329, 353.
5. Sack (n 1).
6. Samuel R Cross, Maurice Possley, and Klara Stephens, *Race and Wrongful Convictions in the United States* (National Registry of Exonerations, Newkirk Center for Science and Society 2017).
7. ibid 1.
8. ibid 11.
9. ibid 26.
10. Frederick L Hoffman, 'The Race Traits and Tendencies of the American Negro' (1896) 11 Publications of the American Economic Association 1.
11. ibid 218.
12. ibid 228.
13. ibid 230.
14. ibid 234.
15. ibid 158.
16. ibid 134.
17. ibid 328.
18. ibid 312.
19. See eg TM Scanlon, *Why Does Inequality Matter?* (OUP 2017) 11–25.
20. ibid 619.
21. ibid 26.
22. Thomas E Starzl, *The Puzzle People: Memoirs of a Transplant Surgeon* (University of Pittsburgh Press 1992) 3.
23. ibid 100.
24. Ali Zarrinpar and Ronald W Busuttil, 'Liver Transplantation: Past, Present and Future' (2013) 10 Nature Reviews Gastroenterology & Hepatology 434.
25. Eunice Lee, Chris JC Johnston, and Gabriel C Oniscu, 'The Trials and Tribulations of Liver Allocation' (2020) 33 Transplant International 1343.
26. Ashwani K Singal and Patrick S Kamath, 'Model for End-stage Liver Disease' (2013) 3 Journal of Clinical and Experimental Hepatology 50.
27. MichaelR Lucey, KimberlyA Brown, and GregoryT Everson, 'Minimal Criteria for Placement of Adults on the Liver Transplant Waiting List: A Report of a National Conference Organized by the American Society of Transplant Physicians and the

American Association for the Study of Liver Diseases' (1997) 3 Liver Transplantation and Surgery 628.
28. Singal and Kamath (n 26) 50.
29. ibid.
30. CynthiaA Moylan and others 'Disparities in Liver Transplantation before and after Introduction of the MELD Score' (2008) 300 Journal of the American Medical Association 2371.
31. Mayo Clinic, 'Transplant Professionals Strive to Correct MELD Score Gender Disparities' Medical Professionals Transplant Medicine (25 May 2022) <https://www.mayoclinic.org/medical-professionals/transplant-medicine/news/transplant-professionals-strive-to-correct-meld-score-gender-disparities/mac-20532132> accessed 20 January 2023.
32. See eg Russell Wiesner and others, 'Model for End-Stage Liver Disease (MELD) and Allocation of Donor Livers' (2003) 124 Clinical-Liver, Pancreas, and Biliary Tract; Bjorn Brandsaeter and others, 'Outcome Following Liver Transplantation for Primary Sclerosing Cholangitis in the Nordic Countries' (2003) 38 Scandinavian Journal of Gastroenterology 1176.
33. Caroline Criado-Perez, *Invisible Women: Exposing Data Bias in a World Designed for Men* (Harry N Abrams 2019) 193–216.
34. ibid 215.
35. Michael Lewis, *Moneyball: The Art of Winning an Unfair Game* (WW Norton & Co 2004) 223.
36. ibid 242.
37. ibid 220.
38. ibid 242.
39. ibid 234.
40. Ehren Wassermann and others, 'An Examination of the Moneyball Theory: A Baseball Statistical Analysis' (2005) The Sport Journal 1.
41. ibid.
42. ibid.
43. ibid.
44. Lewis (n 35) 18.
45. Amos Tversky and Daniel Kahneman, 'Availability: A Heuristic for Judging Frequency and Probability' (1973) 5 Cognitive Psychology 207.
46. ibid 208.
47. Bill James, *The New Bill James Historical Baseball Abstract* (The Free Press 1953) 1775.
48. ibid 330.
49. (Hits + Walks) x Total Bases/ (At-bats + Walks). ibid 609.
50. Lewis (n 35) 128.
51. ibid.
52. ibid 218.
53. ibid 242.
54. ibid.
55. *Moneyball* (Sony Pictures 2011).

56. See generally Miranda Bogen and Aaron Rieke, *Help Wanted: An Examination of Hiring Algorithms, Equity, and Bias* (Upturn 2018).
57. ibid 39.
58. ibid 29.
59. ibid 30, fn 177.
60. Muhammad Ali and others, 'Discrimination through Optimization: How Facebook's Ad Delivery Can Lead to Skewed Outcomes' (2019) 1 Computers and Society 1; Miranda Bigen, 'All the Ways Hiring Algorithms can Introduce Bias' *Harvard Business Review* 6 May 2019 <https://hbr.org/2019/05/all-the-ways-hiring-algorithms-can-introduce-bias> accessed 20 January 2023.
61. Amit Datta, Michael Carl Tschantz, and Anupam Datta, 'Automated Experiments on Ad Privacy Settings: A Tale of Opacity, Choice, and Discrimination' (2015) 1 Proceedings on Privacy Enhancing Technologies 92.
62. Sheridan Wall and Hilke Schellman, 'LinkedIn's Job-Matching AI Was Biased. The Company's Solution? More AI' *MIT Technology Review* (23 June 2021) <https://www.technologyreview.com/2021/06/23/1026825/linkedin-ai-bias-ziprecruiter-monster-artificial-intelligence/> accessed 7 April 2023.
63. Jeffrey Dastin, 'Amazon Scraps Secret AI Recruiting Tool that Showed Bias Against Women' *Reuters* (11 October 2018) <https://www.reuters.com/article/us-amazon-com-jobs-automation-insight-idUSKCN1MK08G> accessed 20 January 2023.
64. See eg Scanlon (n 19) 11.
65. ibid 48.
66. Archibald J Cronin, *The Citadel* (Picador 2019, first published in 1937) v.
67. Marcos Martinez Del Pero, 'The Citadel' (2007) 334 British Medical Journal 855.
68. Cronin (n 66) 460.
69. Ross McKibbin, 'Politics and the Medical Hero: AJ Cronin's 'The Citadel'' (2008) 123 The English Historical Review 651, 661.
70. ibid 651.
71. Jessica Brain, 'The Birth of the NHS' *Historic UK* (30 June 2021) <https://www.historic-uk.com/HistoryUK/HistoryofBritain/Birth-of-the-NHS/> accessed 20 January 2023.
72. Sir William Beveridge, *Social Insurances and Allied Services: Report Presented to Parliament* (His Majesty's Stationer's Office November 1942).
73. ibid 5.
74. ibid 48.
75. Chris Day, 'The Beveridge Report and the Foundations of the Welfare State' *The National Archives Blog* (7 December 2017) <https://blog.nationalarchives.gov.uk/beveridge-report-foundations-welfare-state/> accessed 20 January 2023.
76. ibid.
77. ibid.
78. National Health Service Act 1946.
79. Stephen Duckett, 'How the US Health-Care System Works—and How Its Failures Are Worsening the Pandemic' *The Conversation* (19 November 2020) <https://theconversation.com/how-the-us-health-care-system-works-and-how-its-failures-are-worsening-the-pandemic-150271> accessed 20 January 2023.

80. Jennifer Prah Ruger, Theodore W Ruger, and George J Annas, 'The Elusive Right to Health Care Under US Law' (2015) 372 The New England Journal of Medicine 2558.
81. Clemens S Hong, Allison L Siegel, and Timothy G Ferris, 'Caring for High-Need, High-Cost Patients: What Makes for a Successful Care Management Program?' (2015) 19 Issue Brief (Commonwealth Fund) 1.
82. ibid.
83. Ziad Obermeyer and others, 'Dissecting Racial Bias in an Algorithm Used to Manage the Health of Populations' 366 (2019) Science 447.
84. ibid 451.
85. ibid 453.
86. Scanlon (n 19) 15.
87. Elizabeth Horodowich, *A Brief History of Venice: A New History of the City and its People* (Robinson 2009) 215.
88. Phillip Wilan Rome, 'St Mark's Basilica in Venice is Crumbling after Flood Damage' *The Times* (August 13 2021) <https://www.thetimes.co.uk/article/st-marks-basilica-in-venice-is-crumbling-after-flood-damage-pdzjrbcgr> accessed 7 April 2023.
89. Thomas F Madden, *Venice: A New History* (Penguin 2012) 11: 'While the fish were plentiful, the water was brackish, the soil poor, and the mosquitoes ferocious.'
90. Horodowich (n 87) 9.
91. ibid 17.
92. ibid 18.
93. ibid 17.
94. ibid.
95. Nicholas Angelini and others, *Mapping Underwater Turbulence in Venice: A Major Qualifying Project Report* (Worcester Polytechnic Institute 2006).
96. Water levels in the Venetian lagoon have risen approximately 23 centimetres since 1897: Horodowich (n 87) 14.
97. Fabio Carrera, Stephen Guerin, and JoshuaB Thorp, 'By the People, For the People: The Crowdsourcing of "Streetbump", An Automatic Pothole Mapping App' (2013) XL-4/W1 ISPRS International Archives of the Photogrammetry, Remote Sensing and Spatial Information Sciences 19, 23.
98. Ellen Edmonds, 'AAA: Potholes Pack a Punch as Drivers Pay $26.5 Billion in Related Vehicle Repairs: New Data Shows 2021 was an Expensive Year for Drivers who Sustained Vehicle Damage from Potholes' *Newsroom* (1 April 2020) <https://newsroom.aaa.com/2022/03/aaa-potholes-pack-a-punch-as-drivers-pay-26-5-billion-in-related-vehicle-repairs/> accessed 7 April 2023.
99. As Mathew Mayrl from the City of Boston has put it, 'We probably have 30 to 40 staff out there each day, and one of their responsibilities is to identify potholes': 'Bump App Detects Potholes, Alerts City Official' *Washington Examiner* (20 July 2012) <https://www.washingtonexaminer.com/bump-app-detects-potholes-alerts-city-officials> accessed 7 April 2020.
100. CEA, Digital Innovation and Transformation: MBA Student Perspectives (30 October 2015), 'Street Bump: Crowdsourcing Better Streets, but Many Roadblocks Remain' <https://d3.harvard.edu/platform-digit/submission/street-bump-crowdsourcing-better-streets-but-many-roadblocks-remain/> accessed 11 April 2023.

101. The creators of StreetBump note that it 'may soon be coming full-circle back to its Venetian origins, since the gondoliers' guild has expressed interest in a version of the app to document the moto ondoso that affects the iconic row boats of Venice'. See Carrera, Guerin, and Thorp (n 97) 23.
102. CEA, Digital Innovation and Transformation: MBA Student Perspectives (n 100).
103. ibid. See also Daniel E O'Leary, 'Exploiting Big Data from Mobile Device Sensor-Based Apps: Challenges and Benefits' (2013) 12 MIS Quarterly Executive 179, 181.
104. Carrera, Guerin, and Thorp (n 97) 22.
105. ibid.
106. See City of Boston, New Urban Mechanics <https://www.boston.gov/transportation/street-bump> accessed 11 April 2020.
107. CEA, Digital Innovation and Transformation: MBA Student Perspectives (n 100); Carrera, Guerin, and Thorp (n 97) 22.
108. See City of Boston, New Urban Mechanics (n 106).
109. O'Leary (n 103) 183.
110. ibid.
111. Evelien Tonkens and Imrat Verhoeven, 'The Civic Support Paradox: Fighting Unequal Participation in Deprived Neighbourhoods' (2019) 56 Urban Studies 1595.
112. Maddalena Favaretto, Eva De Clercq, and Bernice Simone Elger, 'Big Data and Discrimination: Perils, Promises and Solutions. A Systematic Review' (2019) 6 Journal of Big Data 1.
113. Kate Crawford, 'The Hidden Biases in Big Data' *Harvard Business Review* (1 April 2013) <https://hbr.org/2013/04/the-hidden-biases-in-big-data> accessed 10 April 2023.
114. Favaretto, De Clercq, and Elger (n 112) 3.
115. Crawford (n 113).
116. 'Najeh Davenport' IMDB: <https://www.imdb.com/name/nm1419906/> accessed 23 January 2023.
117. Eddie Rossell, 'Najeh Davenport Re-Signs with Pittsburgh Steelers: Third Time's a Charm?' *Bleacher Report* (28 November 2008): <https://bleacherreport.com/articles/86810/> accessed 20 January 2023.
118. 'Random Questions with Najeh Davenport' (23 May 2004) <https://www.packers.com/news/random-questions-with-najeh-davenport-2472916> accessed 20 January 2023.
119. *Kevin Henry and Najeh Davenport v National Football League and NFL Properties LLC*, Class Action Complaint No 20-4165 District Court for the Eastern District of Pennsylvania 4.
120. Emphasis original, 4–5.
121. Bennet I Omalu and others, 'Chronic Traumatic Encephalopathy in a National Football League Player' (2005) 57 Neurosurgery 128.
122. Christina D Mack and others, 'Epidemiology of Concussion in the National Football League, 2015–2019' (2021) 13 Sports Health 423.
123. ibid.
124. Jeanne Marie Laskas, *Concussion* (Penguin 2015) 107.
125. ibid.
126. Omalu and others (n 121) 128.
127. ibid.

128. Jesse Mez and others, Clinicopathological Evaluation of Chronic Traumatic Encephalopathy in Players of American Football (2017) 318 Journal of the American Medical Association 360.
129. ibid.
130. Jonathan Abrams, 'Phillip Adams Had Severe CTE at the Time of Shootings' *New York Times* (14 December 2021) <https://www.nytimes.com/2021/12/14/sports/football/phillip-adams-cte-shootings.html> accessed 20 January 2023.
131. ibid.
132. Ken Belson, 'It's Not the Ending He Wanted' *New York Times* (16 December 2021) <https://www.nytimes.com/2021/12/16/sports/football/vincent-jackson-death-cte.html> accessed 20 January 2023.
133. NFL Player Disability & Neurocognitive Benefit Plan <http://www.nflplayerbenefits.com> accessed 20 January 2023.
134. DeanC Delis and others, *California Verbal Learning Test-II* (2nd edn, The Psychological Corporation 2000).
135. Marc A Norman and others, 'Demographically Corrected Norms for African Americans and Caucasions on the Hopkins Verbal Learning Test: Revised, Brief Visupatial Memory Test, Revised Stroop Word Test, and Wisconsin Card Sorting Test' (2011) 33 Journal of Clinical Experimental Neuropsychology 793.
136. ibid 794.
137. ibid.
138. Ken Belson, 'Black Former NFL Players Say Racial Bias Skews Concussion Payouts' *The New York Times* (25 August 2020) <https://www.nytimes.com/2020/08/25/sports/football/nfl-concussion-racial-bias.html?action=click&module=RelatedLinks&pgtype=Article> accessed 20 January 2023.
139. Darshali A Vyas, Leo G Eisenstein, and David S Jones, 'Hidden in Plain Sight—Reconsidering the Use of Race Correction in Clinical Algorithms' (2020) 383 New England Journal of Medicine 874.
140. ibid 874.
141. Darshali A Vyas and others, 'Challenging the Use of Race in the Vaginal Birth after Cesarean Section Calculator' (2019) 29 Women's Health Issues 201.
142. KJ Cox, 'Providers' Perspectives on the Vaginal Birth after Caesarean Guidelines in Florida, United States: A Qualitative Study' (2011) 11 BMC Pregnancy and Childbirth 72.
143. WJ Turner, 'The Index of the Pelvic Brim as a Basis of Classification' (1885) 20 Journal of Anatomy and Physiology 125, 143.
144. Vyas and others (n 141) 202.
145. ibid.
146. ibid.
147. ibid.
148. ibid.
149. Norman and others (n 135) 801.
150. Jennifer J Manly and Diane M Jacobs, *Minority and Cross-cultural Aspects of Neuropsychological Assessment* (Taylor & Francis 2002).

151. Scanlon (n 19) 23.
152. Duff Wilson, 'NFL Executives Hope to Keep Salaries Secret' *The New York Times* (11 April 2008) <https://www.nytimes.com/2008/08/12/sports/football/12nfltax.html> accessed 20 January 2023.
153. *Kevin Henry and Najeh Davenport v National Football League and NFL Properties LLC*, Class Action Complaint No 20-4165 District Court for the Eastern District of Pennsylvania 2.

4
Choice

Born Criminal

On one afternoon in early 1870, experimental physician-criminologist Cesare Lombroso was conducting a routine post-mortem examination of a prisoner in Turin.[1] During that examination, Lombroso discovered an impression at the base of his patient's skull, which he called the 'median occipital fossa'.[2] Lombroso later wrote that this moment was 'a revelation' for him; 'At the sight of that skull, I seemed to see all of a sudden, lighted up as a vast plain under a flaming sky, the problem of the nature of the criminal—an atavistic being who produces in his person the ferocious instincts of primitive humanity and the inferior animals.'[3]

Lombroso used these observations to support his developing theory of criminal 'atavism'.[4] For Lombroso, criminals could be distinguished from non-criminals according to certain physical and hereditary 'stigmata', which showed evidence of a 'revival of the primitive savage'.[5] The physical characteristics that Lombroso singled out included: an asymmetrical face or forehead; wide jaw; high cheekbones; long limbs; or unusually large or small ears.[6] These characteristics gave substance to a broad taxonomy of physical criminal types, which Lombroso used to forecast particular crimes.[7]

Lombroso applied his theory of atavism to a wide range of subjects, from the 'physiognomy of the anarchists'[8] to the 'man of genius'[9] and the 'prostitute'.[10] In an extensive treatise on the moral well-being of Christopher Columbus, devised entirely from portraiture and handwriting samples, Lombroso concluded that Columbus was probably a psychopath of 'disturbed mind', and 'even more defective than the average man of his time in moral sense'.[11]

Lombroso's work had an extensive reach and impact, during his lifetime and in the decades that followed. He coined the term 'criminology' to describe a distinct field of research encompassing crime and criminal behaviour, and founded the Italian School of Positivist Criminology, which came to rival the dominant Classical School of the Enlightenment era. Where the latter placed free will at the heart of penal theory, adherents to positivist criminology promoted a different view—that criminality could be biologically pre-destined and criminologically forecast.[12] For some, Lombroso's views are still evident in the shape and content of the Italian Penal Code.[13]

Lombroso's work underpinned many policies and practices of social exclusion and intolerance that are still in place across the world, including the long-term segregation of those who suffer from serious psychological illnesses, and the 're-education' of left-handed children.[14] His arguments about the link between skin colour and atavism informed sentencing and police practices in urban areas of central Italy, culminating in a series of repeat arrests amongst disadvantaged black communities throughout the late nineteenth and early twentieth centuries.[15]

Just as the popularity of criminal atavism was starting to wane in continental Europe, British statistician Charles Goring took up the mantle of proving the relationship between heredity and crime.[16] Lombroso's supporters and critics alike had aired doubts about his 'sensational anecdotal method' and poor statistical techniques,[17] and Goring set about remedying these methodological defects.[18] For Goring, the nature of the 'criminal type' would be revealed by a road 'paved with statistical facts'[19]—a road that would, he thought, lead us to the correct conclusions with 'the same degree of reliability as the conclusions of an exact science'.[20]

Having conducted extensive studies of prison inmates and (to his own satisfaction) ruled out environmental explanations for habitual crime, Goring felt confident that 'heritable constitutional conditions prevail in the making of criminals'.[21] Some of these characteristics were physical: Goring claimed that 'on average, the criminal of English prisons is markedly differentiated by defective physique—as measured by stature and body weight'.[22] Others were psychological: Goring highlighted a 'defective mental capacity' and a 'decadence in general intelligence'.[23] For Goring, these added up to a 'criminal diathesis'—a diagnosable criminal condition, defined by a set of characteristics that were 'so potent' in some people 'as to determine for them, eventually, the fate of imprisonment'.[24] Goring even linked certain characteristics to specific types of crime—lower intelligence to petty theft, muscular weakness to crimes of violence, and short stature to sexual offences.[25]

This work underpinned a set of policy ambitions. According to Goring, the 'crusade against crime' should be governed by a particular strategy: alongside 'segregation and supervision of the unfit',[26] we should 'regulate the reproduction of those degrees of constitutional qualities—feeble-mindedness, inebriety, epilepsy, deficient social instinct, insanity, which conduce to the committing of crime'.[27]

Goring's research drew an enthusiastic response from the eugenicist lobby. In 1914, Leonard Darwin, son of Charles Darwin, used *The English Convict* to support the claim that there was a 'class of criminals whose seed should not be permitted to contaminate posterity'.[28] He argued for a programme of 'selective breeding',[29] by which criminals would be segregated from the general population throughout the duration of their fertile years.[30] These publications in turn informed a set of high-profile policy recommendations for prison reform, which (mercifully) failed to gain public traction.[31]

There are clear and important egalitarian reasons for objecting to the policies and policy recommendations that arose from criminal atavism and its statistical counterpart. We have already seen that Lombrosian theory had the effect of subjecting certain groups of society to significant burdens, many of whom were already experiencing pervasive disadvantage. But this doesn't seem to capture the full extent of the concerns that we might have with the claim that we should send a person to prison (at all, or for longer) because they are shorter, weaker, or less intelligent than the average person.

This brings us to the role that choice plays in justifying the imposition of burdens. On one view, which treats autonomy as a basic or intrinsic good, we are responsible for actions just when we have chosen to bring them about. According to this 'will-based' view of the justificatory role of choice, an individual 'has an inherent moral power to legitimate outcomes by giving consent, or by voluntarily laying down a right to something'.[32] The idea is that, when we freely choose to perform an action in the knowledge that some undesirable consequence may follow from doing so, we cannot complain when that is exactly what happens; we were warned (so it goes) and gave up our right to have those consequences withheld from us. This is part of what can make the relationship between choice and punishment seem so compelling: we blame an individual for choosing to do wrong, and require them to bear only those burdens that they have willingly forfeit the right not to suffer.

But there is an alternative view of the legitimizing force of choice, which does not require us to treat autonomy as a basic value with this foundational role in blame and punishment. For this 'value of choice' account, there is a distinction between the justifying conditions of moral opprobrium (blame and criticism), and practical burdens (the benefits that we deny people, or the things that we require them to do).[33] The value of choice account is concerned with the second category only, which feeds into questions of justice.

The starting point for this account is to look directly to the reasons that we have for wanting a choice—for wanting what happens to us to depend upon the way in which we respond when presented with a range of options about what to do. The argument is that, where these reasons are sufficiently strong, we may have sound objections to a policy that fails to make the imposition of burdens upon us contingent upon how we behave when we have these choices, or which otherwise fails to ensure that we are sufficiently well equipped to exercise them.[34] Thus, the focus is not upon the choices that we make, but upon the choices that we have—upon the position in which we are placed to influence what happens to us by choosing appropriately.

What, then, are the reasons that we may have for wanting outcomes to depend on our choices? The first and most obvious sort of reason is instrumental: having a choice will often improve aspects of our lives, in small or significant ways. For instance, we may enjoy our meal at a restaurant more if we get to choose what we have to eat,[35] or may derive more satisfaction from a professional or personal relationship that we have chosen to forge.

But there are also non-instrumental reasons to value having a meaningful opportunity to choose. These include what Scanlon terms 'representative' reasons:[36] we may want to be able to choose how to dress or whether to get a tattoo or piercing, how to celebrate important moments with our loved ones, or when and how to protest decisions to which we are opposed. These reasons 'for wanting to see features of ourselves manifested in actions and their results'[37] can apply to us even if exercising these choices does not make our lives go better, as ways of expressing our personality, tastes, and preferences.[38]

Finally, there are many situations in which people are, for better or worse, generally expected to make choices for themselves—for instance, choices about the people with whom they form relationships, which political party to support in a general or local election, or (within certain limits) how to spend their leisure time. Denying these choices to some people can reflect a judgement, or can be seen by others to reflect a judgement, that those people 'are not competent or do not have the standing normally accorded an adult member of the society'.[39]

This sort of 'symbolic'[40] reason formed the lynchpin of arguments for women's suffrage throughout the late nineteenth and early twentieth centuries. In 1867, John Stuart Mill spoke before the UK House of Commons in favour of enfranchising women, to resist the argument that women 'are not capable of a function of which every male householder is capable'—of forming a sensible 'opinion about the moral and educational interests of a people'.[41] There are, as Mill stressed to other Members of Parliament, important symbolic reasons not to categorize women 'with children, idiots, and lunatics, as incapable of taking care of either themselves or others',[42] reasons that count whether or not women suffer any 'practical inconvenience' from their exclusion from the political process.[43]

This last category of reason can be comparative, and has both an instrumental and non-instrumental component. The claim is that there may be reasons to object to a policy that denies the decision-subject the same range of opportunities for choice as other competent members of society, where this labels them as too 'immature or incompetent' to make these choices well.[44] This can be objectionable on its own terms, and where these judgements have the effect of creating unjustified differences in status, by signalling that some people are not competent to manage important privileges or opportunities.[45]

How do these reasons translate into conclusions about the practical burdens to which we can justify subjecting individuals? The argument is that an individual can have good reasons of each of these kinds to want the opportunity to avoid the burden of some social policy by choosing appropriately, and to want to be sufficiently well placed to exercise such a choice. And if they have these reasons, it will be easier to justify a policy that makes that burden contingent upon how they behave when these opportunities arise;[46] vice versa, it will be more difficult to justify a policy that makes these burdens contingent on facts that they cannot influence (easily, or at all).

In his magnum opus *What We Owe to Each Other*, Tim Scanlon exemplifies the role of choice in justifying policies that place some people at a greater risk of harm. I abridge and adapt that example here:[47]

> *Hazardous Waste:* hazardous waste has been identified within a city's most populous residential district. Moving the waste will put local residents at an immediate risk of lung damage by releasing chemicals into the air. However, leaving the waste *in situ*, where it will seep into the water supply, creates a risk of harm to generations of residents, workers, and visitors throughout the wider city. So, officials decide to take the steps needed to excavate and dispose of the waste as safely as possible.

The city officials have an important social goal: they aim to keep inhabitants and visitors as safe as they can. To achieve that goal, they must create a 'zone of danger': there will be certain activities that those who reside in the immediate vicinity of the excavation site cannot perform without serious risk of harm. For some, this might even include quotidian activities, such as residing in or travelling short distances around their homes.

Scanlon argues that, in order to justify their decision to remove the waste in the context of this danger, officials should take steps to minimize the risk of harm—both by carrying out the work with proper precautions, and by equipping residents to adjust their own actions to secure protection against any residual risk.[48] This might include warning people to stay away from the excavation site by providing appropriate information in an accessible format, and supplying families in close proximity with the means to secure alternative accommodation for the duration of the enterprise.

The goal of these steps is to provide those affected with a meaningful opportunity to avoid suffering harm by making appropriate choices about what to do.[49] In this case, the value of that opportunity is instrumental: residents are less likely to suffer harm if they have this opportunity. And making sure that this opportunity is sufficiently valuable for everyone means introducing additional safeguards that increase the likelihood that people will choose well—through clear and appropriate communication, and barriers or disincentives to site access.

So, the claim about the justificatory role of choice is not that we can justify imposing burdens upon those who choose (badly), or (vice versa) that we cannot justify imposing burdens upon those who have failed for whatever reason to exercise a choice. The actual exercise of choice is neither here nor there. What matters is the quality of the opportunity to choose with which an individual is provided, in light their position (eg their knowledge and economic, social, and other resources), the background conditions of their choice, and the safeguards made available to them to encourage good choices.[50] The reasons that we have to value choice can weigh heavily against policies that allocate significant burdens without providing these opportunities, or the safeguards needed to make them sufficiently valuable.

Hazardous Waste provides a helpful point of departure for thinking about criminal punishment.[51] Policies of criminal punishment aim at an important social goal—keeping people safe and their property secure. The chosen strategy for attaining this goal entails the creation of a risk that some people will bear a burden, which may be minor (eg a small fine or demerit points), or extensive (eg the loss of certain rights, privileges, and freedoms, or even loss of life). In consequence, there are some activities that people cannot perform without incurring the risk that they will suffer these costs—a metaphorical zone of danger. So, to justify a policy of criminal punishment, we should equip people to avoid straying into that zone, which includes publicizing the rules, and providing meaningful opportunities for individuals to choose a course of action that does not involve transgression.

There are different kinds of reason to want to have the opportunity to avoid criminal punishment by choosing appropriately. Like the reasons that apply to the residents in *Hazardous Waste*, the most obvious reasons are instrumental:[52] criminal punishment in various forms is amongst the most significant institutional burdens that we can be required to bear. This is particularly true of incarceration, which is attended by the loss of social, political, and economic rights and privileges that play a key role in any individual's ability to thrive as part of society. There is very little evidence that those burdens play a positive short- or longer-term role in the lives of those who suffer them, and a good deal of evidence to the contrary.[53]

So, if punishment is part of the menu of institutional responses to crime, we have instrumental reasons to want it to turn on behaviours in which we can choose not to engage, and to be informed and equipped to exercise these choices well. In the context of criminal punishment, these safeguards include clarifying the bounds of acceptable behaviour (publicizing a set of clear and comprehensible rules) and creating and sustaining socio-economic conditions that enable people to live a meaningful life on the right side of the law.

Criminal punishment in general, and incarceration in particular, can also limit the scope that we have to express ourselves in a variety of ways that may be significant to us. Indeed, incarceration is designed to have this effect—both by mandating similitude in routine, dress, décor and so on, and by closing off a range of typical freedoms and privileges. Accordingly, prisoners have few means of shaping their immediate environment to reflect their personality, and little opportunity to make choices that reflect individual preferences. Where these limitations cause psychological distress or social disengagement, the line between instrumental and non-instrumental may blur.

Finally, we also have symbolic reasons to want to have the opportunity to avoid criminal punishment by choosing well. Giving people these opportunities, by making punishment contingent upon how people behave when confronted with different options, signals that they have a certain sort of rational competence—that they are able to guide their decisions in accordance with the rules, for their own good and the good of others. By contrast, denying these opportunities, by making punishment contingent upon characteristics over which individuals have little or no influence, signals the contrary—that those who have these characteristics are less competent to choose well, and can be denied the privileges held by mature, rational, adults.

These reasons—instrumental, representative, and symbolic—combine to create a powerful case for making punishment contingent upon on how we behave when we are confronted with adequate choices about what to do, and creating a set of background conditions that can support individuals to make these choices well. Yet, we have seen that the criminological vision of biological determinism was that the penal system should be shaped around the idea that an individual's 'hereditary' characteristics could set them on a path of social deviance—a path with an inevitable conclusion.[54] For Lombroso and Goring, there simply were 'born criminals'—'degenerate' individuals who were less capable of choosing well,[55] and less deserving of the foundational rights, privileges, and freedoms that attend healthy powers of self-governance. Thus, Lombroso and Goring each thought that incarceration could be an appropriate institutional response to the presence of characteristics (*simpliciter*) that they perceived to be linked to criminal behaviour.

This, then, is the broader concern with criminal atavism and its statistical counterpart: when we attach some of the most extensive institutional burdens to physical and intellectual characteristics, we fail to give appropriate weight to significant reasons that individuals have to value choice. The claim is not that we have failed to link punishment to the exercise of choice; rather, it is that we have failed to provide affected individuals with a meaningful choice to exercise. As Goring put it, the 'fate of imprisonment' is pre-determined for them by facts that they cannot influence, the characteristics with which they were born.[56]

Goring insisted that the outputs of his statistical enquiry were a matter of 'facts, and facts only',[57] lending an apparent incontrovertibility to his conclusions. No doubt, the existence of some correlation between variables in a given dataset is a fact. But we have already seen that apparent correlations are readily influenced by variations in study design and implementation. Moreover, the explanations that we give for these patterns, and the corresponding decisions that we make about how to treat others in light of the conclusions of any statistical enterprise, are matters of human judgement.

In this respect, there are important decisions to make about the sort of criminal justice system that we want to adopt and sustain. One version of that system gives appropriate weight to the reasons that we have to value the opportunity to avoid or minimize the burdens of criminal punishment by choosing appropriately. Another version treats the 'criminal' as a distinct type of person, with aberrant predispositions that warrant a weaker claim to the legal protections that preserve those opportunities.

An Ideal Crime-Fighting World

'In an ideal crime-fighting world, we would know every convict's criminal proclivities. An offender could be detained for precisely the right amount of time as we effortlessly balanced the many competing interests served by our system of criminal justice.'[58] These are the opening words to an article penned by Brian Netter, Deputy Assistant Attorney General for the Federal Programs Branch of the US Department of Justice. The subject of Letter's article was a sentencing algorithm developed by the Virginia Criminal Sentencing Commission (VCSC), and launched state-wide in 2002.[59] The VCSC awards a risk score to offenders, which is based on ten 'criminogenic' factors, including relationship and employment status. The higher that score, the more likely it is that the defendant will receive a sentence that includes prison time and extended post-release supervision.

A range of risk assessment techniques now support decision-making within criminal justice across the United States. The most widely used is Correctional Offender Management Profiling for Alternative Sanctions (COMPAS), a suite of algorithmic tools developed and owned by Equivant.[60] COMPAS is designed to predict the risk of recidivism for individual offenders and recidivism patterns across wider populations, by drawing upon a range of observations of the relationship between individual characteristics and criminal activity that have emerged from criminology research over the past thirty years. The tools are used by corrections departments, lawyers, and courts to shape decisions throughout the justice system, including: pre-trial plea negotiations, 'jail programming' requirements, community referrals, bail applications, sentencing, supervision, and probation recommendations, and the frequency and nature of post-release contact with the justice system.[61]

Though the literature often refers to 'the COMPAS algorithm',[62] COMPAS is not a single algorithm that produces one type of risk-score; rather, the COMPAS software includes a range of tools that use algorithms to predict risk, which are described by Equivant as 'configurable for the user'.[63] The tools available include: 'Pre-Trial Services',[64] which principally concern the risk that the accused will flee the jurisdiction; and three assessments (the General Recidivism Risk scale (GRR), the Violent Recidivism Risk scale (VRR), and the 'full assessment') which involve predictions about recidivism.[65]

The COMPAS software is a trade secret. Accordingly, the defendant and court see the score, but are not privy to the factors and weightings that inform an individual output. Nevertheless, Equivant's public materials explain that the GRR captures factors such as: 'criminal associates',[66] 'early indicators of juvenile delinquency problems',[67] 'vocational/educational problems',[68] history of drug use,[69] and age.[70] The enquiry into 'vocational/educational problems' in turn includes datapoints that are identified by defendants' responses to questions such as: 'how hard is it for you to find a job above minimum wage'; 'what were your usual grades in school'; and 'do you currently have a skill, trade, or profession at which you usually find work'.[71] Equivant notes that these datapoints are strongly correlated to 'unstable residence and poverty', as part of a pattern of 'social marginalisation'.[72]

The 'full assessment'[73] is designed to assess a much wider set of 'criminogenic' factors.[74] These include: 'anti-social friends and associates';[75] unstable family and/or marital relationships (including whether the defendant was raised by their biological parents, parental divorce or separation, and family involvement in criminal activity, drugs, or alcohol abuse);[76] employment status and prospects;[77] school performance;[78] and 'poor use of leisure and/or recreational time'.[79]

Each set of factors is assessed via a combination of the defendant's own input to a pre-trial questionnaire, subjective observations made by the assessing agent, and objective data such as the nature and frequency of any prior offences. Scores are then incorporated by the agent into an overall narrative, which forms the basis of a sentencing recommendation by the district attorney. Judges have been clear that these scores and recommendations have played a significant role in sentencing and post-release supervisory decisions, and judicial training in many US states now includes the use of COMPAS for these purposes.[80] Put simply, COMPAS can make all the difference to whether an individual spends time in prison, and for how long.

Two criticisms have been levelled at policies that use COMPAS outputs to make these decisions, one of which concerns predictive accuracy. In 2016, investigative journalism non-profit ProPublica published a report detailing recidivism statistics for 10,000 criminal defendants in Broward County, Florida, over a two-year period.[81] They found that COMPAS GRR scores 'correctly predicted an offender's recidivism 61% of the time', but that VRR scores were correct only 20 per cent of the time.[82] In 2018, Julia Dressel and Hany Farid published the results of research comparing the success of COMPAS predictions with those of the general public.[83] They gave individuals without judicial training the task of predicting recidivism from a short description of the defendant—sex, age, and criminal history. They found that participants were correct 62 per cent of the time.

The aim of incorporating these tools into sentencing decisions is to reduce rates of recidivism, or to keep rates of recidivism on a par with non-algorithmic decisions whilst minimizing the time that offenders must spend behind bars.[84] So, what we really need to know to assess the justification for using COMPAS outputs to make sentencing decisions is not just whether the facts that inform these outputs correlate to recidivism, but whether: (1) a policy of awarding more extensive criminal sentences to those with higher COMPAS scores has the effect of reducing rates of recidivism; or (2) COMPAS outputs predict recidivism accurately, given some reliable strategy for reducing rates of recidivism.[85] Yet, the empirical evidence for either association is not just 'beyond thin; it is close to non-existent'.[86]

Several obstacles impede that research. First, there are profound disparities in the way in which judicial officers engage with COMPAS outputs across different states, counties, and intra-county populations.[87] This makes it difficult to control for variations in judicial practice, in turn confounding efforts to rule out other variables that might affect the predictive value of COMPAS scores.

Second, and perhaps most importantly, we cannot measure rates of crime directly; instead, we must base statistical assessments on proxies such as rates of arrest, conviction, prosecution, or some other involvement in the criminal justice process. So, for Equivant, recidivism is 'a finger-printable arrest involving a charge and a filing for any uniform crime reporting (UCR) code'.[88] For Propublica, it is 'a criminal offense that resulted in a jail booking and took place after the crime for which the person was COMPAS scored'.[89]

Yet, proof of a correlation between certain facts about individuals and rates of arrest or other involvement in the criminal justice process may reveal more about the proclivities and practices of those who wield power within these systems than they do about the actual incidence of crime. For instance, a greater police presence in a particular area, or a policing focus on individuals within certain characteristics, will yield a higher rate of arrest for these areas or individuals—regardless of the actual distribution of crime.[90]

This brings us to concerns about inequality—specifically, to the way in which COMPAS distributes the risk of error amongst populations subjected to the assessment process.[91] In 2016, ProPublica reported the results and their conclusions from a two-year study of 10,000 criminal defendants in Broward County, Florida. They found that 'black defendants who did not recidivate over a two-year period were nearly twice as likely to be misclassified as higher risk compared to their white counterparts ... '.[92] More precisely, COMPAS classified black defendants as highly likely to commit another crime in circumstances in which that prediction was not borne out by the evidence during the assessed period twice as often as it did for white defendants. This is a difference in false positive rates, and it reflects the 'fraction of non-recidivating defendants who were ranked as high risk'.[93] By contrast, COMPAS was almost twice as likely to 'misclassify' a white defendant as low risk.[94]

For some, this data regarding the distribution of the risk of error is conclusive evidence of racial bias.[95] Equivant have resisted this criticism on the basis that an equal distribution of the risk of error is not an appropriate goal for population data that displays meaningful differences in incidences of the target variable amongst individuals with different characteristics.[96] If the false positive rate is a ratio of recidivists to non-recidivists who are classified as high risk, and more people are ranked as high risk and fewer as low risk as the risk level goes up, 'higher false positive rates and lower false negative rates are obtained for the high-scoring group'.[97] This, they say, is a 'natural consequence of using unbiased scoring rules for groups that happen to have different distributions of scores'.[98] Instead, they argue, the predictive values for two different groups should be the same *given* a high risk score. They term this 'predictive parity'.[99]

Other researchers have argued that there are a range of ways in which we might accommodate differences in baseline risk rates, and that satisfying predictive parity is incompatible with a balance in error rates at any given risk threshold, where the prevalence of the target variable differs.[100] For recidivism risk assessments, the result is that defendants in the higher prevalence group will generally receive greater penalties than defendants in the lower prevalence group—what the authors term 'disparate impact'.[101] The authors argue that the 'preferred approach' may be to aim at a balance in error rates without predictive parity,[102] or to facilitate predictive parity by allowing the risk threshold at which rates are compared to differ amongst groups.[103]

Whichever calculation is adopted, actual error distribution is extremely difficult to measure in this context, for several reasons. As above, we cannot access true rates of recidivism; we can only use proxies, which are generally rates of arrest or conviction.[104] Again, as above, policing practices have a direct impact on these variables. If police target those who belong to a particular social demographic, or who live in geographical areas that correspond to socioeconomic or racial characteristics,[105] a distribution of the risk of error that is proportionate to rates of rearrest can reflect unjustified differences in treatment between groups.

A fair distribution of the risk of error may be one goal of a justified social policy, but achieving it will not always be enough to show that the policy answers objections that stem from inequality. For instance, the authors of the ProPublica study found that there were slightly higher rates of jail bookings for black people captured by the study. Even if we ignore concerns about the way in which policing practices affect these numbers and assume that this observation does in fact reflect higher rates of offending amongst black people, I have already argued that a justified policy should also respond to concerns that arise from the background conditions that enable, or fail to enable, people to live a meaningful life on the right side of the law.

This brings us to the final consideration, which concerns the value of individual choice. Reuben Binns has written that 'one of the potentially objectionable features of the COMPAS scoring system was not the use of "race" as a variable (which it did not), but rather its use of variables which are not the result of individuals' choices, such as being part of a family, social circle, or neighbourhood with higher rates of crime'.[106] He continues: 'These may be objectionable in part because they correlate with "race" in the U.S., but they are also objectionable more generally to the extent that they are not the result of personal choices.'[107]

Binns' goal, developed in another related piece,[108] was to situate objections to COMPAS within an egalitarian framework, to help us to think more precisely about which differences between people might be tolerable. In particular, his concern was with the relationship between choice and luck egalitarianism—whether and how it matters that a particular departure from equality stems from the exercise of choice.[109] But I think that there is a broader significance to the idea captured by Binns' concerns, that the facts upon which decisions are based should be responsive in the right sort of way to individual choice.

I have argued that there are important reasons to want to have the opportunity to avoid significant burdens by choosing appropriately, which can apply with particular force to policies of criminal punishment. These reasons do not cease to have force once an individual is convicted of some criminal offence, such that we have determined (accurately or otherwise) that they have chosen poorly. Reasons to want the type and duration of any criminal punishment to be sensitive to one's choices apply also to the sentencing decision, and to the burdens that follow from it.

We have seen that some of these reasons are instrumental: they relate to the way in which having and exercising the opportunity to choose can make our lives go better. These reasons are particularly powerful in the context of criminal punishment, in which the impact of punitive decisions can be significant and lasting for the individual. Moreover, they are reasons for putting conditions in place that can facilitate and incentivize good choices, by allowing people to live meaningful lives without breaking the rules that proscribe certain actions.

We have also seen that there are non-instrumental reasons to value the opportunity to act in a way that expresses our personality, preferences, and attitudes, opportunities that can be substantially circumscribed by incarceration.[110] And there are symbolic reasons to want punishment to reflect our status as rational choosers—reasons for providing individuals with opportunities to avoid the burdens of criminal punishment by choosing appropriately, which communicate certain things about our capacity to make those choices well. Giving people the chance to avoid punishment, by making those burdens contingent upon how they respond when confronted with different options, signals that they have the competence and maturity to make these choices. By contrast, denying these opportunities by making punishment contingent upon characteristics over which they have little or no influence, signals the contrary—that those who have these characteristics are less competent to choose well, and less deserving of the privileges this competence entails.

So, there are particularly powerful (instrumental, representative, and symbolic) reasons to want to have the opportunity to avoid criminal punishment by choosing appropriately, and to have background conditions that can support us to exercise these choices well. We deny these opportunities when we attach legal consequences to facts that are beyond the influence of those affected. And this, of course, is precisely the effect of tools like COMPAS, which purport to predict the choices that people will make on the basis of facts that have little or nothing to do with the choices that they have made in the past—the behaviour of their family and friends, their socio-economic circumstances, the characteristics of their neighbourhood, and so on. When we use these algorithmic outputs to determine criminal punishment, we make the burdens of criminal punishment inevitable for those whose characteristics and circumstances correspond to these facts.

Of course, we cannot always justify providing the opportunity to avoid certain significant social burdens by making choosing well amongst a range of alternatives. For instance, if we allocate vaccines or vital organs on the basis of good behaviour, we will fail to save lives that could be saved by a policy that sidelined individual choice in favour of, say, vulnerability and likelihood that the relevant operation will succeed. But policies of criminal punishment are not of this kind; they respond to intentional actions, which follow from our judgements about the world around us. And COMPAS tools are used to predict intentional actions of a particular kind—actions that count as criminal legal transgressions. It is in this context that we should ask and answer questions about the value of having certain outcomes depend upon the way in which we behave when confronted with a range of alternatives.

In this respect, the way in which the COMPAS exercise is framed betrays a particular view of the rationale for predictive punishment. The COMPAS Practitioners' Guide begins with an analogy:

> Think about the different steps taken in the medical field to find a solution
> to an illness or a problem. When you don't feel well and you go to the doctor,

what is the first thing that the doctor does? Asks about symptoms: When did they start? How severe are they? She asks about your medical history: Are you taking any medications? Have you had this or a similar problem before? And, she runs tests, takes your temperature, takes your blood pressure, takes blood samples, orders MRIs, etc. What does she do with all of this information? She makes a diagnosis and prescribes an effective treatment.[111]

This, Equivant tells us, is how we should understand criminal risk assessment: practitioners are 'connecting the dots' that chart the path from facts about individual history to criminal activity,[112] to inform a diagnosis and decision about the most 'effective treatment'.[113]

Like Goring, Equivant takes this 'diagnostic' exercise one step further, drilling down into a set of male and female criminal 'typologies' that correspond to different legal categories: the 'socially marginalized—poor, uneducated, stressed, habitual offenders' tend towards 'instrumental crime for financial gain'; 'young antisocial poorly educated women with some violent offences'; and 'family disorganization and inadequate parenting' lead to 'residential instability and minor non-violent offences'.[114]

But criminal punishment is not medical treatment, and intentional action differs fundamentally from health and medical prognosis. I cannot choose whether a particular course of medical treatment will be effective for me (other than by following any relevant advice for treatment administration), but I can (given suitable conditions) choose how to act in order to stay on the right side of the law. When criminal punishment is presented as a 'diagnostic' exercise—an exercise in identifying the characteristic symptoms of an underlying condition—these distinctions lose prominence. According to policies of criminal punishment that rely upon COMPAS outputs, certain social and economic facts can simply mark people out as belonging to an undesirable social type—a type that is defined by deviant behaviours that (so it goes) can warrant a certain kind of institutional response. This response includes the regulation of access to a range of personal freedoms that are critical to self-expression, and to the satisfaction of various individual goals and preferences.

If this is what's at stake for individuals when we use COMPAS to make sentencing and other critical decisions within the realm of criminal justice, where does this leave us? We have already seen that there are a number of obstacles to measuring rates of recidivism, and that—whilst we have evidence to connect certain characteristics and proxies for recidivism—we lack evidence to show that incarcerating people with these characteristics increases public safety and security. Accordingly, the strongest reasons for wanting to institute a policy of criminal justice that incorporates COMPAS outputs may not be very strong at all.

But let us put the question as a hypothetical: *if* it could be demonstrated that such a policy lowered the risk of recidivism, perhaps in some small but statistically significant way, could reasons of public safety for wanting such a policy outweigh the reasons that defendants have for wanting the sentencing process to be responsive to instrumental, representative, and symbolic reasons from individual choice? If the answer is no (and I think it is), this conclusion has significant implications for policy decisions about the use of wide-ranging algorithmic risk assessments within criminal justice.

The point that I have tried to make here is a simple one, though it matters a great deal to the way in which we approach decision-making within the sphere of criminal justice: an 'ideal crime-fighting world' is not one in which we can make unassailable predictions about criminal activity, for individuals to be 'detained for precisely the right amount of time'; it is a world in which we give everyone the chance to avoid or minimize the significant burdens of punishment, and the benefit of any doubt about their ability to choose well.

Relentless Pursuit

Robert Jones moved to Pasco County, Florida, with his family in early 2015. Shortly after the family arrived, law enforcement officers employed by the Pasco County Sheriff's Office (PCSO) began showing up at their house. Deputies often visited multiple times a day, and sometimes at night. On one occasion, Robert reported coming home from work to find eighteen officers outside his home, hammering on the windows and yelling at his young daughters to let them in.[115] Robert entered the property to find his distraught children hiding under the bed.[116]

The reason for this behaviour became apparent in short order: without any warning or opportunity to challenge the decision, Robert's son had been identified as a threat by the PCSO's predictive policing algorithm, which was rolled out shortly before the family arrived in Pascoe County. That algorithm is not complex. A simple scoring system assigns points for various factors that include: socio-economic deprivation;[117] 'adverse childhood experiences' and 'poor rearing';[118] 'having delinquent friends';[119] and being a victim of personal crime,[120] or even a 'bystander' or the person who reported a crime.[121] Scores are used by police to identify 'at-risk youth who are destined to a life of crime' (so-called 'targets').[122] A target is never formally notified that they have been included within the programme, and they have no opportunity to contest their inclusion.[123]

For the algorithm to 'produce the greatest impact to our bottom line', the PCSO say, potential offenders must 'believe the costs of committing a crime outweigh the benefits'.[124] This, they argue, requires a practice of 'relentless pursuit', to ensure that targets 'feel the pressure'.[125] Accordingly, deputies are sent to visit the target residence repeatedly—often multiple times per day, at any time or day or night, over the course of several years. They scale fences, use flashlights and bullhorns, and approach anyone seen arriving at or leaving the residence. Family and friends are pulled over by police whilst driving, and issued citations for trivial civil code violations. One former PCSO deputy told journalists that deputies would 'literally go out there and take a tape measure and measure the grass if somebody didn't want to cooperate'.[126]

Because officers believed that Robert was not cooperating with surveillance efforts, they became increasingly inventive with citations—uncut grass, missing mailbox numbers, and having a trailer on the property.[127] They failed to notify Robert of those citations, and then obtained arrest warrants when he did not turn up for court hearings.[128] When officers discovered a young employee smoking on his property, Robert was arrested for causing the 'delinquency of a minor', child neglect, and the possession of marijuana.[129] Robert was arrested five times between October 2015 and April 2016. None of these arrests led to a conviction.[130]

One former PCSO deputy described these tactics with the following words: 'Make their lives miserable until they move or sue.'[131] Robert chose to do both. After a confrontation with officers during the early hours of one morning in mid-2016, Robert's family decided that life in Pasco County was no longer tolerable. They left that night—first to a hotel, and then to more permanent accommodation.[132] Nevertheless, the State continued to pursue its retaliatory charges throughout the following year.[133] In April 2017, prosecutors finally asked the court to enter a judgment of *nolle prosequi* on the ground that 'the facts and circumstances revealed to date do not warrant prosecution'.[134] Robert is now party to a civil action against the PCSO, alleging a violation of the First, Fourth, and Fourteenth Amendments to the US Constitution: freedom of association; the right to security of property and person; and the right to adequate and equal procedural safeguards.[135] The action claims damages for (*inter alia*): emotional harm and reputational damage; the loss of property and significant financial and social opportunities; and a number of fines.

The PCSO algorithm is just one example of predictive or 'intelligence-led' policing efforts; there are many others that operate at both local and national levels across the world. For instance, in New South Wales (NSW), Australia, the Suspect Target Management Plan (STMP) has been instituted with the goal of reducing offending in general, and violent offending in particular.[136] Like the PCSO algorithm, the STMP algorithms are used to subject certain individuals to enhanced police surveillance, and targets are unable to challenge their inclusion within the programme. Targets and their families have reported that the programme has caused them to experience social isolation, clinical anxiety, the loss of rental premises, employment, and other financial opportunities.[137] Unlike the PCSO algorithm, the STMP programme includes suspects as young as ten.[138]

There are several reasons to object to the use of predictive policing programmes that target individuals on the basis of facts about their socioeconomic background, upbringing, and interpersonal relationships. The first is an objection of relevance: despite widespread uptake, we lack robust, independent empirical evidence supporting the reduction of personal or violent crime following introduction of these programmes.[139] By contrast, we have clear evidence that they can amplify a range of social problems for those targeted.[140]

The second sort of objection concerns the distribution of policing burdens across populations. For instance, Aboriginal and Torres Strait Islander peoples (hereafter First Peoples) make up 44.1 per cent of STMP programme targets,[141] compared with 3.2 per cent of the national population.[142] Of the seventy-three children under the age of sixteen identified as targets, 73 per cent were indigenous.[143] These are worrying statistics, which evidence comparative and non-comparative failures to discharge state powers appropriately.

As for the latter, the exercise of police search powers in relation to young people under the STMP has been found to be unlawful on several occasions.[144] In these circumstances, individuals do not receive the minimum level of protection that they are entitled to have against this sort of interference.

As for the former, First Peoples do make up a high proportion of the prison population in NSW, which is reflected on a national level: the latest figures (as of June 2022) show that 29 per cent of adults in prison are First Peoples, and 51.5 per cent of the custodial population of young people.[145] For young women, that figure is 69 per cent.[146] But the difference between general population and prison population rates can hardly be used to justify the targeting of heavy-handed police resources. We saw in Chapter 3 that these differences may be attributable to a number of different causes, one of which is the unfair targeting of police resources. There is an egregious circularity to any subsequent attempt to use these differences to justify those practices.

Moreover, I have already argued that the solution to actual or apparent disparities in the perpetration of crime is not to intensify the ways in which individuals experience negative manifestations of state power, thereby aggravating forms of social stratification. Rather, it is to address differences in the social and economic conditions that might affect options for living a meaningful life that does not involve transgressing legal boundaries.[147]

These policies can also give credence to a form of status inequality, which sustains a social and policy environment in which First Peoples are generally regarded as less suitable for certain opportunities, and thus systematically denied important benefits for no good reason. One lawyer representing young people subject to the STMP commented that 'extensive police contact is in and of itself social disadvantageous because [of] the stigma' that this causes.[148] This stigma can operate on an individual level, where those targeted become 'outcasts' or 'marginalised' within their social groups, often causing behaviours that 'manifest in ways in which the police consider to be offending or criminal behaviours'.[149] And it can operate at a systemic level, where society generally regards these groups as less deserving of important social and economic goods.

The final concern relates to the value of individual choice, which is the focus of this chapter. The PCSO tactics target young people on the basis of facts about their individual history, which encompass their social environment and upbringing, and how they have been treated at the hands of others (eg 'adverse childhood experiences', and 'being the victim of personal crime'). As there is nothing that the person affected can do to influence the incidence of these facts, there is nothing that they can do to avoid incurring the burden that follows from them. The child who suffers abuse or neglect cannot avoid being subjected to practices of 'relentless pursuit' and targeted pressure as an adolescent by choosing to conduct themselves well; they never have the chance to make that choice.

There are clear instrumental reasons to want to have the opportunity to avoid this sort of heightened police scrutiny, which (we have seen) can result in social isolation, anxiety, loss of employment, accommodation, and a range of related economic opportunities. And there are important instrumental and non-instrumental reasons to object to the symbolism that attends inclusion within the programme—as the PCSO manual describes it, that an individual with 'adverse childhood experiences' can be 'destined to a life of crime'.

No doubt, we can sometimes justify mandating police engagement for reasons that do not stem from individual choice. Let us suppose that data concerning the rates of crime across a particular population reveal that attendance at certain schools correlates to higher incidences of crime in young people, and that these observations are used to inform a strategy of educational collaboration with law enforcement. This sort of practice, which has far more positive connotations and consequences for those affected, might be easier to justify than targeted surveillance.

For instance, in NSW, Australia, the 'School Liaison Police' (SLP) programme was established to 'increase the positive relationships and remove barriers between the school community and police' by 'developing programs and activities that involve students understanding the law, police role, and their responsibilities to the community'.[150] This sort of practice is not generally seen as reflecting a judgement that these students lack the competence to make good choices. And any negative impact is likely to be minimal (eg drawing much-needed time from the curriculum), with a potential upside of providing an engaging and contextualized learning experience that encourages students to make positive choices.

A more difficult example concerns the use of socio-economic and geographic profiling to concentrate policing resources in certain areas. At their best, these techniques allow police to distribute limited resources effectively, deterring criminal activity and responding quickly to situations of emergency need. At their worst, they increase the risk of social alienation, entrench differences in the level of protection against unwarranted police interference afforded to citizens, and perhaps even cause that protection to fall below minimum acceptable levels.[151]

In each of our examples, those affected experience higher levels of police interaction, for reasons related to facts that do not turn on individual choice. In each case, those affected cannot avoid the costs imposed simply by choosing well. The differences between each example, and the justificatory conclusions that they prompt, turn on what's at stake for individuals—the nature and magnitude of the burdens that they impose, and the symbolism that attends the inclusion of certain individuals within a programme of enhanced police engagement.

The Worst-Case Scenario

At the start of the global COVID-19 pandemic in early 2020, governments across the world were confronted with difficult decisions about whether and how to proceed with standardized school-level assessment. There was no doubt that educational provision had been disrupted in significant ways—both by the virus itself, and by policies introduced to attempt to limit its spread. Nor was there any doubt that the pandemic had affected, and would continue to affect, the well-being of students across the breadth of their lives—including their physical and psychological health, family and social life, and economic resources.[152]

In these circumstances, subjecting students to the examination process—stressful under any circumstances—seemed unduly burdensome, and highly likely to aggravate existing inequalities amongst student cohorts. Moreover, public health guidelines, and a lack of adequate digital alternatives, made the physical demands of mass simultaneous assessment particularly difficult. Gathering hundreds of students together in an examination hall simply was not a viable option, and there was no straightforward way of providing equivalent conditions for accessible, adaptable, and cheat-proof testing.

Yet, for better or worse, standardized assessment is the go-to method across the world for distinguishing between students who are entering a new phase of education, or graduating from school-level education altogether. Higher education providers and employers use exam results as a key criterion for decisions about whether to offer a position to a particular candidate; for the same reasons, students use scores to inform personal ambitions and goals. How then to rank students, if not by requiring them to undergo the typical examination process?

In Europe, responses were mixed. Students in Germany and Hungary sat socially-distanced examinations—assessments that included the typical curriculum requirements, but which were circumscribed by the prevailing medical guidelines concerning physical space and ventilation. Those taking Spain's university entrance exam, the *selectividad*, were offered a range of questions from which to choose, and were not examined on material that they had studied since the national lockdown had begun. Italian students faced hour-long oral exams, whilst Austrian students had the option of an oral exam, or proceeding with written assessment in the ordinary way.

In the United Kingdom, heated discussions were underway about the best approach to take. Roger Taylor, Chair of the Office of Qualifications and Examinations Regulation (Ofqual), gave the British government a list of three options, ranked in order of preference: socially-distanced exams came out on top; delaying exams was the second-favoured option; and 'some form of calculated grades', using a standardized template, was described as the 'worst case scenario'.[153]

On 18 March 2020, the British government's advice was released: all standardized secondary school assessments due to be held in 2020 were cancelled, and a grades standardization algorithm was to be developed by the relevant regulators (Ofqual in England, Qualifications Wales in Wales, Scottish Qualifications Authority in Scotland, and the Council for the Curriculum, Examinations & Assessment in Northern Ireland).[154] Gavin Williamson, then Secretary of State for Education, instructed the regulators to 'ensure, as far as is possible, that qualification standards are maintained and the distribution of grades follows a similar profile to that in previous years'.[155]

In England, the 'Direct Centre Performance Model' (DCPM) was chosen as the model for calculating grades at General Certificate of Secondary Education (GCSE) and Advanced Level (A-Level). The method was relatively simple, though not quite standardized. The school or college ('centre') provided a list of teacher-assessed grades (called 'centre assessed grades', or CAGs) for each subject, ranking students in order of predicted performance.[156] For the vast majority of schools, teacher rankings fed into the final assessment, but the CAGs did not. The DCPM compared assessment data from that school for the three years prior to 2020 to predicted grades for students at the same schools, to provide an assessment of predictive accuracy. Finally, the algorithm took account of students' last-recorded general assessment grades, according to level (SATs for GCSEs,[157] and GCSEs for A-Level).

For small cohorts and minority interest exams (those with assessment groups of fewer than fifteen students), the individual CAG was used unchanged. In his written statement to the Education Select Committee, Roger Taylor later described this as a practical matter: whilst Ofqual had regarded some form of standardization as 'preferable', 'the impossibility of standardising very small classes meant that some subjects and some centres could not be standardised'.[158]

By taking into account the historical grade distribution at the relevant school, the DCPM was able to calibrate individual results by reference to average attainment levels, producing a set of results that were far lower than the CAGs. Indeed, nearly 36 per cent of A-Level grades were lower than the CAGs, and 3 per cent were lower by two or more grades. This was a particularly stark effect of overlaying average centre achievement upon student rankings. For instance, the lowest-ranking students, even if predicted to do well in the exam, might well have their CAG shifted down by multiple grades.[159] As fee-paying (independent) schools generally have smaller cohorts, for whom the CAGs were used without more, this meant in practice that the burden of these negative effects was borne largely by free (state) schools.[160]

This had serious and immediate implications for students affected by the DCPM: in particular, as the media reported widely at the time,[161] a number of students were initially denied university places that were conditional on a certain level of attainment. After a public outcry about the impact of the DCPM and differences between the two modes of assessment (DCPM versus CAG), and a rapid U-turn by the Scottish government under similar conditions,[162] there was a great deal of political and public pressure for the British government to follow suit.[163] The CAG was eventually accepted across the board in place of grades awarded by the DCPM.

Initial resistance to this solution rested on the objection that teachers had handed out 'implausibly high grades',[164] given the difference between CAGs and schools' average performance—this in light of the government's stated objective of ensuring a 'similar profile' between pandemic-context grades and the achievement of students in any other year.[165] Gavin Williamson stated that the use of CAGs across the board would cause 'rampant grade inflation', 'damage' the value of grades, and 'degrade' the system as a whole.[166]

Yet, these allegations seem misplaced. Teachers assess aptitude according to a range of factors, such as class and homework performance over time, whether the student is hard-working and responsive to criticism, and so on. Examination results, by contrast, are affected by a limitless range of possible vicissitudes: the student's emotional and physical well-being; whether they happen to misread a particular question, or time their answers poorly; whether the questions that come up correspond to their revision emphasis, and so on.[167] Some students will be affected detrimentally by these factors, sometimes to devastating effect, and teachers cannot know which. Unless teachers artificially adjust their grades *ex post* to distribute that risk in some way amongst students, teacher-predicted grades *ought* to be higher than the actual grades achieved.

But this raises the question: why was the DCPM, in calibrating grades by reference to the centre's actual spread of grades in previous years, designed to reflect the way in which students at a particular centre would have performed if they had undertaken the (cancelled) examination? The assessment objective that guided the process of policy development was never articulated in clear terms, beyond a broad assertion that any process of grades standardization should correspond to the achievement of students in previous years. But we might express the rationale for standardized assessment as follows: the goal is to provide a set of conditions under which employers and further education providers can distinguish between students, for the purposes of matching them to opportunities for which they are well suited. This can help employers to achieve their own institutional objectives, and can allow students to pursue careers in which they are well equipped to flourish.

If this, or something like it, is the goal of assessment, what does this mean for the kind of information that we are trying to capture? Students may be 'well-suited' for these post-school opportunities because of their natural ability, and/or because they have the characteristics (self-motivation, determination, organization, and so on) to turn their natural ability into practical results. Accordingly, the mechanism for assessment ought to provide some way of capturing these abilities and characteristics, whilst excluding a range of facts that are not relevant to that social goal.

Examinations assess one thing only—the student's performance at a particular moment in time. No doubt, this method may reflect their cognitive skills and the characteristics needed to prepare for an assessment thoroughly at some level, but it suffers from the flaws just outlined; as a method of ranking students, it is highly susceptible to the influence of a range of facts that have nothing to do with the goal of communicating the relative capabilities of students assessed. Thus, by attempting to predict examination results (and doing so by adjusting grades according to the historical achievement of students at the school in question), the DCPM was poorly designed to reflect the social goal in question. More precisely, it allowed a range of irrelevant characteristics to attain decision-making significance in the process of applying the algorithmic rules to individual cases.

It bears emphasis that there are many ways of reflecting relative intellectual capability and self-motivation without mandatory grades deflation. Achieving this goal simply required the ability to distinguish between students in one cohort, and (in context) between students amongst different cohorts. No doubt, a set of higher grades for the 2020 cohort passed some of the decision-making buck to potential employers or higher education institutions, not least where offers had already been made. But this burden, such as it is, seems like a small price to pay in light of the impact of the DCPM.

A full picture of that impact, and of the reasons that lay behind objections to the 2020 dual-algorithm policy, requires us to think about equality—about the differences between the grades allocated to students via the DCPM/CAG approach. At many junctures prior to grade publication, the British government was warned that the DCPM was more likely to downgrade the marks of students from state schools in lower-income areas.[168] Nevertheless they chose to persist with the dual approach—highlighting, as we have seen, the need for systemic integrity.[169] This disparity in treatment may be problematic in each of the ways considered in the previous chapter—because of unequal concern or status between students from different types of school.

First, if the DCPM had the effect of capturing facts that were not related to the social goal in question (and I have suggested that it did), the use of these grades to govern some results but not all will have had the effect of distributing the burden of error unevenly amongst students assessed through different mechanisms, without justification. Moreover, as students from certain backgrounds are likely to be more vulnerable to some of the vicissitudes that can lower examination grades for reasons that have nothing to do with that goal, those facts will also have had an uneven impact upon students attending different schools to whom the DCPM applied.[170]

More simply, the disparity in grading approach—DCPM or CAG, with the consequence of awarding higher grades for students attending private schools—could not be justified by reference to the social goal in question. In Chapter 3, I argued that the duty of equal concern, where applicable, requires agents to justify disparities in treatment between members of the relevant class. So, for instance, a school could justify providing more time in an exam for students with certain educational needs. But it could not justify providing a set of unequal assessment conditions on the basis of considerations that did not bear on the goal of assessing relative capabilities, and the characteristics needed to translate them into outcomes.

In this case, we have seen that the reason for adopting the dual (DCPM/CAG) approach lay simply in the difficulty of applying a standardized approach to small cohorts. As Roger Taylor wrote to the House of Commons: 'the impossibility of standardising very small classes meant that some subjects and some centres could not be standardised, and so saw higher grades on average than would have been expected if it had been possible to standardise their results'.[171] He continued, 'this benefitted smaller schools and disadvantaged larger schools and colleges. It affected private schools in particular, as well as some smaller maintained schools and colleges, special schools, pupil referral units, hospital schools and similar institutions'.[172] This practical difficulty is hardly an adequate justification for adopting a policy that led inexorably and predictably to the disparate outcomes produced by DCPM and CAG; to the contrary, it pointed towards the need to rethink the DCPM approach.

The second egalitarian concern would have been felt less acutely by the students directly affected by the DCPM. Nevertheless, it plays into a set of wider, important, social dynamics that relate to differences in status between individuals. If the result of using the DCPM is to reflect a set of enduring but inaccurate beliefs about the relative intellectual capabilities of students attending certain types of schools, or schools in certain areas, this can feed into systemic beliefs and practices that result in the denial of opportunities to students who graduate (or fail to graduate) from these schools.

Of course, human decision-making is not without its flaws, which affect the conclusions reached with respect to considerations of relevance and equality.

We saw in Chapter 2 that humans display systemic tendencies to make irrational deductive leaps, and are easily influenced by facts that are not directly related to the question at hand. These tendencies are so common and predictable that there is now a large taxonomy of cognitive 'heuristics and biases'.[173] Moreover, a review by Ofqual found evidence of teacher biases in assessment,[174] particularly against those from special educational needs and disadvantaged backgrounds,[175] while a recent study from Russia demonstrated that teachers awarded higher discretionary grades to students with 'more agreeable personalities'.[176] Accordingly, there are reasons to doubt whether using the CAGs for all students would in fact have produced a set of results that corresponded more directly to the social goal in question, without creating unjustified differences between students.

Accordingly, this is not to endorse the alternative approach actually adopted—to use CAGs across the board, in lieu of (some form of) algorithmic assessment, or adapted examination (limited curriculum or different format). Rather, it is to argue that the DCPM, and in particular the dual DCPM/CAG approach, was the worst of both worlds: it neither reflected students' capabilities, nor provided the conditions for equitable assessment.

There is one final consideration, which relates to the focus of this chapter. Students who received the lower DCPM grades had strong reasons to want the opportunity to apply themselves to the task of studying for and sitting the relevant exam, or otherwise to have their grades reflect a set of prior achievements in which they had such a chance. These reasons were predominantly instrumental: they concerned the value of being able to achieve results that would (in addition to being a source of personal pride, a reflection of work well done) open the doors to a range of further, often life-changing, opportunities.

Instead, the DCPM captured facts that included the prior performance of other students attending the relevant centre—facts that had nothing to do with the accomplishments, behaviours, attitude, or character of the student to whom the algorithm was applied in any given case. Thus, by adopting the DCPM, the British government denied students an opportunity that they had significant reason to value—the opportunity to have their assessment outcome turn on a (prior or contemporaneous) process of concerted cognitive effort. And it was this objection that lay at the heart of many of the concerns raised by students and their families at the time of what came to be called the 'grades fiasco'.[177] As Taylor wrote to Parliament on 1 September 2020,[178] neither the moderation nor appeals process instituted 'could make up for the feeling of unfairness that a student had when given a grade other than what they and their teachers believed they were capable of, without having had the chance to sit the exam'.[179] The DCPM denied students 'the ability to affect their fate'.[180]

Every Parent's Nightmare

In February 2018, Megan Johnson left her eight-month-old daughter in the care of her friend, twenty-three-year-old Jacy Mattingly. Jacy would later admit to beating the child, in what the police described 'the worst blunt force trauma in an infant they had seen that had not died or had intercranial bleeding'.[181] At Mattingly's hearing, Johnson told the court that the events of that evening left her daughter's face so swollen that she couldn't hold a pacifier in her mouth. Johnson later told reporters that Mattingly's actions caused deep and lasting trauma to the entire family; in her words, 'our whole world turned upside down'.[182]

But for Predictim, a small company that operated a risk assessment service for anxious parents seeking childcare, the case presented a marketing opportunity—an opportunity of which they took full advantage. At the time of Mattingly's conviction, Predictim used natural language processing and image-recognition software to scan the social media content of potential babysitters, producing risk profiles that parents and primary carers could use to make hiring decisions. Mattingly's case appeared at the heart of Predictim's marketing materials for that month. The company claimed: 'Had the parents of the little girl injured by this babysitter been able to use Predictim as part of their vetting process, they would never have left her alone with their precious child.'[183] A small fee, they said, could prevent 'every parent's nightmare'.[184]

Predictim catered to one of the most risk-averse socio-demographic subgroups in the United States: white, married women, with relatively high economic and educational status.[185] Some of Predictim's marketing materials were geared towards child abuse. As they put it: 'There's people out there who either have mental illness or are just born evil', and 'Our goal is to do anything we can to stop them'.[186] But others played to more subtle social and class-oriented anxieties. A range of blog posts peppered the website, with titles such as 'Children Will Mimic Their Child Care Provider—Who Do You Want Your Child to Act Like?'[187]

Predictim's operational model was straightforward. Clients wishing to use its services could initiate a request for information. This would trigger an email to the potential babysitter, asking for permission to access their social media accounts. Whilst this was presented as an 'opt in' request, the email also informed babysitters that 'the interested parent will not be able to hire you until you complete this request'.[188] The profiles of those who granted access were then graded on a scale of 1–5 (5 being the riskiest) in four categories: 'Bullying/ Harassment', 'Disrespectful Attitude', 'Explicit Content', and 'Drug Use'.[189] Babysitters received an individual score for each component, and an aggregated 'risk level' score.

Predictim was taken offline after Facebook and Twitter prohibited access to their platforms for a violation of their rules against using data 'for surveillance purposes, including performing background checks'.[190] But the model remains in use elsewhere. For instance, algorithmic recruitment company Fama operates a tool that aims to predict which potential employees are likely to engage in sexual harassment, workplace violence, and other 'toxic behaviour' on the basis of public content.[191]

Clearly, these services raise privacy concerns: we have good reasons to want certain aspects of our lives to be free from observation, and to have assurances to that effect.[192] These concerns cannot be answered merely by pointing to the fact that an individual chose to make their data publicly available at a certain point in time; there is a significant difference between the piecemeal public release of information via social media posts, and the aggregation of data to create a new informational product in the form of a risk profile. Nor is it an answer to this concern that potential employees can in theory opt out, if their choices are severely circumscribed by the threat of unemployment.

Other concerns relate to the accuracy of these predictions, not least in circumstances in which corroborating data may be sparse. Linguistic and image-based AI tools, which 'have limited ability to parse the nuanced meaning of human communication, or to detect the intent or motivation of the speaker',[193] simply aren't very good at predicting antisocial language or behaviour, let alone instances of child abuse. There are no studies linking the linguistic habits of caregivers with child safety concerns, nor any connecting Predictim's algorithm in particular to the promotion of desired behaviours in babysitters. Moreover, as individuals are rarely provided with reasons for assessments or mechanisms to challenge assessments, there is no scope to rectify mistakes at an individual or algorithmic level.

Knowledge also feeds into the question of whether the decision-subject has been given an adequate opportunity to avoid the burden in question by choosing appropriately. For instance, in 2013, fifteen-year-old Anthony Stokes was denied a heart transplant by doctors at Children's Healthcare of Atlanta.[194] Stokes met the criteria for need; indeed, he was given a mere six months to live without a transplant. Yet, doctors concluded that his school performance and attendance, and time spent in juvenile detention, were risk factors for 'non-compliance'—the failure to take necessary medications or to attend follow-up appointments. In a letter to Stokes' family, the hospital wrote: 'Anthony is currently not a transplant candidate due to having a history of noncompliance, which is one of the center's contraindications to listing for heart transplant.'[195]

Anthony's situation is not one in which the facts that informed the relevant decision fell completely beyond the scope of his influence. To the contrary, Anthony's intentional actions (albeit actions taken by a child not yet at the age of maturity) formed the basis for the assessment: he had made certain poor choices, which were now the reason for denying him medical treatment. Yet, it should be clear that Anthony did not have a meaningful opportunity to avoid this burden—missing out on life-saving treatment—by choosing appropriately. At the least, this would have required knowledge, or the means to acquire knowledge, that this particular risk existed, and the steps that he would have to take to avoid it. Like the city residents in Scanlon's *Hazardous Waste* example,[196] we are only adequately equipped to avoid some burden if (at least) we are aware both of the circumstances under which that burden will be incurred, and what we need to do to avoid incurring it.

This knowledge may exist (or fail to exist) at two levels: a general understanding that there may be longer-term consequences, including employment consequences, to making antisocial remarks on social media websites; or specific knowledge of precisely what kind of commentary or content is likely to bring about these effects in a particular case.

For Predictim itself, there were no clear parameters for the kind of language that might count as evidence of a 'Disrespectful Attitude'; indeed, those who attempted to reverse-engineer the system to figure this out found a remarkable lack of consistency in categorization.[197] Some of the highest scores were awarded to users whose content appeared innocuous, whilst lower scores were often associated with more controversial, rude, or aggressive content.[198] If it is not possible for users to determine in advance—either on the basis of explicit, situation-specific information provided to them in an accessible and timely way, or on the basis of generally-accessible information that shapes the relevant social context—how they must behave in order to avoid being blacklisted for certain opportunities, they cannot be said to have had a meaningful opportunity to pursue a course of conduct that leaves these opportunities on the table.

A Blizzard of Prescriptions

In 2015, something happened in the United States that had not happened for a century: life expectancy entered a period of sustained decline. According to the World Bank Group, the country's average life expectancy fell from 78.8 years in 2014 to 78.7 years in 2015, and then to 78.5 years in 2016 and 2017.[199] The culprit? A surge of drug overdoses and suicides, both linked to the use of opioid drugs.[200]

'The launch of OxyContin tablets will be followed by a blizzard of prescriptions that will bury the competition. The prescription blizzard will be so deep, dense and white that you will never see their White Flag.'[201] Those were the words of Richard Sackler at Purdue Pharma's launch of OxyContin in 1996. The company had received US Food and Drug Administration (FDA) approval for the drug a few weeks earlier, and the marketing onslaught began immediately.[202] OxyContin was, Purdue told doctors, the drug for patients 'to start with and stay with'.[203]

It appears that Purdue was made aware during or shortly after 1996 that OxyContin had significant potential for abuse.[204] Nevertheless, sales representatives were given explicit instructions to challenge concerns about the potentially addictive properties of opioids, informing doctors that the slow release of OxyContin into the bloodstream made for lower levels of addiction than those demonstrated by comparable pharmaceuticals.[205] By the time Purdue acted, reformulating OxyContin in 2010 to make it harder to abuse, it was too late for many of those who had been given repeat prescriptions for the drug. Some switched to heroin, and later fentanyl—a synthetic analgesic that is up to 100 times more powerful than morphine.[206]

In 2019, a team of economists concluded that the introduction of OxyContin explained 'a substantial share of overdose deaths' in the United States over two decades.[207] Those numbers are high, and climbing: deaths from opioid abuse across the United States increased to 75,673 in the twelve-month period ending in April 2021, up from 56,064 the year before.[208] In 2020, during the height of the pandemic, more people in San Francisco died of opioid overdoses than COVID-19.[209]

Various steps have been taken at both the federal and state level to detect and prevent abuse, one of which is the Opioid Risk Tool (ORT). In 2005, American physician Lynn Webster published an article entitled 'Predicting Aberrant Behaviors in Opioid-Treated Patients: Preliminary Validation of the Opioid Risk Tool'.[210] Having gathered a series of 'known risk factors' from statistical studies into drug misuse, Webster developed a short questionnaire, designed 'to measure the likelihood of whether a patient will abuse opioids in the future'.[211]

The questionnaire consists of ten scorable components, some of which differ by sex.[212] These components include: a family or personal history of substance abuse; the patient's age range; any history of psychological disorder; and (if the patient is female) any history of preadolescent sexual abuse. The ORT was rolled out across the United States shortly after 2005, and is now the second-line medical standard for opioid prescription decisions across the world.

Doctors aim to avoid or minimize opioids where possible as first-line therapeutic agents for chronic pain, prescribing non-opioid painkillers and anti-inflammatories, anti-depressants, and different forms of non-pharmaceutical physical and psychological therapy.[213] Where patients either cannot access or do not respond to these therapies, opioids are deemed to be 'indicated and efficacious in well-selected individuals'.[214] And this is where the ORT comes in, as a way of discriminating between patients who count as 'well-selected': a higher score indicates a higher risk, and contraindicates the prescription of opioid medication.

According to Webster, his goal was 'to help doctors identify patients who might require more careful observation during treatment, not to deny the person access to opioids'.[215] Yet, the ORT is in fact used in clinical practice to decide whether to deny or withdraw medical treatment from patients, and even to terminate doctor-patient relationships[216]—decisions that have a significant impact on patients who suffer from severe and chronic pain.[217] The vast majority of those who have been denied treatment by doctors on the basis of ORT scores are women.[218]

In 2019, a research team led by Martin Cheatle demonstrated that a revised ORT, which eliminates sex-specific questions in favour of a nine-factor questionnaire, is just as accurate as the original ORT.[219] In the same year, Webster publicly acknowledged evidence that 'the ORT has been weaponized by doctors who are looking for a reason to deny patients—particularly, women—adequate pain medication', and urged clinicians to use the revised model. 'Since the question about a woman's sexual abuse history does not provide any additional benefit', he said, 'there is no reason to retain it.'[220]

Yet, the original ORT prevails in medical policy and practice, and those at the forefront of software development in the field medical decision-making have shown no sign of abandoning the datapoint. This includes NarxCare, an automated prescription protocol marketed as a 'substance abuse software solution', which has been adopted by a number of healthcare providers across the United States.[221] Patients subjected to assessment are assigned a 'Narx Score', which is used to inform prescription decisions. The basis for that score is not disclosed to patients or care providers, but NarxCare's public materials reveal that scores may be affected by a range of factors that include 'a patient's criminal and sexual trauma history, number of prescribers, prescription payment method, and distance travelled for treatment'.[222]

In 2020, Kathryn, a thirty-two-year-old psychology student from Michigan, was denied pain relief for endometriosis.[223] The condition, in which cells that normally line the uterus grow outside the uterine walls, can cause chronic and acute pain. Kathryn was experiencing a particularly aggressive form of the condition, and had previously undergone emergency uterine surgery. When her symptoms flared up again, she was admitted to hospital for observation, and given a course of opioid analgesics. She later told reporters that this treatment was abruptly withdrawn on her fourth day of in-patient care, and she was summarily discharged from hospital. As she left, a nurse said: 'It's quite obvious that you need help that is not pain-related'.[224]

Shortly afterwards, Kathryn received a notice from her medical practice indicating that her doctor was no longer willing to provide Kathryn with medical care. In that letter, the practice referenced her high 'Narx Score'. Her own research into the algorithm revealed a possible explanation for that score: Kathryn's two dogs had been prescribed high doses of pain relief medication, which Kathryn was only able to fill by visiting multiple pharmacies in different locations. As Wired reported, it 'looked like Kathryn was seeing many doctors for different drugs, some at extremely high dosages'.[225]

The algorithmic predecessors to the ORT were designed to assess the risk of generalized opioid misuse or aberrant opioid use, which are highly prevalent in patients suffering from chronic pain. By contrast, the ORT has been independently validated for the more serious outcome of opioid use disorders.[226] Thus, the ORT's overall rates of predictive success are relatively good. Yet, there are egalitarian reasons for objecting to policies that continue to capture gender-specific characteristics via the ORT or Narx Score, with the result that medical treatment has been denied to women for reasons that cannot be supported by the goal of minimizing opioid abuse.

Replacing the ORT with its revised successor would be a step in the right direction. But each version of the algorithm, as well as Narx Score, captures a range of other considerations that are not the product of individual choice—facts such as family behavioural history, distance travelled to receive treatment, or whether the individual has access to health insurance. The effect of incorporating these facts into medical decisions is that patients with these characteristics are less able to affect the outcome of those decisions by (for instance) demonstrating that they have a track record of conforming behaviour.

There are important instrumental reasons to want to have the opportunity to choose how to protect oneself against the risk of substance misuse, rather than having medication proscribed in a blanket fashion. In particular, given that patients like Kathryn have exhausted first-line pain treatment options, the ability to access appropriate pain relief is likely to make a significant difference not only to their day to day lives, but also to their ability to make long-term plans on the basis of adequate pain management. Of course, the value of those reasons turns upon the presence of a set of conditions that can encourage good choices, which may include health education, psychological support, and (if the risks of harm are particularly acute) physical monitoring.

We have also seen that denying some people opportunities for choice that are available to others can signal that they are less competent to choose well. This can be the effect of denying much-needed medication to patients on the basis of a prediction about individual behaviour that is based on facts such as family history of substance abuse, or personal experience of sexual abuse—facts over which those affected have little or no influence. In these cases, we treat the individuals who meet these criteria as predisposed to a set of bad choices, which render them less suitable candidates for effective but high-risk medications.

The justification for denying medication is concerned both with the wellbeing of decision-subjects, and the wider interests of others who may be more or less directly affected by the prevalence of substance misuse. As for the former, the 'pejorative ring of paternalism' generally stems from cases in which there is room for substantial doubt about whether the harm is significant, or whether 'poor' choices are really poor, or merely the product of an atypical set of values.[227] In cases governed by opioid risk protocols, there is no doubt that the risks and harms are significant, and that regulating access can mitigate them. Yet, here as elsewhere, there is disagreement about the representative, and symbolic values of unconstrained choices—of 'being self-determining in this way and taking these risks'.[228]

In this context, the question is where we draw the line in terms of preserving or prohibiting access to life-changing second-line medical treatments, given a set of suitable, and suitably affordable, safeguards that can support good choices. This question should be answered by taking appropriate account not only of the instrumental value of having access to appropriate pain management—reasons that can be powerful, not least where other therapies fail or are otherwise unsuitable—but also of reasons that concern the value of being treated as (equally) competent to choose wisely.

Notes

1. Cesare Lombroso, 'Introduction' in Gina Lombroso (ed), *Criminal Man According to the Classification of Cesare Lombroso* (The Knickerbocker Press 1911) 16.
2. ibid.
3. Gina Lombroso, *Criminal Man* (n 1) 24.
4. Cesare Lombroso, 'Introduction' (n 1) 17.
5. ibid 15.
6. Gina Lombroso, *Criminal Man* (n 1) 27–40.
7. ibid.
8. ibid 272–75.
9. ibid 250–55.
10. ibid 258–62.
11. Cesare Lombroso, 'Was Columbus Morally Irresponsible?' *The Forum* (1899) 542.
12. See generally Marvin E Wolfgang, 'Pioneers in Criminology: Cesare Lombroso (1835–1909)' (1961) 52 The Journal of Criminal Law, Criminology, and Police Science 361.
13. Anna Ziliotto, 'Cultural Expertise in Italian Criminal Justice: From Criminal Anthropology to Anthropological Expert Witnessing' (2019) 8 Laws 13.
14. Howard Kushner, 'Deficit or Creativity: Cesare Lombroso, Robert Hertz, and the Meanings of Left-handedness' (2013) 18 Laterality 416.
15. Shaun L Gabbidon and Helen Taylor Greene, *Race and Crime* (5th edn, Sage Publications 2018) 1962.
16. Charles Buckman Goring, *The English Convict: A Statistical Study* (Her Majesty's Stationery Office 1913) 8.
17. Wolfgang (n 12) 374.
18. Earnest Hooton, *The American Criminal* (CUP 1939) 16–17.
19. Goring (n 16) 370.
20. ibid 374.
21. ibid 373.
22. ibid 8.
23. ibid 3.
24. ibid 26.
25. ibid 371.
26. ibid 373.
27. ibid 373, quoted by Gina Lombroso-Ferrero in 'The Results of an Official Investigation Made in England by Dr Goring to Test the Lombroso Theory' (1914) 5 Journal of the American Institute of Criminal Law and Criminology 207, 222.
28. Leonard Darwin, 'The Habitual Criminal' (1914) 6 The Eugenics Review 204, 210.
29. ibid 209.
30. ibid 211.
31. Martin J Weiner, *Reconstructing the Criminal: Culture, Law, and Policy in England, 1830–1914* (CUP 1990) 379.
32. TM Scanlon, 'Responsibility and the Value of Choice' (2013) 12 Think 9, 10.
33. TM Scanlon, *What We Owe to Each Other* (HUP 1998) 251–252; Emmanuel Voyiakis, *Private Law and the Value of Choice* (Bloomsbury 2017) 248–49.

34. Voyiakis (n 33) 128.
35. Scanlon (n 33) 251; Voyiakis (n 33) 106.
36. Scanlon (n 33) 251–52; Voyiakis (n 33) 119–20.
37. Scanlon (n 33) 252.
38. Voyiakis (n 33) 120.
39. Scanlon (n 33) 253. See also Voyiakis (n 33) 120.
40. Scanlon (n 33) 253.
41. John Stuart Mill, 'On the Admission of Women to the Electoral Franchise', Speech in the House of Commons, 20 May 1867.
42. ibid.
43. ibid.
44. Scanlon (n 33) 254.
45. As Mill put it, enfranchising women would eliminate an 'unworthy stigma' obstructing the social and professional advancement of women: Mill (n 41).
46. Voyiakis (n 33) 128.
47. Scanlon (n 33) 256–67.
48. ibid 257.
49. ibid.
50. Voyiakis (n 33) 128.
51. ibid 263.
52. Scanlon (n 33) 251; Voyiakis (n 33) 119.
53. See eg Francis T Cullen, Cheryl Lero Jonson, and Daniel S Nagin, 'Prisons Do Not Reduce Recidivism: The High Cost of Ignoring Science' (2011) 91 The Prison Journal 48S. 'Even for those who are not unusually vulnerable, incarceration can cause long-term detriment to economic opportunity, social integration, psychological wellbeing, and physical health': Lauren Brinkley-Rubinstein, 'Incarceration as a Catalyst for Worsening Health' (2013) 1 Health and Justice 1.
54. Goring (n 16) 26.
55. ibid 24.
56. ibid 26.
57. ibid 373.
58. Brian Netter, 'Using Groups Statistics to Sentence Individual Criminals: An Ethical and Statistical Critique of the Virginia Risk Assessment Program' (2007) 97 The Journal of Criminal Law & Criminology 699, 699.
59. The tool is part of a set of first-generation algorithmic risk-prediction mechanisms, which include the Wisconsin Risk Tool. See eg Faye S Taxman, Meridith Thanner, and David Weisburd, 'Risk, Need, And Responsivity (RNR): It All Depends' (2006) 52 Crime and Delinquency 28.
60. Previously Northpointe.
61. See generally 'COMPAS—Potential Decision Points (County Adult)' in *Electronic Case Reference Manual* (State of Wisconsin Department of Corrections) <https://doc.helpdocsonline.com/arrest-and-adjudication> accessed 23 January 2023. For instance, Wisconsin DOC recommends that probation be imposed if one of the 'eight criminogenic needs' identified by COMPAS is present.

62. See eg Ellora Israni, 'Algorithmic Due Process: Mistaken Accountability and Attribution in *State v Loomis*' *Harvard Journal of Law and Technology Digest* (31 August 2017) <https://jolt.law.harvard.edu/digest/algorithmic-due-process-mistaken-accountability-and-attribution-in-state-v-loomis-1> accessed 20 January 2023; Leah Wisser, 'Pandora's Algorithmic Black Box: The Challenges of Using Algorithmic Risk Assessments in Sentencing' (2019) 56 American Criminal Law Review 1811.
63. Northpointe Institute for Public Management, *Measurement and Treatment Implications of COMPAS Core Scales* (Northpointe Institute 2009) 4.
64. ibid.
65. ibid.
66. ibid 6.
67. ibid.
68. ibid.
69. ibid.
70. ibid 30.
71. ibid 21.
72. Equivant, *Practitioner's Guide to COMPAS Core* (Equivant 2019) 31, 45 and 57.
73. Northpointe Institute for Public Management, *Measurement and Treatment Implications of COMPAS Core Scales* (n 63) 36.
74. ibid.
75. Equivant (n 72) 36.
76. Northpointe Institute for Public Management, *Measurement and Treatment Implications of COMPAS Core Scales* (n 63) 36.
77. ibid 22.
78. ibid 23.
79. Equivant (n 72) 44.
80. Brief of Defendant-Appellant, *State v Loomis*, 2015AP157-CR (Wis Ct App 2015), 2015 WL 1724741, 9.
81. Julia Angwin and others, 'How We Analyzed the COMPAS Recidivism Algorithm' *ProPublica* (23 May 2016) <https://www.propublica.org/article/how-we-analyzed-the-compas-recidivism-algorithm> accessed 20 January 2023.
82. ibid.
83. Julia Dressel and Hany Farid, 'The Accuracy, Fairness, and Limits of Predicting Recidivism' *Science Advances* (17 January 2018) <https://www.science.org/doi/10.1126/sciadv.aao5580> accessed 20 January 2023.
84. Jon Kleinberg and others, 'Human Decisions and Machine Predictions' (2018) 133 The Quarterly Journal of Economics 237.
85. In fact, there are serious doubts about the effectiveness of incarceration as a tool for reducing recidivism. See eg Cullen, Jonson, and Nagin (n 53); Paul Nieuwbeerta, Daniel S Nagin, and Arjan A Blokland, 'The Relationship between First Imprisonment and Criminal Career Development: A Matched Samples Comparison' (2009) 25 Journal of Quantitative Criminology 227.
86. Megan Stevenson, 'Assessing Risk Assessment in Action' (2018) 103 Minnesota Law Review 303.
87. ibid 306.

88. Tim Brennan, William Dieterich, and Beate Ehret, Northpointe Institute for Public Management Inc, 'Evaluating the Predictive Validity of the COMPAS Risk and Needs Assessment System' (2009) 36 Criminal Justice and Behaviour 21, 26.
89. Angwin and others (n 81).
90. See eg Stevenson (n 86) 332.
91. ibid 305.
92. Angwin and others (n 81).
93. Stevenson (n 86) 329.
94. Angwin and others (n 81).
95. ibid.
96. William Dieterich, Christina Mendoza, and Tim Brennan, *COMPAS Risk Scales: Demonstrating Accuracy Equity and Predictive Parity* (Northpointe 2016).
97. ibid 8.
98. ibid.
99. ibid 9.
100. Alexandra Chouldechova, 'Fair Prediction with Disparate Impact: A Study of Bias in Recidivism Prediction Instruments' (2017) 5 Big Data 153.
101. ibid 154.
102. ibid 161.
103. ibid.
104. Brennan, Dieterich, and Ehret, Northpointe Institute for Public Management Inc (n 86) 26.
105. Stevenson (n 88) 332.
106. Rueben Binns, 'Fairness in Machine Learning: Lessons from Political Philosophy' (2018) 81 Proceedings of Machine Learning Research: Conference on Fairness, Accountability, and Transparency 146, 152.
107. ibid.
108. Reuben Binns, 'On the Apparent Conflict between Individual and Group Fairness' (2020) FAT '20: Proceedings of the 2020 Conference on Fairness, Accountability, and Transparency' 514.
109. ibid.
110. Scanlon (n 33) 251–52; Voyiakis (n 33) 119–20.
111. Equivant (n 72) 3.
112. ibid.
113. ibid 3.
114. ibid Ch 5, 52–61.
115. Plaintiffs' Complaint in *Dalanea Taylor, Tammy Heilmanm Darlene Deegan, and Robert A Jones III v Chris Nocco* (2021) 8:21–cv–0055 US DC Middle District of Florida Tampa Division [78].
116. ibid.
117. Pasco County Sheriff's Office, *Intelligence-Led Policing Manual* (Revised edn, PCSO 2018) 13.
118. ibid.
119. ibid.
120. ibid.

121. Plaintiffs' Complaint in *Dalanea Taylor, Tammy Heilmanm Darlene Deegan, and Robert A Jones III v Chris Nocco* (2021) 8:21–cv–0055 US DC Middle District of Florida Tampa Division [128].
122. Pasco County Sheriff's Office (n 117) 12.
123. Plaintiffs' Complaint in *Dalanea Taylor, Tammy Heilmanm Darlene Deegan, and Robert A Jones III v Chris Nocco* (2021) 8:21–cv–0055 US DC Middle District of Florida Tampa Division [256].
124. Pasco County Sheriff's Office (n 117) 17.
125. ibid 18.
126. Plaintiffs' Complaint in *Dalanea Taylor, Tammy Heilmanm Darlene Deegan, and Robert A Jones III v Chris Nocco* (2021) 8:21–cv–0055 US DC Middle District of Florida Tampa Division [178].
127. ibid [79].
128. ibid [81].
129. ibid [84]–[90].
130. ibid [91].
131. Kathleen McGrory and Neil Bedi, 'Targeted: Pasco's Sheriff Created a Futuristic Program to Stop Crime Before It Happens' *Tampa Bay Times* (3 September 2020) <https://projects.tampabay.com/projects/2020/investigations/police-pasco-sheriff-targeted/> accessed 20 January 2023.
132. Plaintiffs' Complaint in *Dalanea Taylor, Tammy Heilmanm Darlene Deegan, and Robert A Jones III v Chris Nocco* (2021) 8:21–cv–0055 US DC Middle District of Florida Tampa Division [93].
133. ibid [95].
134. ibid.
135. ibid.
136. Steve Yeong, 'An Evaluation of the Suspect Target Management Plan' 233 (2021) NSW Bureau of Crime Statistics and Research, Crime and Justice Bulletin.
137. Vicki Sentas and Camilla Pandolfini, *Policing Young People in NSW: A Study of the Suspect Targeting Management Plan* (Youth Justice Coalition 2017) 23.
138. ibid 61.
139. ibid 52–53.
140. ibid.
141. ibid 11.
142. Australian Bureau of Statistics, 'Aboriginal and Torres Straight Islander People: Census' *Australian Bureau of Statistics* (28 June 2022) <https://www.abs.gov.au/statistics/people/aboriginal-and-torres-strait-islander-peoples/aboriginal-and-torres-strait-islander-people-census/2021> accessed 20 January 2023.
143. Michael McGowan, 'NSW Police Accused of 'Oppressive' Tactics Against Subjects on Secretive Blacklist' *The Guardian* (4 July 2022) <https://www.theguardian.com/australia-news/2022/jul/04/nsw-police-accused-of-oppressive-tactics-against-subjects-on-secretive-blacklist> accessed 20 January 2023.
144. Sentas and Pandolfini (n 137) 23.
145. NSW Bureau of Crime Statistics and Research, *Aboriginal Over-representation in the NSW Criminal Justice System (Quarterly Report): March 2022 – Aboriginal Adults* (2022).

146. ibid.
147. Scanlon (n 33) 264.
148. Sentas and Pandolfini (n 137) 32.
149. ibid.
150. NSW Government, 'School Liaison Police' <https://www.police.nsw.gov.au/safety_and_prevention/crime_prevention/young_people/young_people/schools> accessed 20 January 2023.
151. See generally Will Douglas Heaven, 'Predictive Policing Algorithms Are Racist. They Need to Be Dismantled' *MIT Technology Review* (17 July 2020) <https://www.technologyreview.com/2020/07/17/1005396/predictive-policing-algorithms-racist-dismantled-machine-learning-bias-criminal-justice/> accessed 20 January 2023.
152. See eg Wayne Deeker, 'The Covid Generation: The Effects of the Pandemic on Youth Mental Health' *Horizon: The EU Research and Innovation Magazine* (20 January 2022) <https://ec.europa.eu/research-and-innovation/en/horizon-magazine/covid-generation-effects-pandemic-youth-mental-health> accessed 11 April 2023 and Aparajita Ashwin, Satya D Cherukuri, and Ashwin Rammohan, 'Negative Effects of COVID-19 Pandemic on Adolescent Health: Insights, Perspectives, and Recommendations' (2022) 21 Journal of Global Health 12.
153. Richard Adams, 'Gavin Williamson to Blame for England Exams Fiasco, Says Ofqual Chair' (3 September 2020) <https://www.theguardian.com/education/2020/sep/02/gavin-williamson-to-blame-for-england-exams-fiasco-says-ofqual-chair> accessed 7 April 2023.
154. Andrew Sparrow, 'All schools to close from Friday; GCSE and A-level exams cancelled—UK Covid-19, as it happened' *The Guardian* (18 April 2020) <https://www.theguardian.com/politics/live/2020/mar/18/uk-coronavirus-live-boris-johnson-pmqs-cbi-urges-government-pay-businesses-directly-saying-350bn-loangrant-package-not-enough> accessed 14 April 2023.
155. Ben Quinn and Richard Adams 'England Exams Row Timeline: Was Ofqual Warned Of Algorithm Bias?', *The Guardian* (21 August 2020) <https://www.theguardian.com/education/2020/aug/20/england-exams-row-timeline-was-ofqual-warned-of-algorithm-bias#:~:text=With%20schools%20closed%20and%20the,to%20that%20in%20previous%20years%E2%80%9D> accessed 7 April 2023.
156. Anthony Kelly, 'A Tale of Two Algorithms: The Appeal and Repeal of Calculated Grades Systems in England and Ireland in 2020' (2021) 47 British Education Research Journal 725, 726.
157. Standardised Assessment Tasks, or 'SATs' are undertaken by students prior to GCSE level in British secondary schools.
158. Roger Taylor, Chair, Ofqual Board, *Getting the grades they've earned: COVID-19: the cancellation of exams and 'calculated' grades: Response to the Committee's First Report: Annex 2, Written statement from Chair of Ofqual to the Education Select Committee on this year's GCSE, AS, A level, extended project and advanced extension award qualification results* (1 September 2020) <https://publications.parliament.uk/pa/cm5801/cmselect/cmeduc/812/81205.htm> accessed 22 June 2022.
159. Rosemary Bennett and Ryan Watts, 'A-Level Results: Gove's Reforms Fail to Prevent Rise in Top Grades' *The Times* (5 September 2020) <https://www.thetimes.co.uk/arti

cle/a-level-results-goves-reforms-fail-to-prevent-rise-in-top-grades-wr80tvb3m> accessed 14 April 2023.

160. Richard Adams and Niamh McIntyre, 'England A-Level Downgrades Hit Pupils from Disadvantaged Areas Hardest' *The Guardian* (13 August 2020) <https://www.theguardian.com/education/2020/aug/13/england-a-level-downgrades-hit-pupils-from-disadvantaged-areas-hardest> accessed 14 April 2023.

161. Sean Coughlan, Katherine Sellgren, and Judith Burns, 'Anger over 'Unfair' Results This Year' *BBC News* (13 August 2020) <https://www.bbc.com/news/education-53759832> accessed 11 April 2023; Steven Swinford, 'Gavin Williamson Interview: "In Scotland there were no checks ... it degrades every single exam result"' *The Times* (5 September 2020) <https://www.thetimes.co.uk/article/gavin-williamson-interview-in-scotland-there-were-no-checks-it-degrades-every-single-exam-result-gwrhx8ztx> accessed 14 April 2023.

162. Alan McGuinness, 'Tens of thousands of Scottish pupils have exam results reinstated after outcry: Scotland's education secretary says the 124,564 results affected will revert to the grades estimated by the pupils' teachers' *Sky News* (11 August 2020) <https://news.sky.com/story/downgraded-scottish-exam-results-to-be-withdrawn-after-moderation-controversy-12047226> accessed 11 April 2023.

163. Fiona McIntyre and Chris Parr, 'Triple Lock' for A Level Results after "Humiliating" Scottish U-turn' *ResearchProfessional News* (12 August 2020) <https://www.researchprofessionalnews.com/rr-he-government-education-2020-8-triple-lock-for-a-level-results-after-humiliating-scottish-u-turn/> accessed 11 April 2023.

164. Aubrey Allegretti, 'A-level results: Government accused of "baking in" inequality with "boost" for private schools' *Sky News* (13 August 2020) <https://news.sky.com/story/35-of-a-level-results-downgraded-by-one-grade-figures-reveal-12048251> accessed 11 April 2023.

165. Ben Quinnand Richard Adams, 'England Exams Row Timeline: Was Ofqual Warned of Algorithm Bias?' *The Guardian* (21 August 2020) <https://www.theguardian.com/education/2020/aug/20/england-exams-row-timeline-was-ofqual-warned-of-algorithm-bias#:~:text=With%20schools%20closed%20and%20the,to%20that%20in%20previous%20years%E2%80%9D> accessed 7 April 2023.

166. Swinford (n 161).

167. Sam Freedman summarized it well in a Twitter Post: 'The reason teacher predicted grades were much higher than exam results is not because teachers (on the whole) were being unethical or unprofessional but because teachers are assessing their view of capability and exams assess actual performance. For instance, imagine I'm a maths teacher in a normal year and I have 5 pupils who I know are all capable of getting an A. They sit the exam and only 3 get an A, for whatever reason, e.g. a tough question they weren't prepared for etc ... Now this year I have to give an assessed grade for those 5. What do I do—well I know they're all capable of an A so I put them down as an A. That happens across the system so overall now there are far more students predicted an A than in a normal exam year. But as the teacher I've done nothing wrong or unprofessional. How could I possibly tell which of those 5 would not perform on the day? All I can possibly judge on is whether they are capable based on their work to date. It is literally impossible for individual teachers and schools to anticipate exam results and moderate

accordingly so it's really wrong to try and somehow indicate they are to blame for this' *Twitter* (14 August 2020) <https://twitter.com/Samfr/status/1294033335237455878> accessed 7 April 2023.
168. <https://www.theguardian.com/education/2020/aug/20/england-exams-row-timeline-was-ofqual-warned-of-algorithm-bias> accessed 23 January 2023.
169. Swinford (n 161).
170. Moreover, schools in the least affluent areas also had a higher number of teacher assessments downgraded than those in the wealthiest: Rosemary Bennett, Oliver Wright, and Nicola Woolcock, 'Tory MPs Revolt over "Shambolic" A Levels' *The Times* (14 August 2020) <https://www.thetimes.co.uk/article/tory-mps-revolt-over-shambolic-a-levels-208xb3tsh> accessed 14 April 2023.
171. Taylor (n 158).
172. ibid.
173. See generally Daniel Kahneman, *Thinking, Fast and Slow* (Penguin 2012); Keith E Stanovich and Richard F West, 'Individual Differences in Reasoning: Implications for the Rationality Debate?' (2000) 23 Behavioral and Brain Sciences 645 and Jonathan Evans, 'Heuristic and Analytic Processes in Reasoning' (1984) 75 British Journal of Psychology 451.
174. Jake Anders and others, 'Pupils with Graduate Parents Received an Unfair Advantage in Their A-Level Results Last Year' *LSE British Politics and Policy* (10 June 2021) <https://blogs.lse.ac.uk/politicsandpolicy/a-level-results-unfair-advantage/> accessed 10 April 2023.
175. Ofqual, 'Systematic Divergence between Teacher and Test-Based Assessment: Literature Review' https://ofqual.blog.gov.uk/2021/05/17/bias-in-teacher-assessment-results/> accessed 10 April 2023.
176. Sean Coughlan, 'Teachers' Grades Biased to More "Agreeable" Pupils, Claim Psychologists' *BBC News* (20 May 2021) <https://www.bbc.com/news/education-57178473> accessed 10 April 2023.
177. Daan Kolkman, 'F**k the Algorithm?: What the World Can Learn from the UK's A-Level Grading Fiasco' *LSE Blogs* (26 August 2020) <https://blogs.lse.ac.uk/impactofsocialsciences/2020/08/26/fk-the-algorithm-what-the-world-can-learn-from-the-uks-a-level-grading-fiasco/> accessed 14 April 2020.
178. Taylor (n 158).
179. ibid.
180. ibid.
181. Jeff D'Alessio, 'Mother Describes Frantic Moments after Child Abused by Sitter' *The News Enterprise* (20 February 2019) <https://www.thenewsenterprise.com/news/crime_and_courts/mother-describes-frantic-moments-after-child-abused-by-sitter/article_2a4ec24d-c79d-5d06-b245-932a856135ff.html> accessed 20 January 2023.
182. ibid.
183. Drew Harwell, 'Wanted: The 'Perfect Babysitter'. Must Pass AI Scan for Respect and Attitude' *The Washington Post* (23 November 2018) <https://www.washingtonpost.com/technology/2018/11/16/wanted-perfect-babysitter-must-pass-ai-scan-respect-attitude/> accessed 20 January 2023.
184. ibid.

185. Allison B Rosen, Jerry S Tsai, and Stephen M Downs, 'Variations in Risk Attitude across Race, Gender, and Education' (2003) 23 Medical Decision Making 511.
186. Harwell (n 183).
187. Brian Merchant, 'Predictim Claims Its AI Can Flag 'Risky' Babysitters. So I Tried it on the People Who Watch my Kids' *Gizmodo* (6 December 2018) <https://gizmodo.com/predictim-claims-its-ai-can-flag-risky-babysitters-so-1830913997> accessed 20 January 2023.
188. Harwell (n 183).
189. Merchant (n 187).
190. Harwell (n 183).
191. See generally Miranda Bogen and Aaron Rieke, *Help Wanted: An Examination of Hiring Algorithms, Equity, and Bias* (Upturn 2018).
192. Scanlon (n 33) 203–04.
193. Natasha Duarte and Emma Llansó, 'Mixed Messages? The Limits of Automated Social Media Content Analysis' *Center for Democracy and Technology* (28 November 2017) <https://cdt.org/insights/mixed-messages-the-limits-of-automated-social-media-content-analysis/> accessed 20 January 2023.
194. Elizabeth Landau, 'Teen Put on Heart Transplant List After Earlier Denial' *CNN* (14 August 2013) <https://edition.cnn.com/2013/08/14/health/georgia-heart-transplant/index.html> accessed 20 January 2023.
195. ibid.
196. ibid 257.
197. Merchant (n 187).
198. ibid.
199. Sarah De Weerdt, 'Tracing the US Opioid Crisis to Its Roots' *Nature Outlook* (11 September 2019) <https://www.nature.com/articles/d41586-019-02686-2> accessed 20 January 2023.
200. ibid.
201. Patrick Radden Keefe, *The Secret History of the Sackler Dynasty: Empire of Pain* (Pan Macmillan 2021) 206.
202. ibid 208.
203. ibid.
204. Barry Meier, 'Origins of an Epidemic: Purdue Pharma Knew its Opioids Were Widely Abused' *New York Times* (29 May 2018) <https://www.nytimes.com/2018/05/29/health/purdue-opioids-oxycontin.html> accessed 20 January 2023.
205. Keefe (n 201) 208.
206. 'Patrick Radden Keefe Traces the Roots of America's Opioid Epidemic' *The Economist* (13 May 2021) <https://www.economist.com/books-and-arts/2021/05/13/patrick-radden-keefe-traces-the-roots-of-americas-opioid-epidemic> accessed 23 January 2023.
207. Keefe (n 201) 408.
208. Centers for Disease Control and Prevention, National Center for Health Statistics, 'Drug Overdose Deaths in US Top 100,000 Annually' (17 November 2021) <https://www.cdc.gov/nchs/pressroom/nchs_press_releases/2021/20211117.htm> accessed 20 January 2023.

209. 'Last year, more people in San Francisco died of overdoses than of covid-19' *The Economist* (15 May 2021) <https://www.economist.com/united-states/2021/05/15/last-year-more-people-in-san-francisco-died-of-overdoses-than-of-covid-19> accessed 20 January 2023.
210. Lynn R Webster and Rebecca M Webster, 'Predicting Aberrant Behaviors in Opioid-Treated Patients: Preliminary Validation of the Opioid Risk Tool' (2005) 6 Pain Medicine 432.
211. ibid 433.
212. The tool does not specify whether this is biological sex or identified gender.
213. Martin D Cheatle and others, 'Development of the Revised Opioid Risk Tool to Predict Opioid Use Disorder in Patients with Chronic Non-Malignant Pain' (2019) 20 Journal of Pain 842, 851.
214. ibid.
215. Lynn Webster, 'Another Look at the Opioid Risk Tool' *Pain News Network* (29 June 2022) <https://www.painnewsnetwork.org/stories/2022/6/29/another-look-at-the-opioid-risk-tool> accessed 20 January 2023.
216. See eg Nathan R Brott, Elisha Peterson, and Marco Cascella, *Opioid Risk Tool* (StatPearls Publishing 2022).
217. Jennifer D Oliva, 'Dosing Discrimination: Regulating PDMP Risk Scores' (2022) 110 California Law Review 47.
218. Webster (n 215).
219. Cheatle and others (n 213) 851.
220. Webster (n 215).
221. Oliva (n 217) 97–102.
222. ibid.
223. Maia Szalavitz, 'The Pain Was Unbearable. So Why Did Doctors Turn Her Away?' *Wired* (11 August 2021) <https://www.wired.com/story/opioid-drug-addiction-algorithm-chronic-pain/> accessed 20 January 2023.
224. ibid.
225. ibid.
226. See generally Cheatle and others (n 213).
227. Scanlon (n 33) 254.
228. ibid.

5
Transparency

A Chilling Conclusion

Dr John Yelenic, a dentist in Blairsville, Pennsylvania, was brutally assaulted and murdered in his home in the early hours of 13 April 2006.[1] Yelenic had suffered multiple stab wounds and partial decapitation. Police found blood on the walls, floors, and furniture. A sample was recovered from underneath Yelenic's fingernails, which contained DNA from Yelenic and another unidentified person. Yelenic was at the end of bitter divorce proceedings with his wife Michelle Yelenic, and the police took a DNA sample from Michelle's new partner, Kevin Foley.

Those samples were sent for processing by the FBI's forensic lab, and by TrueAllele, Cybergenetic's probabilistic genotyping software. Each result implicated Foley, but the match statistics varied widely. At trial, a forensic scientist employed by the FBI testified to a 1 in 13,000 chance that the DNA found at the crime scene belonged to someone other than Foley, selected at random from the population (the Random Match Probability, or RMP). Dr Mark Perlin, CEO and CSO of probabilistic genotyping company Cybergenetics, testified to an RMP of 1 in 189 billion. The jury found Foley guilty of first-degree murder, and he was sentenced to life imprisonment in 2009.[2]

In 2018, a team led by analytical chemist and geneticist John Butler published the results of 'Mix13', a study assessing the ability of forensic labs to process DNA mixtures derived from multiple sources (so-called 'complex mixtures').[3] The Mix13 team contrived a range of scenarios, one of which involved DNA recovered from a ski-mask at the site of a gang-related bank robbery. The sample contained DNA from four unrelated individuals, and labs were given swabs from two suspects (5A and 5B), and one red herring (5C), whose DNA was not part of the sample. The purpose of Case 5 was 'to explore whether laboratories would consider this mixture too complex to interpret, and whether they would include the non-contributing reference profile and provide a matching statistic'.[4]

One hundred and eight labs across the United States and Canada supplied results, including a range of federal forensic labs. Almost three quarters provided an RMP for 5C, ranging from 1 in 9 to 1 in 344,000. Twenty-seven labs declared the mixture 'inconclusive', and only seven were able to exclude 5C.[5] Greg Hampikian, biologist and founder of the Idaho Innocence Project, describes this as a 'chilling conclusion':[6] the result, he says, is 'equivalent to an innocent person being wrongly tied to a crime by DNA' in an overwhelming majority of lab-processed samples.[7]

In previous chapters, we saw that jurors often overestimate the accuracy and significance of DNA evidence, even when faced with single-source samples that admit a much lower rate of predictive error. But Mix13 revealed just how misplaced that confidence may be for DNA match results in the context of complex mixtures, which have traditionally required the interposition of human judgement, and return much lower rates of accuracy.

TrueAllele, developed by Cybergenetics and launched in 2001,[8] is an algorithmic tool that uses probabilistic genotyping software to process complex mixtures of DNA. In their own studies, Cybergenetics has demonstrated much higher rates of accuracy for TrueAllele match statistics than existing techniques in mixtures of up to ten individuals.[9] Independent studies have yet to verify these results, though Cybergenetics was part of the small minority of institutions that were able to discount 5C in Mix13.[10]

The company's genotyping success has been met with support by the Innocence Project, a non-profit organization dedicated to the goal of exonerating defendants who have been wrongfully convicted. A partnership between the two organizations produced five exonerations in the United States between 2016 and 2019.[11] But TrueAllele is used on both sides of the criminal justice process, and many others have raised concerns about the rapidity with which TrueAllele DNA match statistics have been rolled out to support evidence of guilt. These concerns have prompted a number of procedural challenges to the use of TrueAllele to make predictive assertions in the context of criminal justice,[12] one of which was instigated by Kevin Foley.

In *Commonwealth v Foley*, Foley appealed his murder conviction, arguing that the trial court had erred in admitting the evidence generated by TrueAllele and communicated to the court by Perlin.[13] Specifically, Foley argued that the evidence failed to meet the procedural thresholds for admissibility of expert evidence.[14] In Pennsylvania, that threshold is the *Frye* test,[15] under which 'novel scientific evidence' must have attracted 'general acceptance in the relevant scientific community'.[16] The defendant argued that TrueAllele failed this test, on the basis that 'no outside scientist can replicate or validate Dr Perlin's methodology because his computer software is proprietary'.[17] Affirming the sentencing judgment, Panella J concluded that the defendant's argument was 'misleading', because 'scientists can validate the reliability of a computerized process even if the "source code" underlying that process is not available to the public'.[18]

Perlin has publicly welcomed this conclusion. He argues that counsel should be satisfied with the ability to access and test the software themselves; in his words, 'Here's the car, here's the keys—drive it'.[19] Others have been less enthusiastic. For instance, Erin Murphy has argued that 'Just as courts would not accept opinions from witnesses not shown to have qualifications as an expert, so, too, should courts not accept opinions from digital "experts" without probing the "qualifications" of the technology'.[20] For Murphy, this process of verification requires access to the code itself, in order to rule out certain kinds of technological failure.

But Murphy's argument begs the question: what sort of evidence about an individual should we accept when we are trying to work out whether they are sufficiently competent to make a reliable assessment about the facts at hand? The best evidence is proof that their judgements are accurate—that they make assessments that are demonstrably correct. As Raz has put it, 'Sometimes we can tell that we or others are good at judging matters of a certain kind by the results of our judgements. That would suggest that we, or they, should be trusted'.[21] 'This is especially so', he says, 'when understanding of matters in that area is slight'.[22]

In the absence of such empirical data, we might resort to professional qualification as an imperfect proxy for accuracy. But this second method lacks the same pertinence to the goal of identifying a set of sufficiently reliable insights into the question at hand. There are many highly qualified people—including the experts engaged to perform forensic assessments in the *Willingham* and *Brewer* cases, considered in Chapter 2—who get things systematically and seriously wrong.

Predictions made using statistical algorithms can be assessed using the first method. We need not resort to some next-best source of information about professional qualification, such as the credentials of protocol-developers; instead, we can look directly to statistical indicia of algorithmic performance—how accurate the algorithm's predictions are overall, and how it distributes the risk of error. The more extensive, independent, and well-constituted that evidence is, the more confident we can be in drawing conclusions about predictive accuracy; vice versa, the weaker the evidence, the less confident we can be that the algorithm's outputs are reliable enough to form the basis of policy decisions.

This brings us to two different types of assessment that we might use to evaluate statistical algorithms. The first is technical: it involves understanding the mechanics of the algorithm, or 'opening the black box'. This is the kind of assessment most typically associated with the field of so-called 'explainable AI',[23] and it was the type of access that Foley claimed was necessary to render the TrueAllele evidence admissible, which was—due to the proprietary status of the algorithm—unobtainable on the facts. The second is a statistical assessment: we apply the algorithm to a predictive task, and record overall rates of accuracy (success at predicting which facts will coincide with the target variable) and the distribution of error amongst the assessed population.

The judge was correct to conclude that the second method sufficed to 'validate the reliability of a computerized process'[24] for the purposes of admitting its outputs into evidence. If, as Murphy puts it, 'courts should not accept opinions from digital "experts" without probing the "qualifications" of the technology',[25] the relevant 'qualifications' of statistical algorithms are output-oriented: they concern predictive accuracy and the distribution of error amongst members of the assessed group. No doubt, there are important questions about where we ought to place the threshold in terms of the quality and independence of evidence required to prove overall and in-group performance. But we can assess these things statistically—by driving the car, not by taking apart its engine.

The Determinative Factor

In 2013, Eric Loomis was convicted of two charges relating to a drive-by shooting in La Crosse, Wisconsin: 'attempting to flee a traffic officer and operating a motor vehicle without the owner's consent'.[26] Loomis' pre-sentence investigation (PSI) included COMPAS risk and needs assessments,[27] which were used to inform the trial court's conclusion that the 'high risk and the high needs of the defendant' warranted a six-year prison sentence with extended supervision.[28]

We met COMPAS (the 'Correctional Offender Management Profiling for Alternative Sanctions') in Chapter 4. COMPAS is a suite of algorithmic tools that are used to predict recidivism risk at an individual and population level for a range of purposes, including sentencing and supervision requirements.[29] So-called 'risk' and 'needs' assessments incorporate a range of facts about the decision-subject, from the nature and frequency of any prior offences to the decision-subject's family and social circumstances, educational background, and employment status.

In Wisconsin, PSI guidelines direct assessing agents to capture these factors through the COMPAS PSI-builder. Guidance highlights the importance of a narrower set of facts that relate directly to the defendant's criminal history, and a broader range of background considerations that include the defendant's intellectual ability, financial means, residential stability, whether they were raised by an adoptive family, the marital status of their parents, and family involvement in criminal activity.[30] Each category informs an overall 'criminogenic' picture, and an attendant sentencing recommendation. Defendants have access to the COMPAS report, but cannot ascertain how factors interact to inform a particular score and recommendation.

Following the sentencing decision, Loomis filed a motion for post-conviction relief. Amongst other things, Loomis argued that the use of COMPAS obstructed his right to due process.[31] Specifically, he argued that it was impossible to demonstrate that COMPAS produced accurate, equal, and individualized decisions, because the algorithm was a trade secret.[32] One of those arguments concerned the type of algorithmic transparency to which decision-subjects were entitled; Loomis' argument, which mirrored Foley's, was that 'the proprietary nature of COMPAS prevents him from assessing its accuracy'.[33]

The trial court denied the post-conviction motion, and the Wisconsin Court of Appeals certified the appeal to the Supreme Court of Wisconsin (SCW). Giving the majority judgment for the SCW, Walsh Bradley J concluded that the proprietary status of COMPAS made no difference to considerations of due process: in her view, sufficient overall predictive accuracy had been established by 'statistical validation studies' that applied the algorithm to independent datasets.[34] The judge acknowledged studies concluding that COMPAS assessments 'disproportionality classify minority offenders as having a higher risk of recidivism'.[35] Nevertheless, she felt that this risk could be dealt with by the application of judicial discretion in sentencing.[36]

According to Walsh Bradley J, this balance between the algorithmic and human components of judicial decisions also disposed of Loomis' arguments about 'individualism'. In the judge's opinion, COMPAS assessments could not be 'the determinative factor considered at sentencing';[37] instead, they should be used to 'enhance a judge's evaluation'.[38] Moreover, she said, the court should feel empowered to disagree with algorithmic predictions as and where necessary.[39] In the instant case, the judge felt that the COMPAS assessments had been used correctly,[40] and Loomis' motion was denied.

For present purposes, two key questions arise from these conclusions: (1) what do we need to know about the algorithm to determine whether we can justify using it to make decisions about how to treat others, and to explain those decisions to those affected? And (2) if this enquiry reveals shortcomings in the way in which an algorithm produces predictive outputs, should human discretion be used to override those outputs in a given case?

Above, I distinguished two kinds of assessment: technical (unpacking the code), and statistical (assessing the algorithm's performance empirically across datasets). But there is also a third kind of assessment that is pertinent to the predictive task in *Loomis*. This third kind of assessment, which has been called 'counterfactual',[41] is a matter of figuring out which factors affect the algorithmic output. We can achieve this by adjusting inputs to isolate statistically significant variables—those which have a noticeable effect on algorithmic outputs—via the interface through which the algorithm gathers the data needed to make a predictive assessment in any given case.

One of the most helpful expositions of this third category has been provided by Wachter, Mittelstadt, and Russell,[42] writing on the topic of algorithmic 'explainability' in the context of the EU General Data Protection Regulation (GDPR). The authors argue that counterfactual explanations can satisfy the legal requirement (such as it is) to provide an explanation of 'automated decisions' for the purposes of the GDPR. We do not, they say, need to 'convey the internal state or logic of an algorithm that leads to a decision'; rather, we need only identify 'a specific, limited set of dependencies between variables and the decision'.[43]

I have already endorsed the broader claim, that we do not need to give technical expositions of an algorithm's code to garner sufficient information about what it does—information that will allow us to determine how the reasons considered thus far apply to a particular policy of algorithmic decision-making. But do we also need to engage in the sort of enquiry for which Wachter, Mittelstadt, and Russell advocate—providing counterfactual assessments to source this information?

Answering this question requires us to understand precisely what it is that we are trying to explain, when we talk about explanations of algorithmic 'decisions'. There are two sorts of explanation that we might give of actions that we take, which depend upon the nature of that action. To the question 'why did you sneeze?', I might answer 'because of the pollen in the air', or 'because I have hay fever'. The action is involuntary, and the reasons to which we point when we explain it are causal.

I will give a different sort of answer to the question 'why did you write this book?'—perhaps that I think that there is something worth saying, a way in which I can contribute to the overall state of knowledge and understanding in the field of algorithmic justice. This time, the action is intentional, and the explanation identifies normative reasons for action: I identify the value that I perceive in acting (whether or not I am correct), which the action is designed to serve.

The second sort of explanation does not just tell us what caused the book to be written; it also shows why that action was something that it made sense for me to choose.[44] It singles out the facts that (I think) count in favour of the action,[45] which have the potential to justify it. These reasons—normative reasons—'provide the standard explanations of beliefs and of actions done with an intention or a purpose'.[46] They explain not only how the action can have come about, but also what made it an 'intelligible object of choice' for the chooser.[47]

So, there are two kinds of explanation—causal (how an action came about) and normative (the value of action, which can justify performing it). Within the field of 'explainable AI' (XAI), the focus has been upon explaining how a particular algorithm came to produce a particular output. Accordingly, the type of explanation that has dominated discussion is causal. As Tim Miller has put it, XAI is concerned with 'revealing underlying causes' behind a particular output.[48] But the focus of the GDPR's provisions about automated decisions,[49] and our focus here, is not merely upon the output of an algorithmic process, but rather upon how that algorithmic process informs some ultimate decision about what to do.

This is important, and gives shape to the final mode of assessment that we might usefully distinguish: a 'normative' assessment is not a mode of assessing the algorithm, but rather a mode of assessing the algorithmic *decision*—a decision about how to treat others, which is informed by algorithmic outputs. 'Decision', here, is not a proxy for the algorithmic output itself, though it may be informed by one (but, under the GDPR, must not be supplanted by one). So we are not merely aiming at a causal account (how did the output come to be?). Rather, 'decision' describes the culmination of a process of reasoning about what to do, which precipitates some intentional action. Accordingly, we go about assessing the decision by looking for normative reasons—the value associated with this policy of algorithmic decision-making, which can ground the decision to adopt it.

Moreover, the claim in a case like *Loomis* is not just this—that there is some value in action, which can create reasons for performing it. It is also a claim that the decision is justified—that those reasons are sufficient to ground the decision, in light of countervailing considerations. The claim is either (as in *Loomis*) that there is a sound legal basis for the decision, or (for our wider purposes) that it is morally defensible. Our concern throughout this book has been of this sort—with figuring out whether we are justified in adopting a particular policy of algorithmic decision-making. So, we are looking both for normative reasons—the value that we perceive in action—and for how those reasons bear up against the case for some alternative policy.

How then do we perform this normative task? Specifically, what information do we need to have about the algorithm, in order to figure out whether we are justified in using it to make decisions about how to treat others? It bears emphasis that the answer to this question will not tell us all we need to know in order to figure out whether a policy of algorithmic decision-making can be justified; we will also need to address a range of considerations that include the magnitude of the costs imposed on those affected, the relative magnitude of costs that this policy allows others to avoid, and alternative routes to achieving these benefits. The focus of this part is merely upon the information that the algorithmic component can reveal, or fail to reveal, on our way to performing that justificatory task.

The claim here is a simple one: the information that we need, and the type of assessment that we will accordingly need to perform, will vary according to the predictive task to which that algorithm is directed, on the basis of which we make decisions about how to treat others. In many cases, the relevant algorithm is not used to make predictions about intentional action. Rather, our question may be, for instance, how an individual will respond to a particular medical approach (such as the Vaginal Birth after Caesarean (VBAC) calculator),[50] or what will happen if we fail to provide it (such as the Model for End Stage Liver Disease (MELD)).[51] In these cases, the goal of our decisions is to improve medical outcomes. And the justification for using the algorithm to help us just is that the algorithm is better at making the predictions that will serve this goal than we would be if left to our own devices.

So, what we need to know about the algorithm in order to satisfy the normative requirement is whether it produces more accurate predictions overall, and whether it does so without concentrating the burden of error on any one group. And that, of course, is something that we can measure statistically. We do not also need to know precisely which facts influence the output, or some technical aspect of the algorithm's code, which might inform an assessment of how the output came to be. It is enough that we know how the algorithm performs.

But I have argued that a distinct concern arises from the use of statistical algorithms to allocate burdens by making certain kinds of prediction—'actuarial' predictions about intentional action. This concern stems from the value of having meaningful opportunities to avoid the burdens of policy decisions by choosing appropriately. I have argued that making these predictions on the basis of facts that individuals cannot (or cannot easily) influence limits the ways in which decision-subjects can affect the outcome by making appropriate choices, which is something that they have good reasons to want to be able to do.

In these circumstances, figuring out whether we can justify using the algorithm to make decisions about how to treat others not only requires us to assess the algorithm's predictive accuracy and error-distribution; it also requires us to look at which factors have informed that output. Specifically, we need to know whether those factors pertain to the choices that an individual has made. This will not, on its own, tell us whether the policy can be justified; rather, it will help us to determine the way in which that policy interacts with reasons that stem from the value of choice.

This information—about how facts inform a particular output—is precisely the information that a counterfactual assessment can reveal. So, we always need a statistical assessment, and we sometimes need a counterfactual assessment—where the decision involves an algorithmic prediction about individual conduct, which was the sort of question at the heart of *Loomis*. We do not in any case need to 'open the black box'—to unpack the mechanics of the code itself.

This brings us to the second question that arises from the judge's conclusions in *Loomis*: if the human decision-maker has doubts about the accuracy of that prediction, or otherwise feels that the prediction has been made on the basis of a set of factors that ought not to inform the decision in question, should human judgement override the algorithmic prediction in a given case? Or, if there is evidence that the algorithm does in fact underperform (relative to unaided human discretion) in one of these ways, can the ad hoc intervention of human discretion make up for this shortcoming?

Those tasked with developing and implementing algorithmic decision-making policies have broadly agreed that the answer to each question is 'yes'. In *Loomis*, the judge considered the impact of COMPAS risk factors upon individual defendants, drawing upon evidence from the Wisconsin Department of Corrections (DOC) to the effect that using a wide range of factors about the decision-subject's circumstances can lead to counterintuitive results.[52] Specifically, the DOC have emphasized that 'an offender who is young, unemployed, has an early age-at-arrest and a history of supervision failure, will score medium or high on the Violence Risk Scale even though the offender never had a violent offense'.[53] Citing this statement, Walsh Bradley J continued:

> To ameliorate this problem, the DOC explains that 'staff are predicted to disagree with an actuarial risk assessment (e.g. COMPAS) in about 10% of the

cases due to mitigating or aggravating circumstances to which the assessment is not sensitive.' Thus, 'staff should be encouraged to use their professional judgment and override the computed risk as appropriate ... '. Just as corrections staff should disregard risk scores that are inconsistent with other factors, we expect that circuit courts will exercise discretion when assessing a COMPAS risk score with respect to each individual defendant.[54]

The judge not only thought that decision-makers are permitted to override algorithmic outputs where predictions seemed aberrant; she also though that the willingness to do so might be a condition of the justification for adopting a particular policy of algorithmic decision-making.[55] This might be because the prediction appeared to include factors that were not relevant in the individual case, or to exclude, overweight, or underweight factors that were relevant. Or it might be because the prediction appeared to underweight the defendant's prior behaviours, as a fact relevant to considerations about the value of choice.

This raises important questions about the interaction between algorithmic predictions and human discretion. Clearly, we need human judgement to shape algorithmic design and development, and to translate algorithmic outputs into decisions about what to do. But the judge's suggestion in *Loomis* was that human discretion could and ought to be deployed to override the algorithmic output in an individual case, in order to produce a justified decision.[56]

This policy of ad hoc engagement with algorithmic outputs is troubling. Our goal is to determine whether a particular policy of algorithmic decision-making is justified, which requires us to think (amongst other things) about the implications of using that algorithm for relevance and equality: how well does the algorithm fare at figuring out which facts bear on our target variable (and how), and how does it distribute the burden of error amongst our target population? As far as the algorithmic component of that policy is concerned, these questions produce binary answers: either the relevant algorithm produces predictions that have a better rate and distribution of error than unaided human decision-making, or it does not.

No matter the relative success of the algorithm, we will bear in mind predictive error when we determine how much weight to give the output. But if those predictions outstrip their human alternative with respect to considerations of relevance and equality, we should not be tempted to override them by applying a clinical assessment on the basis of suspicions that the algorithm is producing an inaccurate prediction for an individual case. We have already seen that statistical algorithms can do a far better job of determining which facts bear on our target variable and how—and may do so precisely when we, as human decision-makers, would be unable to counteract the influence of our prejudices. So, these situations—in which the output *seems* aberrant—may be precisely the cases in which we should be particularly wary of human prejudice.

There is, of course, another objection to the use of facts about social background to determine sentencing requirements, which concerns the value of choice; this may be part of the reason why it seemed inappropriate to the judge in *Loomis* that a high risk score for violent crime could be generated from facts that had nothing to do with a prior crime of this nature. We have already seen that the value of choice may ground powerful reasons not to use a particular output to make decisions about how to treat someone.

So, the allegation that gives us cause for concern in a particular case might be that the algorithm underperforms relative to unaided human decision-making—that it has a worse rate and/or distribution of error. Or it might be the case that there are other reasons to object to the range of considerations upon which the output is based. But the answer to these objections is not to adopt the approach for which the Wisconsin DOC and judge in *Loomis* advocated—giving the output less weight and hoping that humans can make up the difference on a case-by-case basis. Rather, it is to give the output no weight at all.

In short, there is no room for the application of ad hoc human discretion to algorithmic predictions, when we aim at justified decisions about how to treat others. If the algorithm does a better job of making the predictions that help us to achieve some social goal, and does so without concentrating the risk of error on particular groups of people, we should not be tempted to override those predictions in individual cases. But if the algorithm does not have this effect, or if there are reasons from the value of choice for objecting to the range of considerations captured by it, nothing short of a comprehensive and systematic effort to revise the algorithm can justify using it. Picking and choosing how to use the algorithm's outputs on a case-by-case basis is not a recipe for just decisions.

Notes

1. *Commonwealth v Foley* (2012) Pa Super Ct 31; 71 38 A 3d 882. See also Andrea Peirano, 'The Murder of John Yelenic' *Odd Murders and Mysteries* <https://www.oddmurdersandmysteries.com/the-murder-of-john-yelenic/> accessed 20 January 2023.
2. *Commonwealth v Foley* (2012) Pa Super Ct 31; 71 38 A 3d 882, 885–87.

3. John M Butler, Margaret C Kline, and Michael D Coble, 'NIST Interlaboratory Studies Involving DNA Mixtures (MIX05 and MIX13): Variation Observed and Lessons Learned' (2018) 37 Forensic Science International: Genetics 81.
4. ibid 90.
5. ibid.
6. Greg Hampikian, 'Correcting Forensic DNA Errors' (2019) 41 Forensic Science International: Genetics 32, 33.
7. ibid.
8. Mark W Perlin and Beata Szabady, 'Linear Mixture Analysis: A Mathematical Approach to Resolving Mixed DNA Samples' (2001) 46 Journal of Forensic Science 1372.
9. David W Bauer and others, 'Validating TrueAllele Interpretation of DNA Mixtures Containing up to Ten Unknown Contributors' (2020) 65 Journal of Forensic Science 380. See also Katherine Kwong, 'The Algorithm says you did it: The Use of Black Box Algorithms to Analyse Complex DNA Evidence' (2017) 31 Harvard Journal of Law & Technology 275, 283.
10. Butler, Kline, and Coble (n 3) 90.
11. Greg Hampikian and Mark Perlin, *The First Five Exonerations Using TrueAllele Statistical Software: How Labs Can Review and Correct Old Cases* (American Academy of Forensic Sciences 71th Annual Meeting, Baltimore, MD, 23 February 2019).
12. Including recently *People v HK* (2020) NY Slip Op 50709(U).
13. *Commonwealth v Foley* (2012) Pa Super Ct 31; 71 38 A 3d 882.
14. ibid 888.
15. *Frye v United States*, 293 (1923) F 1013 (C Cir).
16. See eg *Betz v Pneumo Abex LLC* (2010) Pa Super; 998 A.2d 962, 972.
17. *Commonwealth v Foley* (2012) Pa Super Ct 31; 71 38 A 3d 882, 888–89.
18. ibid.
19. Lauren Kirchner, 'Where Traditional DNA Testing Fails, Algorithms Take Over' *ProPublica* (4 November 2016) <https://www.propublica.org/article/where-traditional-dna-testing-fails-algorithms-take-over> accessed 20 January 2023.
20. Erin Murphy, *Inside the Cell: The Dark Side of Forensic DNA* (Bold Type Books 2015) 299.
21. Joseph Raz, *Engaging Reason: On the Theory of Value and Action* (OUP 2002) 246.
22. ibid.
23. It has been described as 'revealing underlying causes' behind a particular output: Tim Miller, 'Explanation in Artificial Intelligence: Insights from the Social Sciences' (2019) 267 Artificial Intelligence 1, 2.
24. *Commonwealth v Foley* (2012) Pa Super Ct 31; 71 38 A 3d 882, 5.
25. Murphy (n 20) 299.
26. See eg Brief of Defendant-Appellant, *State v Loomis* (2015) Ws Ct App AP157-CR, 2015 WL 1724741, 1–3.
27. See eg *State v Loomis*: 'Wisconsin Supreme Court Requires Warning Before Use of Algorithmic Risk Assessments in Sentencing' (2017) 130 Harvard Law Review 1530.
28. See eg Brief of Defendant-Appellant, *State v Loomis* (2015) Ws Ct App AP157-CR, 2015 WL 1724741, 10.
29. Previously Northpointe.

30. State of Wisconsin Department of Corrections <https://doc.helpdocsonline.com/arrest-and-adjudication> accessed 20 January 2023.
31. *State v Loomis* (2015) Ws Ct App AP157-CR, 2015 WL 1724741 [6].
32. ibid.
33. ibid [34].
34. ibid [58].
35. ibid [61] and [100].
36. ibid [100].
37. ibid [104] and [120].
38. ibid [92] and *Malenchik v State* (2010) Ind 928 NE 2d 564, 573, emphasis added.
39. *State v Loomis* (2015) Ws Ct App AP157-CR, 2015 WL 1724741 [71]. Wisconsin Department of Corrections guidance states that 'staff should be encouraged to use their professional judgment and override the computed risk as appropriate': 'COMPAS—Potential Decision Points (County Adult)' in *Electronic Case Reference Manual* (State of Wisconsin Department of Corrections) <https://doc.helpdocsonline.com/arrest-and-adjudication> accessed 20 January 2023.
40. *State v Loomis* (2015) Ws Ct App AP157-CR, 2015 WL 1724741 [104].
41. See generally Sandra Wachter, Brent Mittelstadt, and Chris Russell, 'Counterfactual Explanations Without Opening the Black Box: Automated Decisions and the GDPR' (2018) 31 Harvard Journal of Law and Technology 841.
42. ibid 845.
43. ibid 872.
44. Raz (n 21) 23.
45. ibid.
46. Joseph Raz, *From Normativity to Responsibility* (OUP 2011) 26.
47. Raz (n 21) 23.
48. Miller (n 23) 2.
49. See eg art 22: 'The data subject shall have the right not to be subject to a decision based solely on automated processing, including profiling, which produces legal effects concerning him or her or similarly significantly affects him or her.'
50. Darshali A Vyas and others, 'Challenging the Use of Race in the Vaginal Birth after Cesarean Section Calculator' (2019) 29 Women's Health Issues 201.
51. Ashwani K Singal and Patrick S Kamath, 'Model for End-stage Liver Disease' (2013) 3 Journal of Clinical and Experimental Hepatology 50.
52. *State v Loomis* (2015) Ws Ct App AP157-CR, 2015 WL 1724741 [69].
53. 'COMPAS Assessment Frequently Asked Questions' in *Electronic Case Reference Manual* (State of Wisconsin Department of Corrections) <https://doc.helpdocsonline.com/arrest-and-adjudication> accessed 20 January 2023.
54. *State v Loomis* (2015) Ws Ct App AP157-CR, 2015 WL 1724741 [69]–[71].
55. *State v Loomis* (2015) Ws Ct App AP157-CR, 2015 WL 1724741 [71].
56. ibid.

6
Concluding Remarks

Summary

The goal of this book has been to unpack the different reasons at play in conversations about 'algorithmic justice'—specifically, the justification for policies that use statistical algorithms to try to achieve certain desirable outcomes. These reasons are not all, or not merely, egalitarian. In particular, I have argued they include reasons that stem from the value of choice—the reasons that we have for wanting the chance to affect what happens to us, by choosing appropriately from a range of options about what to do.

These reasons are often instrumental: they relate to the way in which having a choice can improve our lives, in small or more significant ways.[1] But not all of them; for instance, there are situations in which denying choices to some people can reflect a judgement, or can be seen by others to reflect a judgement, that those people 'are not competent or do not have the standing normally accorded an adult member of the society'.[2] This can be objectionable for its own sake, and where—by reinforcing stigmatizing differences in status—it results in the unjustified exclusion of some people from important benefits.

These reasons can ground a powerful case for wanting policies to be responsive to the way in which we behave when confronted with different choices, and to be placed in an adequate position to make these choices well.[3] What it means to put someone in an adequate position to choose varies according to the circumstances. At the least, it means providing the sort of information that can equip someone to understand the consequences of their choices, and to understand the actions that they need to take in order to avoid incurring those consequences. But it often also means ensuring that these consequences only kick in at the point at which they have adequate (financial, social, psychological, physical, and so on) resources that can enable them to exercise their choices well, in light of the prevailing conditions.[4]

The focus of this book has been wider than criminal punishment, but I have reserved much of the discussion for policies that fall within this sphere. The reason for this is simple: the burdens of criminal punishment are extensive, and the reasons we have for wanting to get things right—for making sure that the burdens that we impose on individuals are acceptable, in light of the costs that others avoid when we adopt one policy rather than another—are particularly strong. And in this respect, the value of choice points towards a more general claim: if we can justify criminal punishment at all, it is only when we have provided those affected with a meaningful chance to avoid it by choosing appropriately, and a set of safeguards that can help them to exercise these choices well.[5]

Accordingly, I have argued that we have powerful reasons to object to policies that make the burdens of criminal punishment inevitable for some people—those who are born with, or otherwise acquire, characteristics that they cannot influence, which correlate to the incidence of crime. This, I have argued, is the effect of basing our decisions on tools like the 'Correctional Offender Management Profiling for Alternative Sanctions' (COMPAS) system.

The use of these tools to make decisions about how to treat others can raise significant concerns of relevance, which relate to the way in which a particular policy advances, or fails to advance, some social goal at which we aim. It can raise egalitarian concerns, which relate to the duty of certain actors to have and show equal concern for all members of a particular group, and unjustified differences in status that can cause certain people to be excluded from benefits for no good reason. But I have argued that a full picture of what's at stake for individuals also includes concerns that stem from the value of choice.

In particular, these tools purport to make actuarial predictions—to predict the choices that people will make in the future, the (aberrant) actions that they will perform—which are used to allocate significant burdens within the realm of criminal punishment. But these predictions are not necessarily limited to facts that relate to their prior choices; they may also be informed by a range of facts that relate to the conditions under which an individual was born or raised, or the way in which they have been treated at the hands of others.[6] And if individuals cannot influence the incidence of characteristics that affect decisions within this sphere, they cannot avoid the burdens of criminal punishment by making appropriate decisions about what to do. For those affected, these burdens are made inevitable.

Thus, I have argued for a proscriptive approach to the use of predictive tools like COMPAS to allocate some of the most significant burdens of criminal punishment—incarceration (of a particular type or duration), and correctional supervision. I have also argued that we should think carefully about the way in which we allocate policing resources, particularly where this concerns targeted surveillance. For instance, we cannot justify a policy of targeting certain 'at-risk' young people for police practices of 'relentless pursuit', on the basis of relative social disadvantage.[7]

Where we allocate the burdens of criminal justice in this way, we not only deny individuals opportunities that they have significant instrumental reason to value; we also mark them out as less competent to choose well, and less deserving of the social privileges that attend this competence. We treat them as if they are 'destined to a life of crime'[8]—as if they belong to a criminal 'type' whose antisocial proclivities simply warrant a certain sort of institutional response.

Finally, I have made certain recommendations about transparency—about the information that we need to have about the relevant algorithm, in order to determine how each of these reasons applies to a particular policy of algorithmic decision-making. And I have made certain recommendations about human oversight—in particular, about the limits to ad hoc human intervention in algorithmic predictions.

I have argued that we need to be able to gather information about the algorithm's overall performance and distribution of error, via a statistical assessment of its outputs. Where the algorithm makes a prediction about how individuals will behave, we also need to perform a counterfactual assessment—to isolate statistically-significant variables by adjusting inputs via the algorithmic interface.[9] But in no case need we 'open the black box'—unpack the code itself, or 'convey the internal state or logic of an algorithm that leads to a decision'.[10]

Clearly, we need human judgement to guide the processes of algorithmic design and development, and to translate algorithmic outputs into decisions about what to do. But I have argued that we should not endorse a practice of overriding algorithmic outputs in individual cases, on an ad hoc basis.[11] If the relevant algorithm has a better rate and distribution of error than unaided human decision-making, we should not be tempted to override those outputs by applying a clinical assessment on the basis of suspicions that the algorithm is producing an inaccurate prediction for an individual case.

If it does not, or if there are other reasons to object to the range of facts upon which the output is based, the solution is not to give the output less weight and hope that humans can make up the difference on a case-by-case basis; it is to give the output no weight at all. Unaided human decision-making should prevail unless and until a comprehensive and systematic effort can be made to produce an algorithm that can be justified.

So, there are different reasons to object to the use of statistical algorithms to make policy decisions, which concern both the task of figuring out whether and how certain tools serve some policy objective at which we aim, and the nature and magnitude of the burdens that we can reasonably expect people to bear along the way. These reasons point towards certain limits—areas of decision-making in which the costs to some people of using algorithmic tools are out of proportion with the benefits that accrue to others. And, vice versa, they help us to figure out where human discretion should yield.

The English Convict

I began this book with the work of Charles Goring—pioneering statistician and criminologist, whose research played a key role in the development of British criminological theory. Goring believed that those engaged in evidence-based assessment could open the door to a range of 'hitherto obscure phenomena related to the lives and conditions of human beings',[12] via a path 'paved with statistical facts'.[13] He is best known for advancing a particular case about criminal wrongdoing: there was, he argued, a 'criminal diathesis', defined by a set of hereditary psychological and physical characteristics that were 'so potent' in some people 'as to determine for them, eventually, the fate of imprisonment'.[14]

The term 'diathesis' describes the tendency to suffer from a particular condition—typically a medically-diagnosable condition, and especially one that is considered 'abnormal or diseased'.[15] Goring thought that this 'diathesis', once sufficiently defined, would allow us to predict and pre-empt criminal activity. It would no longer be necessary to wait and see—to try to reduce antisocial activity by responding to wrongs *ex post*. Rather, we could pinpoint the criminal in advance, and put in place a set of measures aimed at 'modifying opportunity for crime by segregation and supervision of the unfit'.[16]

Thus, Goring's thesis had two parts: first, there was a distinct and identifiable criminal condition, which could be diagnosed from a range of individual characteristics that had nothing to do with evidence of prior wrongdoing; second, we should incarcerate those who exhibit these characteristics *simpliciter*, rather than waiting for them to transgress the bounds of acceptable behaviour.

I have argued that there are echoes of this thesis in policy practices that now shape critical aspects of our public and private lives. The focus of this book has been upon statistical algorithms—decision-making rules developed on the basis of insights gleaned from patterns in population data. And I have argued that statistical algorithms have allowed us to move towards a widespread practice of 'diagnosing'[17] individuals as criminal, antisocial, or otherwise unsuitable for certain important benefits because of the circumstances into which they were born, or other facts over which they have little or no influence. Individuals who display these characteristics are treated as being 'destined to a life of crime'[18] or other antisocial behaviour, and (as such) subjected to a range of significant institutional burdens.

The mechanism behind this shift is straightforward, and beguiling in its promises of predictive accuracy.[19] Statistics and statistical algorithms are helpful in situations of rational uncertainty—when we are not sure precisely which facts do or will correspond to a certain outcome, our target variable. In the absence of sufficient information to draw a deductive conclusion, we can rely upon statistical inferences to guide our decisions—for our purposes, decisions about how to treat others.

Perhaps a physician is trying to decide how to allocate a limited set of medical resources amongst a group of patients, all of whom have a high short-term mortality risk. She cannot know in advance precisely how patients will fare without medical intervention, or whether a particular patient will respond well or poorly upon receipt. Instead, she relies upon treatment guidelines that have emerged from statistical observations about how other patients with this condition have responded to the presence or absence of (this sort of) intervention.[20]

Or perhaps our goal is to keep people safe and their property secure, and we have decided that an appropriate way of achieving this goal is to incarcerate those criminal wrongdoers who are at a high risk of recidivism—of committing another crime in future, especially a violent crime. We cannot know in advance precisely who will recidivate, so we may decide to look to the statistical evidence: which facts about people correlate to high rates of criminal activity? Those indicia may be reduced to a set of rules for humans or computers to follow—a sentencing algorithm, perhaps along the lines of the COMPAS system, which we met in Chapter 5.[21]

In this way, statistics, and statistical rules, can (for better or worse) help us to make predictions about which facts will coincide with our target variable: how will a patient respond to a particular course of treatment, and what will happen if they are left untreated? Will this person reoffend, and (if so) will the nature of a future offence be violent or non-violent? Of a given pool of candidates, who is likely to do the best job, if hired for a specific role? We use these outputs, in turn, to divvy up the burdens of certain social policies—to decide whether to send someone to prison, which course of medical treatment to prescribe, which candidate to hire, and so on.

Yet the range of facts that inform these predictions is broad, often open-ended. Sentencing algorithms like COMPAS make predictions about recidivism on the basis of facts such as whether an individual was raised by their 'natural' parents,[22] the involvement of family or friends in 'antisocial' activities, neighbourhood crime rates,[23] access to medical insurance,[24] residential instability,[25] and financial stress.[26] In Florida, the Pasco County Sheriff's Office uses a predictive policing algorithm to subject 'targets' within the community to a practice of 'relentless pursuit'.[27] Predictions are based on facts such as socio-economic deprivation,[28] 'adverse childhood experiences',[29] being a victim of personal crime,[30] or even a 'bystander' or the person who reported a crime.[31]

In consequence, these facts feed directly into the decisions that we make about whether and when to impose some of the most significant institutional burdens—the loss of social, political, and economic rights and privileges that play a key role in any individual's ability to thrive as part of society.[32] Where Goring advocated for lengthy or indeterminate prison sentences for the physically or psychologically 'degenerate',[33] judges and judicial officers now use algorithmic tools to prescribe lengthy prison sentences for those who are born into social or economic disadvantage.[34] Police officers use predictive algorithms to target those who, because of 'adverse childhood experiences'[35] or an experience of personal crime,[36] are thought to be 'destined to a life of crime'.[37]

And we have seen that these effects are not limited to criminal justice. Medical protocols, such as the Opioid Risk Tool and Narx Score, make predictions about aberrant drugs-related behaviours, which are used to inform decisions about whether to prescribe effective pain-relieving medication for chronic and acute medical conditions.[38] Yet, these predictions are not limited to evidence of past behaviours. Instead, they include facts such as family history of substance abuse, access to health insurance, and even personal experience of sexual abuse—facts that have nothing to do with evidence of past non-compliant behaviours.[39]

In this way, statistical algorithms perform a role that corresponds to Goring's criminal diathesis: we use these diagnoses to impose significant burdens upon people—not because of what they have done, but rather because of the social or economic circumstances into which they were born, the privileges that have been made available to them, or the way in which they have been treated by others.

Algorithmic Justice

Why does this matter? The answer that most often appears in the literature on algorithmic justice is that it matters just when the effect of using algorithms to make decisions about how to treat others is to create or exacerbate unjustified differences between people.[40] Thus, the focus has been upon egalitarian reasons to object to policies of algorithmic decision-making, typically captured through the language of 'discrimination' or 'bias'.[41]

The aim of this book has been to unpack the reasons at play in assessments about the justice of decision-making policies that rely upon the outputs of statistical algorithms. I have argued that egalitarian reasons—reasons that concern the differences between the benefits to which people have access, and for trying to reduce those differences[42]—are important, and warrant the extensive intellectual and financial resources that have been applied to them. But there are also important non-comparative reasons at play when we consider what's at stake for those to whom we apply policies of algorithmic decision-making.

I have argued that the umbrella of algorithmic justice encompasses reasons of relevance, equality, and individual choice. These reasons arise from the need to show a rational link between the policy and some worthwhile social goal, from the demands of equal concern and status, and from the value of having the opportunity to avoid the burdens of a social policy by choosing appropriately. Each of these reasons is significant, but only some of them concern unjustified differences between people.

We may be able to justify adopting a policy that requires some people to bear certain costs, if this will bring about some benefit—perhaps by allowing others to avoid the weightier costs that they would suffer under a different policy. Thus, Chapter 2 was concerned with the demands of 'relevance'—the requirement to demonstrate that there is a rational link between the selection criteria that we use to divvy up burdens, and the cost that we avoid by making the decision on the basis of these criteria.

Meeting these demands does not require us to show a clear understanding of the causal mechanism that connects some set of facts with our target variable. It is enough that we have either: (1) retrospective evidence that a policy based on these criteria is in fact associated with some avoided cost amongst that population (the gold standard); or (2) a sound basis for believing that these correlations between certain facts and the cost that we want to avoid will hold true amongst our target population, and a reliable prospective strategy for avoiding that cost.

There is no doubt that statistics and statistical rules can help us to conduct more rigorous assessments about the likelihood that our target variable will coincide with certain facts, and therefore to reach better decisions about how to treat others when we are otherwise unsure about the rational significance of certain facts. But we have also seen that there are no guarantees: whether they do have this effect in practice depends upon our techniques for gathering and processing data, and translating our predictions into conclusions about what to do.

Chapter 3 discussed two egalitarian reasons that we might have to object to the use of statistical algorithms to make policy decisions, which relate to the way in which we take into account the interests of others, the social status that they occupy, and the attitudes and treatment that follow from that status. The first reason concerns the duty of equal concern—the duty of certain individuals and institutions to have and show equal regard for the interests of everyone within a certain group,[43] which requires that departures from equal treatment be justified by some sufficiently compelling reason. The second is status inequality: a set of persistent beliefs about the characteristics or capabilities of certain people may lead others to treat them as less entitled to important social or economic benefits. This is the distinctive feature of 'discrimination', as that term is often used, and it is a problem of justice when it results in the exclusion of those affected from benefits without justification.[44]

I have argued that statistical algorithms can generate inequalities of both kinds. Even if an algorithm produces outcomes that correlate to a worthwhile social goal at a population level, it may nevertheless concentrate the risk of error unjustly upon certain individuals or groups, with the result that those individuals or groups are more likely to be denied benefits for no good reason. This may evidence a failure of equal concern, and/or an underlying set of stigmatizing beliefs and practices that have the effect of excluding certain individuals from important benefits without justification. And an algorithm that distributes the risk of error fairly can nevertheless advance the goals of a social policy that is unjust in these ways.

Finally, Chapter 4 considered reasons that stem from the value of choice—the value of having, and being seen to have, a meaningful opportunity to influence what happens to us, by responding appropriately when presented with different options about what to do.[45] These reasons can, I suggested, create a powerful case for wanting to have the opportunity to avoid the burdens of a policy decision by choosing appropriately. Yet, we have seen that these choices can be attenuated or denied altogether by the use of statistical algorithms to allocate policy burdens. In particular, where these algorithms make actuarial predictions—predictions about how people will behave in the future—on the basis of facts that have nothing to do with their past choices, we can make these burdens inevitable for those to whom these facts apply.

The Value of Choice

We have seen that the value of choice is conceptualized in different ways, which correspond to different views about two aspects of the relationship between choice and responsibility: the role that autonomy plays in justifying the consequences of voluntary action; and the relationship between moral blame and the imposition of practical burdens upon those whose actions fail to meet some threshold.

According to the 'will-based' view of the justificatory role of choice, we blame an individual just when they have chosen to do wrong, and require them to bear only those burdens that they have willingly forfeit the right not to suffer.[46] Following Scanlon, I have argued that there is an alternative view of the legitimizing force of choice, according to which we can distinguish between the justifying conditions of moral blame and criticism, and practical burdens.[47] This 'value of choice' account is concerned with responsibility of the second sort only, which is a matter of justice.

The argument is that there can be important reasons to value having adequate opportunities to affect what happens to us, by choosing appropriately when confronted with a range of options about what to do. Thus, the focus is not upon the choices that we make—upon the way in which exercising our autonomy can legitimate certain responses to our actions. Rather, it is upon the choices that are made available to us, and how well we are equipped to exercise these choices.

So, for this account, the starting point is to look directly to the reasons we have for wanting a choice—for wanting what happens to us to depend upon the way in which we respond when presented with a range of plausible alternatives. These reasons are instrumental, where they concern the way in which having a choice can improve aspects of our lives.[48] They are representative, where they are reasons for 'wanting to see features of ourselves manifested in actions and their results'.[49] And they are symbolic, where they concern the signals that are sent by denying some people the opportunity to make certain choices[50]—signals that those people 'are not competent or do not have the standing normally accorded an adult member of the society'.[51]

This last category of reason can be comparative, and has both an instrumental and non-instrumental component. The claim is that there may be reasons to object to a policy that denies the decision-subject the same range of opportunities for choice as other competent members of society, where this labels them as too 'immature or incompetent' to make these choices well.[52] This can be objectionable on its own terms, and where these judgements have the effect of creating stigmatizing differences in status that result in the unjustified exclusion of some people from important benefits.[53]

I argued in Chapter 4 that, where these (instrumental, representative, and symbolic) reasons are sufficiently strong, we may have sound objections to a policy that fails to make the imposition of burdens upon us contingent upon how we behave in the face of adequate opportunities to choose.[54] Whether those opportunities are adequate will depend (*inter alia*) upon our own position, the background conditions of our choice, and the safeguards made available to us to encourage good choices.[55] And providing adequate safeguards means providing us with information about the nature of the risk and the steps that we can take to avoid it, and, in many cases, ensuring that the risk of harm is only encountered by those who have sufficient (economic, social, physical, psychological, etc) resources to avoid it.

We have seen that statistical algorithms are used in a range of spheres to make predictions about the choices that people will make in the future, which in turn affect the policy burdens that are assigned to them. Yet, we have also seen that these predictions may be informed by a range of facts that have nothing to do with the choices they have made, or could have made, in the past. Decisions about whether someone should go to prison, or whether they should be subjected to high-intensity police surveillance, are made on the basis of socio-economic circumstances, access to stable housing, or the behaviour of friends or family.[56] Decisions about which grade to award a student are based upon the prior accomplishments of other students at the same institution.[57] And decisions about whether to deny someone a medical privilege are based upon whether the decision-subject has been the victim of abuse.[58]

Accordingly, when we use these predictions to assign burdens to certain people, we deny those affected the chance to influence what happens to them by choosing appropriately—a chance that may be of significant value to them. The strength of the objections they can raise to a policy that has this effect, and the conclusions that we draw from the process of weighing them against the objections that others might raise to some alternative policy, will vary according to the policy in question. But these objections are often at their strongest in a particular context, upon which much of the discussion in this book has focused—criminal justice in general, and criminal punishment in particular.

Criminal Justice

I have argued throughout this book that reasons of relevance, equality, and choice apply to many different circumstances in which algorithms are used to make significant decisions about how to treat others. This encompasses decisions about healthcare, employment, education, and social welfare. Why, then, dwell on criminal justice—on the use of tools like COMPAS to make decisions such as whether to send an individual to prison, and (if so) for how long?

The short answer is that these reasons are often at their most powerful in the context of criminal punishment, which includes the targeted application of police surveillance, pre-trial detention, sentencing, parole, and post-release supervision. Criminal punishment in various forms is amongst the most significant institutional burdens that we can be required to bear. This is particularly true of criminal incarceration, which is attended by the loss of social, political, and economic rights and privileges that play a key role in any individual's ability to thrive as part of society.[59] Accordingly, we have clear instrumental reasons to want punishment to turn on behaviours in which we can choose not to engage, and to be informed and equipped to exercise these choices well.

We also have representative reasons, to want to have and maintain a range of opportunities for individual expression, which can be curtailed in significant ways by certain forms of punishment. And we have symbolic reasons to want criminal punishment to be related to our status as rational choosers. Giving people these opportunities, by making punishment contingent upon how people behave when confronted with different options, signals that they have a certain sort of rational competence—that they can be trusted to choose well. Denying these opportunities, by making punishment contingent upon characteristics over which individuals have little or no influence, signals the contrary—that those who have these characteristics are less competent to choose well, and less deserving of the trust that this competence justifies.

These reasons make a powerful case for wanting our policies of criminal punishment to be responsive to the way in which we behave when we are presented with adequate choices about what to do. The claim is not that we can justify punishing someone who chooses badly, or (vice versa) that we cannot justify punishing someone who has failed for whatever reason to exercise a choice. Rather, it is that we can have good reasons for wanting meaningful opportunities to choose to avoid the burdens of criminal punishment, in light of the various background (social and economic) conditions that shape the availability of routes to a satisfactory life on the right side of the law.[60]

This, I have suggested, is why we should be particularly concerned about the way in which individuals are treated by the use of COMPAS to make sentencing decisions. When we attach some of the most extensive institutional burdens to facts over which individuals can exert little or no influence, we not only deny people opportunities that they have significant instrumental reason to value; we also mark them out as less capable of choosing well, and (in light of this shortcoming) less deserving of certain privileges to which others are entitled. According to policies of criminal punishment that rely upon COMPAS outputs, certain social and economic facts can simply mark people out as belonging to an undesirable social type—a type that is defined by deviant behaviours that (so it goes) can warrant a certain kind of institutional response. That response includes the regulation of access to a range of personal freedoms that are critical to self-expression, and to the satisfaction of various individual goals and preferences.

All of this, I have argued, gives individuals a powerful reason to object to their treatment that cannot be met by looking to reasons that derive from public safety and security. And the policy implications can be put simply. There is a good case for taking a proscriptive approach to the use of tools like COMPAS to make decisions about how to distribute the burdens of criminal punishment, which includes decisions about whether to send someone to prison (and for how long), the conditions of early release from a custodial sentence, and the nature and duration of post-release supervision.

Transparency

Chapters 2, 3, and 5 dealt with the substantive reasons that arise under the umbrella of algorithmic justice—reasons of relevance, equality, and choice. Chapter 5 dealt with two questions that concern how we assess the justification for adopting a particular policy of algorithmic decision-making, and what role (if any) humans play in supervising the outputs that algorithms produce in particular cases. First, what do we need to know about an algorithm, in order to determine how these reasons apply to a particular policy of decision-making that uses it? Second, what scope is there for decision-makers to override algorithmic predictions in a given case, in which we have doubts about the output that it generates? The second question feeds into a wider discussion about keeping humans 'in the loop' in algorithmic decisions.[61]

In order to give a satisfactory normative account of an algorithmic decision,[62] we need (*inter alia*) to have certain information about the algorithmic component of that decision. That information, and the kind of assessment in which we need to engage to acquire it, varies according to the kind of prediction that we use the algorithm to make. In Chapter 5, I argued that we do not, in any case, need to engage in a technical assessment—to identify the mechanics of the algorithm,[63] to understand how it came to generate a particular output.[64] Rather, we need to understand just how good the algorithm is at making the prediction that helps us to achieve some social goal, and how it distributes the risk of error. So, we need to engage in a statistical assessment—to record overall rates of accuracy (success at predicting which facts will coincide with the target variable) and the distribution of error amongst the assessed population.

This will be enough when we use statistical algorithms to make predictions about facts other than what an individual will do, such as predictions about infrastructural or medical need, or how an individual with certain characteristics will respond to a course of medical treatment. But I have argued that a distinct concern arises from the use of statistical algorithms to allocate burdens by making predictions about intentional action, which stems from the value of choice. In these circumstances, figuring out whether we can justify using the algorithm to make decisions about how to treat others not only requires us to assess the algorithm's predictive accuracy and error-distribution; it also requires us to look at which factors have informed that output. This requires us to be able to perform a counterfactual assessment, by adjusting inputs to isolate statistically-significant variables—those which have a noticeable effect on algorithmic outputs—via the interface through which the algorithm gathers the data needed to make a predictive assessment in any given case.[65]

So, in all cases, we need to know how accurate the algorithm is, and how it distributes the risk of error. We can measure these things statistically, by assessing the algorithm's performance empirically across datasets. If the prediction is about what the decision-subject will do, we also need to know which facts influence that output. We can assess this counterfactually, by adjusting inputs to isolate statistically significant variables. In neither case do we need to 'open the black box', in the sense of unpacking the code itself.

In Chapter 5, we saw that institutional guidance often instructs decision-makers to override algorithmic predictions in particular cases, if they have doubts about the accuracy of those outputs.[66] Indeed, judges have concluded that the justification for a particular policy of algorithmic decision-making could well turn on the willingness of judicial decision-makers to take this step.[67]

Clearly, we need human judgement to shape algorithmic design and development, and to translate algorithmic outputs into decisions about what to do.

There is no doubt that human decision-makers are and ought to be 'in the loop' in some sense,[68] when we use statistical algorithms to determine how to treat others. But I have argued that we should not endorse a practice of overriding algorithmic outputs in individual cases, on an ad hoc basis.

Either the relevant algorithm produces predictions that have a better rate and distribution of error than unaided human decision-making, or it does not. If it does, we should not be tempted to override those outputs by applying a clinical assessment on the basis of suspicions that the algorithm is producing an inaccurate prediction for an individual case. Indeed, these—situations in which the output *seems* aberrant—may be precisely the cases in which we should be particularly wary of the subtleties of human prejudice.

If, by contrast, the algorithm has a worse rate and distribution of error, or if there are other concerns about the justification for using the algorithm to make decisions about how to treat others (including the range of considerations that feed into predictive outputs), the solution is not to give the output less weight and hope that humans can make up the difference on a case-by-case basis. Nothing short of a comprehensive and systematic effort to revise the algorithm can justify using it.

Policy and Prediction

Statistical algorithms are hardly the only component of criminal justice, or policy-making more widely, that can raise concerns of the kind discussed in this book. Whenever we make policy decisions that impose burdens upon some people for the sake of some desirable outcome, we have reasons to want to establish a clear relationship between that policy and goal—reasons that I have described in terms of 'relevance'. If policy decisions arise in the context of some allocative responsibility owed to all members of a particular class, we have reasons to want to be able to point to some clear justification for treating members of that class differently from one another—reasons that stem from the duty that the relevant agent owes to have and show equal concern for those individuals. And we always have reasons to ensure that policy decisions do not exacerbate systemic differences in status between people, with the result that certain groups are excluded from important benefits for no good reason.

Similarly, reasons to want policies to be responsive to the way in which we behave when confronted with adequate options about what to do apply whether or not those policies involve the sort of algorithmic practices considered throughout this book.[69] This is also true of the more specific context of predictive decision-making: we have seen that there can be significant reasons from the value of choice to object to policies that allocate burdens on the basis of actuarial predictions, where those predictions are based on facts over which the decision-subject has little or no influence. But these objections arise whether or not the predictive practice stems from statistical observations that have been reduced to a set of precise decision-making rules.

For instance, judges across the United States are permitted to draw upon various facts about the defendant to inform sentencing decisions. These typically include a range of facts that relate to the nature and seriousness of the crime, and the defendant's past criminal record. But they may also include facts such as educational background, and the results of any pre-sentence investigation (PSI).[70] Depending on the rules that prevail in the relevant state, that PSI may in turn include factors such as: intelligence ('mental ability', contributing to the individual's 'ability to function independently in society'); physical health and appearance; hygiene and nutrition; use of social security benefits or other public financial assistance; the nature of their peer group; and 'common interests with gang-affiliated members'.[71] These facts can be captured without the use of statistical algorithms.

In a different context, we have seen that algorithmic healthcare tools can have the effect of compounding inequalities for reasons that stem from broader policy considerations, rather than from the algorithmic component of decision-making. Studies have found that the Model for End-Stage Liver Disease (MELD), which we met in Chapter 3, has decreased racial differences in wait-times experienced by patients once they are included on the wait-list, but that black patients are only listed at a more advanced stage of liver disease.[72] One study found that black patients made up 14.1 per cent of referrals in one US state, despite making up 25.6 per cent of the relevant population.[73] The authors of these studies note that barriers faced by black patients in obtaining referrals for liver transplantation are 'perplexing and troubling',[74] and consistent over time.[75]

There is a risk that technological advances towards predictive accuracy obscure the significant justice implications of outsourcing key aspects of our public and private decision-making to predictive tools.[76] For instance, where COMPAS is used to make predictions about recidivism that inform sentencing decisions, the PSI acts as a gateway to the consideration of a wide range of factors that are more or less obscured from judicial oversight at the point of decision-making. Rather than consciously addressing the question of which facts ought to influence the decisions that we make about how to treat others, the use of algorithmic tools can shield that influence from open examination.

So, statistical algorithms are merely part of a broader set of policy decisions about how to treat individuals that can raise the sorts of concerns discussed in this book. But they are an important part of that picture, and a part that is growing in significance as algorithms are used to make more, and more important, decisions about the way in which we are treated across various aspects of our public and private lives. Unless we think carefully about the reasons why we might wish certain facts to influence decisions about the burdens to which we subject others, gains in predictive accuracy may come to obscure the more significant task at the heart of algorithmic justice—to determine the limits to the burdens that we can reasonably expect people to bear for the sake of certain desirable results.

Conclusion

Against this backdrop, there are good reasons to want to have a complete picture of what's at stake for individuals when we use the outputs of predictive tools to guide our policy decisions. When we engage in conversations about algorithmic justice, our goal is not just to figure out which tools best serve some policy objective, but also to determine the nature and magnitude of the burdens that we can reasonably expect people to bear along the way.

I have argued that we cannot achieve this goal if these conversations begin and end with equality. Egalitarian reasons are significant, particularly when they concern the systemic and long-term effects of unjustified differences in status between groups of individuals, which can have a pervasive impact upon the benefits to which they have access across the breadth of their lives. But they are not the only kind of reason to which we must pay heed when we consider the justification for using a particular statistical algorithm to make decisions about how to treat others.

In particular, I have argued that those who would design and implement policies of algorithmic decision-making must not only ask and answer important questions about differences between the way in which people are treated, and the benefits to which they have access. They must also turn their minds to the value of choice—to reasons that we have to want the chance to influence what happens to us by choosing appropriately.

We have seen that decision-making policies that use tools like COMPAS to allocate some of the most significant institutional burdens, far from providing these opportunities, allocate burdens on the basis of facts over which individuals have little or no influence. The effect is not only to deny people opportunities that they have significant instrumental reason to value; it is also to mark them out as less competent to choose, less deserving of the trust that attends this competence, and less entitled to important privileges that are available to others as a matter of course.

Better predictions about how individuals will behave are rarely cost-free for decision-subjects. Whether or not these costs are acceptable requires us to think carefully about a range of considerations, which include the reasons that we have to want meaningful opportunities to influence what happens to us by choosing appropriately. The stronger these reasons are, the more powerful the case will be for making these policy decisions responsive to the way in which we behave when we are presented with adequate choices about what to do. COMPAS—like other tools that we use to punish people on the basis of facts such as social circumstance, educational opportunity, or childhood disadvantage—is not a route to that end.

Notes

1. TM Scanlon, *What We Owe to Each Other* (HUP 1998) 261; Emmanuel Voyiakis, *Private Law and the Value of Choice* (Bloomsbury 2017) 106.
2. Scanlon (n 1) 253. See also Voyiakis (n 1) 120.
3. See generally Scanlon (n 1) 256-67. This focus upon the adequacy of opportunities to choose distinguishes the value of choice account from the 'will-based' theory of choice.
4. For instance, we generally do not subject people to criminal punishment if, because of mental illness or incapacity, they are 'unable to regulate their conduct in accordance with the law': Scanlon (n 1) 264.
5. ibid 265.
6. Northpointe Institute for Public Management, *Measurement and Treatment Implications of COMPAS Core Scales* (Northpointe Institute 2009); Pasco County Sheriff's Office, *Intelligence-Led Policing Manual* (Revised edn, PCSO 2018); Lynn R Webster and Rebecca M Webster, 'Predicting Aberrant Behaviors in Opioid-Treated Patients: Preliminary Validation of the Opioid Risk Tool' (2005) 6 Pain Medicine 432.
7. Pasco County Sheriff's Office (n 6) 17; Plaintiffs' Complaint in *Dalanea Taylor, Tammy Heilmanm Darlene Deegan, and Robert A Jones III v Chris Nocco* (2021) 8:21-cv-0055 US DC Middle District of Florida Tampa Division.
8. Pasco County Sheriff's Office (n 6) 14.
9. ibid 845.
10. Sandra Wachter, Brent Mittelstadt, and Chris Russell, 'Counterfactual Explanations Without Opening the Black Box: Automated Decisions and the GDPR' (2018) 31 Harvard Journal of Law and Technology 841, 872.
11. cf eg 'COMPAS—Potential Decision Points (County Adult)' in *Electronic Case Reference Manual* (State of Wisconsin Department of Corrections) <https://doc.helpdocsonline.

com/arrest-and-adjudication> accessed 20 January 2023; *State v Loomis* (2015) Ws Ct App AP157-CR, 2015 WL 1724741 [71].
12. Charles Buckman Goring, *The English Convict: A Statistical Study* (Her Majesty's Stationery Office 1913) 26.
13. ibid 370.
14. ibid 26.
15. See <https://www.merriam-webster.com/dictionary/diathesis> accessed 9 April 2023. See also <https://www.oed.com/view/Entry/52119?redirectedFrom=diathesis#eid> accessed 9 April 2023.
16. Goring (n 12) 373.
17. Here, I use the language of Equivant: Equivant, *Practitioner's Guide to COMPAS Core* (Equivant 2019) 3.
18. Pasco County Sheriff's Office (n 6) 12.
19. See eg Bernard E Harcourt, *Against Prediction* (University of Chicago Press 2008) 31.
20. The more precise those rules, and the less room for discretion they leave, the closer we are to something that would typically be described as an 'algorithm'—something like the Model for End-Stage Liver Disease (MELD), which we met in Chapter 3. See eg Cynthia A Moylan and others, 'Disparities in Liver Transplantation before and after Introduction of the MELD Score' (2008) 300 Journal of the American Medical Association 2371.
21. Northpointe Institute for Public Management (n 6) 13.
22. ibid.
23. ibid 10.
24. ibid 22.
25. ibid 10, 16.
26. See generally Equivant (n 17) and Northpointe Institute for Public Management (n 6).
27. Pasco County Sheriff's Office (n 6) 18.
28. ibid 13.
29. ibid.
30. ibid.
31. Plaintiffs' Complaint in *Dalanea Taylor, Tammy Heilmanm Darlene Deegan, and Robert A Jones III v Chris Nocco* (2021) 8:21–cv–0055 US DC Middle District of Florida Tampa Division [128].
32. There is very little evidence that those burdens play a positive short- or longer-term role in the lives of those who suffer them, and a good deal of evidence to the contrary. See eg Francis T Cullen, Cheryl Lero Jonson, and Daniel S Nagin, 'Prisons Do Not Reduce Recidivism: The High Cost of Ignoring Science' (2011) 91 The Prison Journal 48S. Even for those who are not unusually vulnerable, incarceration can cause long-term detriment to economic opportunity, social integration, psychological well-being, and physical health: Lauren Brinkley-Rubinstein, 'Incarceration as a Catalyst for Worsening Health' (2013) 1 Health and Justice 1.
33. Goring (n 12) 24.
34. Equivant (n 17); Northpointe Institute for Public Management (n 6); *State v Loomis* (2015) Ws Ct App AP157-CR, 2015 WL 1724741.
35. Pasco County Sheriff's Office (n 6) 72.
36. ibid 17.

37. ibid 14.
38. Webster and Webster (n 6); Maia Szalavitz, 'The Pain Was Unbearable. So Why Did Doctors Turn Her Away?' *Wired* (11 August 2021) <https://www.wired.com/story/opioid-drug-addiction-algorithm-chronic-pain/> accessed 20 January 2023.
39. Webster and Webster (n 6).
40. See eg Cathy O'Neil, *Weapons of Math Destruction: How Big Data Increases Inequality and Threatens Democracy* (Broadway Books 2016); Solon Barocas and Andrew D Selbst, 'Big Data's Disparate Impact' (2016) 104 California Law Review 671; Sara Wachter-Boettcher, *Technically Wrong: Sexist Apps, Biased Algorithms, and Other Threats of Toxic Tech* (WW Norton & Co 2017); Virginia Eubanks, *Automating Inequality: How High-Tech Tools Profile, Police and Punish the Poor* (St Martin's Press 2018); Safiya Noble, *Algorithms of Oppression: How Search Engines Reinforce Racism* (NYU Press 2018); Matthew Le Bui and Safiya Umoja Noble, 'We're Missing a Moral Framework of Justice in Artificial Intelligence: On the Limits, Failings, and Ethics of Fairness' in Markus D Dubber, Frank Pasquale, and Sunit Das (eds), *The Oxford Handbook of Ethics of AI* (OUP 2020); Annette Zimmermann, Elena Di Rosa, and Hochan Kim, 'Technology can't Fix Algorithmic Injustice' *Boston Review* (9 January 2020) <http://bostonreview.net/science-nature-politics/annette-zimmermann-elena-di-rosa-hochan-kim-technology-cant-fix-algorithmic> accessed 20 January 2023.
41. cf on the topic of bias as a solution-oriented label: Julia Powles, 'The Seductive Diversion of "Solving" Bias in Artificial Intelligence' *Medium* (8 December 2018) <https://onezero.medium.com/the-seductive-diversion-of-solving-bias-in-artificial-intelligence-890df5e5ef53> accessed 9 April 2023.
42. Scanlon (n 1) 1.
43. ibid ch 2.
44. ibid 26.
45. ibid 255.
46. TM Scanlon, 'Responsibility and the Value of Choice' (2013) 12 Think 9, 10.
47. Scanlon (n 1) 251–52; Voyiakis (n 1) 248–49.
48. Scanlon (n 1) 251; Voyiakis (n 1) 106.
49. Scanlon (n 1) 252.
50. ibid 253. See also Voyiakis (n 1) 120.
51. Scanlon (n 1) 253. See also Voyiakis (n 1) 120.
52. Scanlon (n 1) 254.
53. As Mill put it, enfranchising women would eliminate an 'unworthy stigma' obstructing the social and professional advancement of women. John Stuart Mill, 'On the Admission of Women to the Electoral Franchise', Speech in the House of Commons, 20 May 1867.
54. Voyiakis (n 1) 128.
55. Scanlon (n 1) 256–67; Voyiakis (n 1) 128.
56. See eg 'COMPAS—Potential Decision Points (County Adult)' (n 11); Equivant (n 17); Northpointe Institute for Public Management (n 6); *State v Loomis* (2015) Ws Ct App AP157-CR, 2015 WL 1724741.
57. Roger Taylor, Chair, Ofqual Board, *Getting the grades they've earned: COVID-19: the cancellation of exams and 'calculated' grades: Response to the Committee's First Report: Annex 2, Written statement from Chair of Ofqual to the Education Select*

Committee on this year's GCSE, AS, A level, extended project and advanced extension award qualification results (1 September 2020) <https://publications.parliament.uk/pa/cm5801/cmselect/cmeduc/812/81205.htm> accessed 22 June 2022

58. Webster and Webster (n 6); Szalavitz (n 38).
59. There is very little evidence that those burdens play a positive short or longer-term role in the lives of those who suffer them, and a good deal of evidence to the contrary. See eg Cullen, Jonson, and Nagin (n 32). Even for those who are not unusually vulnerable, incarceration can cause long-term detriment to economic opportunity, social integration, psychological well-being, and physical health: Brinkley-Rubinstein (n 32).
60. Scanlon (n 1) 264.
61. See eg Ge Wang, 'Humans in the Loop: The Design of Interactive AI Systems' iStanford University Human-Centered Artificial Intelligence' (20 October 2019) <https://hai.stanford.edu/news/humans-loop-design-interactive-ai-systems> accessed 9 April 2023.
62. Joseph Raz, *Engaging Reason: On the Theory of Value and Action* (OUP 1999) 23.
63. The first question is often approached from the lens of determining whether and how we should 'open the black box'—whether we should, or need to be able to, access the internal workings of the algorithm. This is the terminology and subject of enquiry often associated with the field of 'explainable AI' (XAI), and it is this type of access that proprietary algorithms can prohibit. See eg *Commonwealth v Foley* (2012) Pa Super Ct 31; 71 38 A 3d 882, 888–89, and *State v Loomis* (2015) Ws Ct App AP157-CR, 2015 WL 1724741 [6].
64. Tim Miller, 'Explanation in Artificial Intelligence: Insights from the Social Sciences' (2019) 267 Artificial Intelligence 1.
65. *Commonwealth v Foley* (2012) Pa Super Ct 31; 71 38 A 3d 882, 845.
66. See eg 'COMPAS—Potential Decision Points (County Adult)' (n 11); *State v Loomis* (2015) Ws Ct App AP157-CR, 2015 WL 1724741 [71].
67. *State v Loomis* (2015) Ws Ct App AP157-CR, 2015 WL 1724741 [71].
68. See eg Wang (n 61).
69. Scanlon (n 1) 256–67.
70. *State v Harris* (1984) 119 Wis2d 612, 623, 350 NW 2d 633.
71. See eg Wisconsin Department of Corrections guidance: *Electronic Case Reference Manual* (State of Wisconsin Department of Corrections) <https://doc.helpdocsonline.com/arrest-and-adjudication> accessed 20 January 2023.
72. Moylan and others (n 20).
73. Devin Eckhoff and others, 'Race: A Critical Factor in Organ Donation, Patient Referral and Selection, and Orthotopic Liver Transplantation' (1998) 4 Liver Transplantation and Surgery 499.
74. ibid 505.
75. Moylan and others (n 20).
76. See eg Harcourt (n 18) 31.

Index

For the benefit of digital users, indexed terms that span two pages (e.g., 52–53) may, on occasion, appear on only one of those pages.

Introductory Note

References such as '178–9' indicate (not necessarily continuous) discussion of a topic across a range of pages. Wherever possible in the case of topics with many references, these have either been divided into sub-topics or only the most significant discussions of the topic are listed. Because the entire work is about 'artificial justice', the use of this term (and certain others which occur constantly throughout the book) as an entry point has been restricted. Information will be found under the corresponding detailed topics.

Aboriginal and Torres Strait Islander peoples, *see* First Peoples
abuse 89, 100–1, 138
   alcohol 80
   child 28, 34–35, 97, 98
   sexual 4, 101, 103, 134
   substance 4, 100–1, 102, 103, 134
accelerants 21, 22–23, 24
   liquid 21, 22–23
accuracy 35, 36, 116, 117, 118, 119, 140–41
   predictive 15, 80, 92, 117, 118, 119, 123, 133
actuarial assessments 31, 123–24
actuarial methods 31
actuarial predictions 15, 130, 136, 142–43
acute pain 102
ad hoc basis 131, 141–42
Adams, Phillip 59
adjectival features 12–13, 50
adults 14, 74, 77, 88, 129, 137
adverse childhood experiences 3–4, 15, 86–87, 89, 133–34
advertising, algorithms 50
age 9, 25–26, 28, 29–30, 59, 60–61, 79–80
age range, patients 4, 101
A-Levels 92
algorithmic bias 8, 50–51
algorithmic decisions 9, 140–41
algorithmic design 124, 131, 141–42

algorithmic justice 4–5, 6–15, 120–21, 129–48
   addressing 7
algorithmic outputs 36, 120, 121, 124, 125, 131, 141–42
algorithmic predictions 11, 119, 123, 124, 125, 131, 140, 141
algorithmic rules 94
algorithmic tools 2, 79, 116, 118, 131–32, 134, 143
algorithmic transparency 119
algorithms 53–54, 119–20, 122, 124–25, 131, 140–41, 142
   advertising 50
   COMPAS 2, 79
   hiring 49–50
   learning 6
   PCSO 4, 87–88
   predictive policing 86–87, 133–34
   race-corrected 61–62
   sentencing 78–79, 133–34
   statistical 2, 4–7, 12–13, 117–18, 129–48
   STMP 87–88
   treatment 60
allocative responsibility 11, 57, 142
Amazon 12–13, 50
American Football 58;, *see also* NFL
analysis, statistical 28, 48–49
antisocial activities 2, 132–34

anxiety 59, 87–88, 89
apps 56–57
aptitudes 31, 51, 93
arrests 21–22, 27, 72, 81, 82, 87
arson 21, 22, 24, 25, 26–27
　indicators 21, 22–23, 24, 25
　investigation 21–22, 24, 25
　investigators 22, 24
　mythology 29
assessments 91, 92, 93–94, 98, 99, 118, 120, 122
　actuarial 31, 123–24
　algorithmic 86, 96
　clinical 124–25, 131, 142
　counterfactual 120, 123, 131, 141
　criminal risk 3, 85
　full 2, 79, 80
　Individual 29–30, 31
　predictive 120, 141
　standardized 90–92, 93
　statistical 42, 81, 118, 123, 131, 140–41
atavism 71, 72
　criminal 72, 73, 78
at-risk youth 3–4, 86–87, 130–31
Australia 87–88, 90
automated decisions 120, 121
autonomy 13, 73, 137

babysitters 97–98
　potential 97–98
background
　conditions 76, 77–78, 82, 84, 138
　educational 118, 143
baseball 48–49
base-rate statistics 35
batters 49
Bayes' theorem 35
Beane, Billy 48–49
beliefs 12–13, 31, 44, 57, 121
　persistent 12, 136
　stigmatizing 12, 136
　unjustified 12, 44
benefits 4–5, 8–9, 26, 31, 136, 144
　economic 12, 136
　social 6–7, 8–9, 30
Bennet, Omalu 58–59
Beveridge, Sir William 52
bias 4–5, 7, 23, 134–35
　algorithmic 8, 50–51

cognitive 48
　teacher 95–96
bilirubin 46
Binns, Reuben 83
biological/natural parents 2, 80, 133–34
birth 61
　vaginal 6, 60–61, 122
black defendants 7, 42, 81
black patients 53, 143
black people 42–43, 44, 53, 58, 62, 82
black players 60, 61–62
black women 61
blame 26–32, 73, 137
　lure of 26–32
　moral 137
blood 34, 45, 46, 115
　pressure 3, 53, 84–85
　samples 3, 27, 34, 84–85
　spatter 33–34
　types 35, 41
BMI 60–61
born criminals 71–78
Boston 54–57
Bradford, Chad 48, 49
brain 10, 27, 28
　function 10, 27
　scan 59
Brewer, Kennedy 25, 26
Broward County 80, 81
burden of error 94–95, 122, 124
burdens, institutional 7–8, 76–77, 78, 132–33, 134, 139, 140, 144–45
burdens of criminal punishment 15, 78, 83–84, 129–30, 139, 140
burn patterns 24, 26–27
Butler, John 115
bystanders 86–87, 133–34

Caffey, John 28
CAGs (centre assessed grades) 92–93, 95–96
canals 55
candidates 5, 14, 49–51, 103, 133
　male 12–13, 50
　passive 12–13, 50
　pool 5, 49–50, 133
capabilities 12, 95, 96, 136
　relative 94, 95
capital punishment 21, 28

care 27, 29, 45–46, 52, 53, 54, 61, 74–75
  medical 54, 102
careers 48, 51, 58, 59, 93
case-by-case basis 125, 131, 142
causal explanations 23, 24, 30
causal mechanisms 10, 23, 135
Cheatle, Martin 101
chicken 30–31
child abuse 28, 34–35, 97, 98
child safety 98
childhood experiences, adverse 3–4, 15, 86–87, 89, 133–34
children 10–11, 27–28, 86, 87, 88, 97
  young 21, 59
choice
  exercise of 13, 76, 78, 83
  individual 83, 86, 89–90, 102–3, 135
  opportunities for 75, 137–38
  value of 14, 73, 76, 78, 137, 142–43
choices 8, 13–15, 71–113, 125, 129–48
  adequate 15, 77–78, 139, 145
  good 76, 83, 90, 103, 138
  making appropriate 8, 76, 122–23
chronic pain 101, 102
chronic traumatic encephalopathy, *see* CTE
cities 35, 55–56, 57, 75
city officials 55–56, 57, 75
clinical assessments 124–25, 131, 142
clinical methods 31
Columbus, Christopher 71
co-morbidities 6, 9, 25–26, 29–30
COMPAS (Correctional Offender Management Profiling for Alternative Sanctions) 2, 7–8, 79, 81, 118–19, 130, 144–45
  assessments 119
  outputs 80–81, 85–86, 140
  Practitioners' Guide 3, 84
  software 2, 79–80
  use 80, 119, 140
compensation 58, 60, 61–62
competence 12, 14, 83–84, 90, 131, 139, 144–45
  rational 14, 77, 139
complex mixtures 115, 116
computers 4, 6, 34, 133
concussions 58, 59
Conrad, HS 31
contractualism 8

control groups, appropriate 10–11, 28–29
convictions 10–11, 28, 32, 33–34, 42, 81, 82, 87
Correctional Offender Management Profiling for Alternative Sanctions, *see* COMPAS
correlations 10, 32, 78, 81, 135
  apparent 11, 32, 78
  perceived 5, 23
costs 8, 9, 10, 26, 30, 53–54, 122, 135
  avoided 10, 26, 135
  intolerable 8, 30
  weightier 9, 25, 135
counterfactual assessments 120, 123, 131, 141
courts 24, 79–80, 87, 97, 116–17, 118, 119
  trial 116–17, 118, 119
COVID-19 43, 90–91, 100
  vaccination 9, 26, 29–30
  vaccines 9, 25, 30
CPS (Crown Prosecution Service) 10–11
creatinine 46
Criado-Perez, Caroline 47
crime
  crusade agains 1–2, 72
  instrumental 3, 85
  personal 3–4, 86–87, 89, 133–34
  scenes 33, 34–35, 115
  violent 88, 125, 133
criminal activity 3–4, 42, 79, 80, 85, 86, 119, 133
criminal atavism 72, 73, 78
criminal behaviours 71–72, 77–78, 89
criminal diathesis 1–2, 72, 132
criminal justice 2, 78–79, 85–86, 116, 131, 134, 139–40, 142
  process 81, 116
criminal punishment 14, 76–77, 83, 84, 85, 129–31, 139–40
  burdens of 15, 78, 83–84, 129–30, 139, 140
  policies 14, 15, 76, 83, 84, 85, 139–40
criminal risk assessment 3, 85
criminality 3, 15, 42, 71–72
criminology
  positivist 71–72
  research 79
criteria, selection 9, 10, 26, 30, 135
Cronin, AJ 51–52

Crown Prosecution Service (CPS) 10–11
crusade against crime 1–2, 72
CTE (chronic traumatic encephalopathy) 59
Cybergenetics 115, 116

Darwin, Leonard 73
data, sample 10, 11
datasets 6, 10–11, 32, 56, 78, 119, 120, 141
Davenport, Najeh 58, 60, 62
DCPM (Direct Centre Performance Model) 92–93, 94–95, 96–97
decision-makers, human 123, 124–25, 141–42
decision-making policies 13, 30, 47, 135, 144–45
decision-making rules 2, 132–33, 142–43
decisions
　algorithmic 9, 140–41
　automated 120, 121
　individualized 119
　justified 31, 124, 125
　non-algorithmic 80–81
　policy 8–9, 11, 136, 142, 144, 145
　recruitment 12–13, 48, 49
　sentencing 80–81, 83, 119, 140
decision-subjects 29, 30, 118, 119, 137–38, 141, 142–43
defendants 34, 35, 78–80, 82, 116–17, 118, 119
　black 7, 42, 81
　individual 123–24
　white 7, 42, 81
Delis Norms 60
deoxyribonucleic acid, *see* DNA
Department of Corrections (DOC) 123–24
DePodesta, Paul 48–49
depression 58, 59
deprivation, socio-economic 3–4, 86–87, 133–34
design, algorithmic 124, 131, 141–42
determinative factor 118–25
diagnosable criminal conditions 1, 72
diagnosis 3, 47, 59, 84–85, 134
diathesis, criminal 1–2, 72, 132
differences
　stigmatizing 12–13, 43, 62, 137–38
　unjustified 7, 51, 54, 75, 82, 95–96, 134–35

discretion
　human 48, 119–20, 123, 124, 125, 131–32
　judicial 119
discrimination 4–5, 7, 12–13, 134–35, 136
　institutional 43
disorganization, family 3, 85
disparities 35, 53, 57, 81, 89, 94, 95
distribution of error 82, 118, 123, 124, 125, 131, 140–41, 142
DNA (deoxyribonucleic acid) 33–35, 41, 115–16
　evidence 34, 116
　match statistics 35
　matching 27, 34, 35
　profiles 33
　samples 33, 34, 115
　transfer 34–35
DOC, *see* Department of Corrections
doctors 3, 27–28, 84–85, 98–99, 100, 101, 102
Donohoe, Mark 28–29
Dressel, Julia 80
drugs 80, 100, 102
dual-algorithm policy 94
duty of equal concern 11, 12, 43–44, 54, 62, 95, 136

economic benefits 12, 136
economic rights 76–77, 134, 139
economic segregation 42–43
education 1–2, 4, 91–92, 93, 139
educational background 118, 143
egalitarian objections 44
egalitarian reasons 7–8, 11, 43, 73, 102, 135, 136, 144
employees 12, 33, 53
　potential 50, 51, 98
employers 51, 91, 93, 94
employment 87–88, 89, 99, 139
　opportunities 50, 51
　status 52, 53, 78–79, 80, 118
end-stage liver disease 46, 47, 143
England and Wales 51–52, 53, 91–92
English Convict, The 1–5, 73, 132–34
equal concern
　duty of 11, 12, 43–44, 54, 62, 95, 136
　failures of 11–12, 43, 51, 136
equal treatment 11–12, 43, 47, 136

INDEX

equality 7, 8–9, 11–13, 41–69, 94, 95–96, 124–25, 139
equivalently qualified women 12–13, 50
Equivant 2–3, 15, 79–80, 81–82, 85
error
   burden 94–95, 122, 124
   distribution 82, 118, 123, 124, 125, 131, 140–41, 142
   predictive 116, 124–25
   rates 82
   risk 7, 12, 46–47, 81–82, 136, 140–41
errors, processing 34–35
evidence 21–22, 24–25, 28–29, 35, 42, 61–62, 116–17
   clear 21, 35, 42, 88
   of racial bias 7, 81–82
   retrospective 10, 135
   statistical 29–30, 133
examinations 11–12, 92, 95, 96–97
   process 91
   results 93, 94
excavation site 75–76
exclusion 12, 44, 51, 57, 74–75, 136
   social 72
   unjustified 129, 137–38
exercise of choice 13, 76, 78, 83
experiments 23–24, 31, 33–34, 36
experts 27, 117, 118
   forensic 25, 26
extended supervision 118

Facebook 50, 98
facts, statistical 29, 32, 72, 132
failures, systemic 47
failures of equal concern 11–12, 43, 51, 136
false positives 56, 81–82
families 2, 3–4, 83, 86–88, 96–97
family disorganization 3, 85
family history 3–4, 103, 134
family involvement 2, 15, 80, 119, 133–34
family members 41, 52
Farid, Hany 80
FBI 115
financial resources 7–8, 135
fingerprints 33
First Peoples 88, 89
flashover 21–22
Florida 3–4, 80, 81, 86, 133–34
Fogg, Douglas 24, 26–27

Foley, Kevin 115, 116–17, 118, 119
forensic experts 25, 26
forensic labs 115–16
forensic methods 25, 33–34
forensics 25, 27, 33
freedoms 13, 42–43, 76, 77–78, 87
   personal 26, 85, 140
Frye test 116–17
full assessment 2, 79, 80

GCSE (General Certificate of Secondary Education) 92
GDPR (General Data Protection Regulation) 120, 121
General Recidivism Risk scale (GRR) 2, 79–80
genetic profiles 33, 34–35
goals 12, 30, 50–51, 93–95, 122, 129–48
   policy 4, 42–43, 44, 54
   social 57, 75, 76, 93–96, 135, 136
Goring, Charles Buckman 1, 2, 3, 72, 77–78, 85, 132, 134
grades 79–80, 91–93, 94–95, 96–97, 138
   A-Level 92
   higher 94, 95
Green, Arthur 41
GRR (General Recidivism Risk scale) 2, 79–80
guilt 35–36, 41, 116
   proxy for 10, 28
Guthkelch, AN 27–28

Hampikian, Greg 116
handwriting, samples 71
harm 9–10, 32, 75–76, 103
   intermediate 9, 25
   risk of 9, 26, 75, 103, 138
hazardous waste 75–77, 99
health 42, 54, 61, 85
   insurance 53, 102–3, 134
healthcare 4, 47, 53, 139
   outcomes 47, 54, 61
   private 53
   providers 53, 101–2
   public 47
heart 25, 45, 71–72, 96–97, 123, 144
   transplants 98–99
Heaton, Robert 60
Heaton Norms 60, 61–62

154　INDEX

Heilbronn 33–36
hiring 49–51
　algorithms 49–50
　success 12–13, 50
history 1–2, 4, 49, 79–80, 98–99, 101, 123
　individual 3, 85, 89
　medical 3, 61, 84–85
　personal 4, 101
Hoffman, Frederick Ludwig 42–43, 44
Horodowich, Elizabeth 55
hospital care 42–43
hospitals 27, 53, 98–99, 102
human decision-makers 123, 124–25, 141–42
human discretion 48, 119–20, 123, 124, 125, 131–32
Hurst, Gerald 21–22, 25

ideal crime-fighting world 78–86
illness 3, 29–30, 84–85
　acute 53
　mental 59, 72, 97
impressions 31, 71
　dental 26–27
　interview 31
imprisonment 1, 41, 72, 78, 115, 132
inaccuracy, predictive 54
inaccurate predictions 124–25, 131, 142
incarceration 2, 26–27, 42, 76–78, 83–84, 85–86
inclusion 54, 86–88, 89, 90
income groups, lower 56–57
indicators of arson 21, 22–23, 24, 25
individual choice 83, 86, 89–90, 102–3, 135
inductive basis 9, 26
inequalities 4–5, 8, 12, 23, 42, 51–52, 81, 82
　status 12, 44, 51, 89, 136
inequities 8, 43, 52
infant mortality 61
inferences 5, 6, 24, 29, 30
　causal 32
　false 11
　statistical 9–10, 27, 31, 133
information 9–10, 31, 35, 120, 122, 123, 131, 140–41
innocence 21, 35, 41
Innocence Project 25, 116
institutional burdens 7–8, 76–77, 78, 132–33, 134, 139, 140, 144–45
institutional responses 15, 77, 85, 131, 140

institutions 11, 43, 51, 95, 116, 136, 138
instrumental crime 3, 85
instrumental reason, significant 15, 131, 140, 144–45
insurance, medical 2, 60, 133–34
intentional actions 84, 85, 99, 121, 122–23, 141
interests 11, 12, 13, 43–44, 48–49, 136
intermediate harm 9, 25
intolerable costs 8, 30
investigation 22–23, 25, 34–35
　pre-sentence 118, 143
investigators 21, 22–23, 24–25, 33

Jackson, Christine 25
Jackson, Vincent 59
James, Bill 49
Jeffreys, Alec 33–34
Jim Crow era 42–43, 44
jobs 10, 12, 31, 36, 50, 51, 124–25
Johnson, Megan 97
Jones, Robert 86–87
judgements 35, 74, 75, 84, 90, 117, 129, 137–38
judges 3, 118, 119, 123, 124, 125, 141, 143
judicial process 26, 27
judicial training 80
Julius 23, 24
juries 24, 31, 41, 115
jurors 35, 116
justice 8, 12, 25, 29, 73, 135, 136, 137
　algorithmic 6–15, 129–48
justified decisions 31, 124, 125
justified policies 26, 30, 82

Kay, Adam 51–52
knowledge 5, 26, 31, 47, 73, 76, 98–99, 120–21
　electrical 31

labels 57, 75, 137–38
　anthropomorphic 24
laboratories 21, 34, 115–16
lagoon 55
language 50–51, 58, 98, 99, 134–35
law 15, 42–43, 44, 77, 82, 85, 90, 139
learning algorithms 6
legal protections 42, 43, 44, 78
Lentini, John 22–23, 24–25, 29
Letter, Brian 78–79

Lewis, Gerald Wayne 22
Lewis, Michael 48, 49
Lime Street fire/experiment 21–23, 24
links, rational 9, 26, 135
liquid fire accelerants 21, 22–23
liver 45, 46
   disease, end-stage 46, 47, 143
   transplants 12, 45, 46, 143
Lombroso, Cesare 71–72, 77–78
Loomis, Eric 118, 119, 120, 121–22, 123, 124, 125

Mahan brothers 41–42
Major League Baseball (MLB) 48–49
Mattingly, Jacy 97
maturity 14, 83–84, 99
Mayor's Office of New Urban Mechanics (MONUM) 56
media 4–5, 41, 92–93
medical care 54, 102
medical history 3, 61, 84–85
medical insurance 2, 60, 133–34
medical protocols 4, 6, 134
medical resources 9–10, 43, 133
medical treatment 5, 12, 52, 53, 61, 85, 101, 102
MELD (Model for End State Liver Disease) 12, 46–47, 57, 122, 143
   Score 46
memory loss 58, 59
mental illness 59, 72, 97
method, statistical 1–2, 31
Mill, John Stuart 74–75
misuse, substance 100–1, 102, 103
Mittelstadt, Brent 120
Mix13 115, 116
mixtures 115–16
   complex 115, 116
MLB (Major League Baseball) 48–49
Model for End State Liver Disease, *see* MELD
models 12, 92, 97–98, 101, 122
MONUM (Mayor's Office of New Urban Mechanics) 56
moral blame 137
morbidity 10, 25–26
mortality 10, 29–30
   infant 61
   risks 9, 25, 133
   waitlist 12, 46

murder 10, 21, 25, 33, 34, 115, 116–17
Murphy, Erin 117, 118
myths 22–23

Narx Scores 101–3, 134
NarxCare 101–2
National Football League, *see* NFL
National Registry of Exonerations 42
natural language processing 12–13, 50, 97
New South Wales (NSW) 87–88, 90
NFL (National Football League) 58, 59, 60, 61, 62
   players 58–59, 60, 61–62
non-algorithmic decisions 80–81
non-comparative failures 44, 88
non-comparative reasons 7–8, 135
noncompliance 98–99, 134
non-profit organizations 62, 116
normative reasons 120–22
NSW (New South Wales) 87–88, 90

Oakland As 48–49
officials 75–76
Ofqual (Office of Qualifications and Examinations Regulation) 91–92, 95–96
opioid prescription decisions 4, 101
Opioid Risk Tool, *see* ORT
opioids 100, 101, 102
opportunities 14–15, 75, 76–77, 83–84, 96–97, 99, 139
   adequate 98–99, 137, 138
   for choice 75, 137–38
   employment 50, 51
   professional 12–13, 51
   social 14, 62, 87
Optum 53, 54
organs 6, 45–46, 84
   allocation 45, 46
ORT (Opioid Risk Tool) 4, 100–3, 134
outcomes 5, 8, 9–10, 12, 84, 95, 102–3, 122–23, 129–48
   healthcare 47, 54, 61
   individual 29, 30
outputs 119–20, 121, 122, 123, 124–25, 131, 140–41, 142
   algorithmic 36, 120, 121, 124, 125, 131, 141–42
   individual 79–80
   predictive 119–20, 142

OxyContin 100

pain
  acute 102
  chronic 101, 102
parents 2, 11, 27–28, 29, 43, 119
  biological/natural 2, 80, 133–34
  nightmare 97–99
parity, predictive 81–82
parole 25, 41, 139
Pasco County Sheriff's Office, *see* PCSO
patients 4, 5, 9–10, 45–46, 53–54, 100–3, 133
  black 53, 143
  white 54
patterns 2, 6, 22, 23, 24, 33, 78, 79–80
  burn 24, 26–27
  hallucinating 32
  pour 21
  recidivism 79
PCSO (Pasco County Sheriff's Office) 3–4, 86–87, 89, 133–34
  algorithm 4, 87–88
people opportunities 15, 103, 140
perceptions 14, 24, 35, 61
performance, school 80, 98–99
Perlin, Mark 115, 116–17
personal crime 3–4, 86–87, 89, 133–34
personal freedoms 26, 85, 140
personal history 4, 101
personality 14, 31, 74, 77, 83–84
physical characteristics 1, 71, 132
pigeons 23–24
players 48–49, 58, 59, 61–62
  black 60, 61–62
  former 59, 60
  just-in-case 48
  white 62
Poche, Howard 34
police 10, 33–34, 41, 42, 86–87, 89, 90, 115
  practices 72, 130–31
  surveillance 87–88, 138, 139
policies 7–8, 9, 25–26, 43, 44, 129–48
  of criminal punishment 14, 15, 76, 83, 84, 85, 139–40
  decision-making 13, 30, 47, 135, 144–45
  objecting to 5, 7–9, 102, 142–43
  race-based 44
  social 4–5, 8, 12, 75, 133, 135, 136

policing
  practices 82
  resources 2, 90, 130–31
policy burdens 13, 136, 138
policy decisions 8–9, 11, 136, 142, 144, 145
policy goals 4, 42–43, 44, 54
policy recommendations 9, 52, 73
policymakers 4, 42–43
policymaking 6
  and prediction 142–44
Pope, Pamela 41
population 5, 7, 29, 34, 35, 42, 88
  assessed 118, 140–41
  data 2, 81–82, 132–33
positives, false 56, 81–82
positivist criminology 71–72
post-flashover burning 22, 26–27
post-release supervision 2, 78–79, 139, 140
potential employees 50, 51, 98
potholes 55–56
practitioners 3, 4, 23, 85
Predictim 97–98, 99
  marketing materials 97
predictions 4, 122–23, 124, 133–34, 138, 140–41
  actuarial 15, 130, 136, 142–43
  algorithmic 11, 119, 123, 124, 125, 131, 140, 141
  inaccurate 124–25, 131, 142
  making 31, 141
  and policymaking 142–44
predictive accuracy 15, 80, 92, 117, 118, 119, 123, 133
predictive assessment 120, 141
predictive error 116, 124–25
predictive inaccuracy 54
predictive outputs 119–20, 142
predictive parity 81–82
predictive policing algorithms 86–87, 133–34
predictive rules 4, 5
predictive success 53, 102
predictive tasks 49–50, 118, 120, 122
predictive tools 6–7, 130–31, 143, 144
predictive values 81–82
prescriptions 4, 100–3
pre-sentence investigation (PSI) 118, 119, 143
Pre-Trial Services 2, 79

priority vaccination 9, 26
prison 5, 25, 41, 73, 80, 138, 139, 140
prisoners 1, 71, 77
privileges 15, 75, 76–78, 134, 139, 140
probability 27, 34–36, 48
   background 35
processing errors 34–35
professional opportunities 12–13, 51
professional qualifications 117
profiles 49–50, 91–92, 97–98
   genetic 33, 34–35
   reference 115
proof 11–12, 81, 117
property 26, 42–43, 76, 86, 87, 133
proprietary status 118, 119
ProPublica 7, 80, 81, 82
prosecution 22, 41, 81
prosecutor's fallacy 35
protection 26, 75–76, 88, 90
   legal 42, 43, 44, 78
proteins 45
protocol-developers 117
protocols, medical 4, 6, 134
proxies 11, 32, 45–46, 53–54, 61, 81, 85–86, 121
   for guilt 10, 28
   imperfect 117
   predictive 61
   reliable 60
PSI (pre-sentence investigation) 118, 119, 143
public safety 85–86, 140
puddle configurations 22, 24
punishment 2, 3, 14, 26, 73, 83–84, 86, 139
   capital 21, 28
Purdue Pharma 100
pursuit, relentless 3–4, 86–90, 130–31, 133–34
puzzle people 45–47

qualifications 50, 51, 91, 117, 118
   professional 117
   standards 91–92
quasi-parental roles 11

race 42, 44, 60, 61, 83
Race Traits and Tendencies of the American Negro 42
race-based policies 44

race-corrected algorithms 61–62
racial bias, evidence 7, 81–82
rape 41
rational choosers 14, 83–84, 139
rational competence 14, 77, 139
rational links 9, 26, 135
recidivism 2, 3, 79, 80–81, 85–86, 133–34
   patterns 79
   rates/statistics 2, 80–81, 82
   risk 79, 82, 86, 118
recommendations
   policy 9, 52, 73
   sentencing 80, 119
recruiters 12–13, 50
recruitment 4, 6
   decisions 12–13, 48, 49
   practices 49, 50
reference profiles 115
relative capabilities 94, 95
relentless pursuit 3–4, 86–90, 130–31, 133–34
relevance 8–11, 21–40, 88, 95–96, 135, 139, 140, 142
reliability 72, 116–17, 118
representative reasons 14, 74, 139
resources 54, 57, 76, 129, 138
   financial 7–8, 135
   medical 9–10, 43, 133
   policing 2, 90, 130–31
responses, institutional 15, 77, 85, 131, 140
responsibility 47, 59, 90, 137
   allocative 11, 57, 142
rewards 23
rights
   civil-service 42–43
   economic 76–77, 134, 139
   foundational 77–78
risk 2, 9–11, 27, 54, 61–62, 76, 103
   of error 7, 12, 46–47, 81–82, 136, 140–41
   factors 9, 29–30, 98–99
   of harm 9, 26, 75, 103, 138
   high 7, 81–82, 118, 133
   higher 4, 81, 101, 119
   low 7, 81–82
   of recidivism 79, 82, 86, 118
   scores 2, 49–50, 78–79, 81–82, 123–24, 125
RMP (Random Match Probability) 34, 35, 36, 115, 116

Roberts, Carla 27
rules 6, 14, 25, 27, 31, 76, 77
  algorithmic 94
  decision-making 2, 132-33, 142-43
  predictive 4, 5
  statistical 31, 32, 133, 135-36
Russell, Bertrand 30
Russell, Chris 30, 120

Sackler, Richard 100
safeguards 76, 77, 87, 103, 129-30, 138
safety
  child 98
  public 85-86, 140
samples 31, 34-35, 41, 60, 115
  blood 3, 27, 34, 84-85
  data 10, 11
  DNA 33, 34, 115
  handwriting 71
  semen 41
  single-source 116
Sarbin, Theodore R. 31
Satter, GA 31
SBS (Shaken Baby Syndrome) 10-11, 27-29, 32
Scanlon, Tim 8, 29, 44, 74, 75-76, 99
school performance 80, 98-99
schools 11-12, 79-80, 89-90, 92, 93, 94-95
scores 2, 3-4, 78-80, 81-82, 101-2
  risk 2, 49-50, 78-79, 81-82, 123-24, 125
  VRR 80
scouts 48
security 85-86, 87, 140
segregation 1-2, 44, 72, 132
  economic 42-43
  racial 42
selection criteria 9, 10, 26, 30, 135
self-motivation 93-94
sentencing 3, 6, 79, 80, 85-86, 118, 119, 139
  algorithms 78-79, 133-34
  decisions 80-81, 83, 119, 140
  process 86
  recommendations 80, 119
sex 46-47, 80, 101
sexual abuse 4, 101, 103, 134
Shaken Baby Syndrome, *see* SBS
signals 14, 77, 83-84, 103, 137, 139
Skinner, Burrhus Frederic 23-24

social benefit 6-7, 8-9, 30
social goals 57, 75, 76, 93-96, 135, 136
social insurance 52
social opportunities 14, 62, 87
social policies 4-5, 8, 12, 75, 133, 135, 136
  burdens of 8-9, 13, 15
social status 11, 136
socio-economic circumstances 15, 84, 138
socio-economic deprivation 3-4, 86-87, 133-34
spalling 22-23
standardized assessments 90-92, 93
Starzl, Thomas 45
statistical algorithms 2, 4-7, 12-13, 117-18, 129-48
  use 4-5, 11, 50, 122-23, 136, 141, 143
statistical analysis 28, 48-49
statistical assessments 42, 81, 118, 123, 131, 140-41
statistical evidence 29-30, 133
statistical facts 29, 32, 72, 132
statistical inferences 9-10, 27, 31, 133
statistical method 1-2, 31
statistical rules 31, 32, 133, 135-36
statistics 27, 29, 30, 32, 35, 88, 133, 135-36
  base-rate 35
status 12-13, 43, 44, 94, 95, 129, 130, 135
  employment 52, 53, 78-79, 80, 118
  inequality 12, 44, 51, 89, 136
  proprietary 118, 119
  social 11, 136
stigmatizing beliefs 12, 136
stigmatizing differences 12-13, 43, 62, 137-38
Stillwell, Craig 27
STMP (Suspect Target Management Plan) 87-88, 89
Stokes, Anthony 98-99
Street Bump 56-57
students 90-91, 92-97, 138
  achievement 93
  ranking 6, 91, 92, 94
substance abuse 4, 100-1, 102, 103, 134
substance misuse 100-1, 102, 103
success, predictive 53, 102
suicidal ideation 59
suicides 59, 100
summary justice 42

INDEX

superstition 23–24
supervision 1–2, 9, 72, 79, 132
   correctional 130–31
   extended 118
   failure 123
   post-release 2, 78–79, 139, 140
surgeons 45
surveillance, police 87–88, 138, 139
Suspect Target Management Plan (STMP) 87–88, 89
suspicions 43, 124–25, 131, 142
symbolic reasons 14, 74–75, 77, 83–84, 86, 139
symptoms 3, 10, 27–28, 58, 59, 84–85, 102
   acute 58
   triad of 10–11, 27, 28, 29, 32

target populations 5, 9–10, 11, 32, 47, 124, 135
target variables 5, 31, 32, 81–82, 124–25, 133, 135–36
Taylor, Roger 91, 92, 95, 96–97
teachers 43, 93, 95–97
   biases 95–96
test scores 31
Texas 24, 25
thresholds 3–4, 47, 50, 59, 116–17, 118, 137
tools 2, 4, 6, 79, 98, 130, 144
   algorithmic 2, 79, 116, 118, 131–32, 134, 143
   predictive 6–7, 130–31, 143, 144
   use 15, 139, 140, 144–45
training
   judicial 80
   professional 27
   specialist 25
transparency 115–27, 131, 140–42
   algorithmic 119
   and determinative factor 118–25
transplants, liver 12, 45, 46, 143
treatment 11, 12, 45–46, 94, 95, 101–3
   algorithms 60
   effective 3, 84–85
   equal 11–12, 43, 47, 136
   medical 5, 12, 52, 53, 61, 85, 101, 102
   unequal 57
triad of symptoms 10–11, 27, 28, 29, 32
trials 21, 24, 35, 41, 115

TrueAllele 115, 116–17
trust 14, 139, 144–45
two-variable regression equation 31
typologies 2–3, 85

UCR (uniform crime reporting) 81
United States 28, 42–43, 53, 97, 100, 101
unjustified beliefs 12, 44
unjustified differences 7, 51, 54, 75, 82, 95–96, 134–35
unjustified exclusion 129, 137–38

vaccination 9–10, 30
   COVID-19 9, 26, 29–30
   priority 9, 26
vaccines 9, 25, 29–30, 43, 84
   COVID-19 9, 25, 30
vaginal birth 6, 60–61, 122
Vaginal Birth after Caesarean, *see* VBAC
value 8, 96–97, 103, 121–23, 125, 129–48
   basic 13, 73
   of choice 14, 73, 76, 78, 137, 142–43
   instrumental 103
variables 6, 9–10, 31, 46, 49, 81, 82, 83
   objective 46
   statistically-significant 120, 131, 141
   subjective 46
   target 5, 31, 32, 81–82, 124–25, 133, 135–36
Vasquez, Manuel 24, 26–27
VBAC (Vaginal Birth after Caesarean) 6, 60–61, 122
VCSC (Virginia Criminal Sentencing Commission) 78–79
Venice 54–55
   lagoon 55
Verret, Roy 34
victims 3–4, 21, 41, 86–87, 89, 133–34, 138
   black 42
violence 1, 72
   physical 27–28
   white 43
   workplace 98
Violence Risk Scale 123
violent crime 88, 125, 133
Violent Recidivism Risk, *see* VRR
Virginia Criminal Sentencing Commission (VCSC) 78–79

160   INDEX

VRR (Violent Recidivism Risk) 2, 79
   scores 80

Wachter, Sandra 120
waitlist mortality 12, 46
Wake Turbulence Mapping
   vdevice 55–56
waste, hazardous 75–77, 99
Webster, Lynn 100–1
whiplash-shaking 28
white defendants 7, 42, 81
white women 60–61

Willingham, Cameron Todd 21–22, 24–25,
   26–27, 117
women 12–13, 14, 46–47, 60–61, 74–75, 101
   black 61
   equivalently qualified 12–13, 50
   white 60–61
   young antisocial poorly educated 3, 85
worst-case scenarios 90–97

Yelenic, Dr John 115
Yelenic, Michelle 115
youth, at-risk 3–4, 86–87, 130–31